This study of Andrei Platonov (1899–1951) focuses on the interrelation of philosophical themes, imagery and verbal devices in his prose. Platonov's intellectual roots lie in Russian utopian thought of the late nineteenth and early twentieth centuries. He was particularly influenced by the writings of Fedorov and Bogdanov, but may also be seen as belonging to a broader tradition of efforts to overcome epistemological dualism that includes such figures as Solov'ev, Bakhtin, and Pasternak.

The world view expressed in Platonov's literary works is a peculiar blend of idealist longings and materialist convictions. At its center stands his dominant image of being's vulnerable residence in the physical body. At the same time, Platonov's world view was significantly shaped by his implicit dialogue with Soviet Marxism–Leninism, and later Stalinism, both of which claimed to be building utopia.

Platonov's unique literary style embeds the high-flown rhetoric of Soviet propaganda, Marxism–Leninism, and the technical jargon associated with 'socialist construction' in the deforming medium of the speech of Russia's unlettered masses. In its use of deformation as a trope, this style represents a development of the Russian tradition of *skaz* narration in the direction of Modernism; its inner workings are closely related to those of the pun.

In Platonov's masterpieces of the late 1920s and early 1930s, linguistic parody comes together with existential *angst* and dystopian doubts about the course of Soviet history, and in them he reveals the extent to which the Soviet mindset is itself a linguistic phenomenon. Thomas Seifrid concludes his study by considering the works Platonov wrote between 1934 and 1951. In these, he maneuvered to preserve some of the essentials of his earlier poetic while fusing them with the expected formulae of socialist realism.

CAMBRIDGE STUDIES IN RUSSIAN
LITERATURE

ANDREI PLATONOV

# CAMBRIDGE STUDIES IN RUSSIAN LITERATURE

A complete list of books in this series
is given at the end of the volume.

# ANDREI PLATONOV

*Uncertainties of spirit*

BY

THOMAS SEIFRID

*Associate Professor, Department of Slavic Languages and Literature,
University of Southern California*

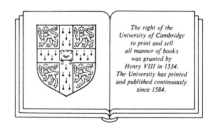

*The right of the
University of Cambridge
to print and sell
all manner of books
was granted by
Henry VIII in 1534.
The University has printed
and published continuously
since 1584.*

CAMBRIDGE UNIVERSITY PRESS

*Cambridge*
*New York   Port Chester*
*Melbourne   Sydney*

Published by the Press Syndicate of the University of Cambridge
The Pitt Building, Trumpington Street, Cambridge CB2 1RP
40 West 20th Street, New York, NY 10011-4211, USA
10 Stamford Road, Oakleigh, Victoria 3166, Australia

First published 1992

Printed in Great Britain at the University Press, Cambridge

*A catalogue record for this book is available from the British Library*

*Library of Congress cataloguing in publication data*
Seifrid, Thomas.
Andrei Platonov, uncertainties of spirit / by Thomas Seifrid.
p.     cm. – (Cambridge studies in Russian literature)
Includes bibliographical references (p.     ) and index.
ISBN 0-521-40522-X (hardback)
1. Platonov, Andreï Platonovich, 1899–1951 – Criticism and interpretation.
2. Philosophy in literature. 3. Socialist realism in literature. I. Title. II. Series.
PG3476.P543Z778    1992
891.73′42 – dc20    91-16969 CIP

ISBN 0 521 40522 X hardback

UP

*Книга посвящается любимой моей жене Ленуле.*

From the start the "spirit" is afflicted with the curse of being "burdened" with matter, which here makes its appearance in the form of agitated layers of air, in short, of language.

(Marx, 'The German Ideology' in Robert C. Tucker, ed., *The Marx–Engels Reader*, 2nd edn, New York: W. W. Norton, 1978, p. 158)

# Contents

# Preface

This study of Platonov's prose has its origins in my doctoral dissertation (Cornell University, 1984), though the basic premises of that text have here been significantly reworked and expanded upon. Segments of Chapter Two appeared in somewhat different form as "On the Genesis of Platonov's Literary Style in the Voronež period," *Russian Literature* 23–4 (1988): 367–86. A substantial portion of Chapter Four appeared as "Writing Against Matter: On the Language of Andrej Platonov's *Kotlovan*," *Slavic and East European Journal* 3 (1987): 370–87.

I am indebted to the International Research and Exchanges Board (IREX) and the Fulbright-Hays Faculty Research Abroad program for support that enabled me to spend ten months conducting research in Moscow and Leningrad in 1985–1986. For invaluable assistance I am grateful to the Central State Archive of Literature and Art in Moscow (TsGALI), and regret only that their delay in admitting me and their veto on my access to many documents made our contact so brief. I am also grateful to the staffs of the reading rooms to which I was assigned in the Lenin Library and the Institute for Scientific Information in the Social Sciences (INION), both in Moscow, and in the Library of the Academy of Sciences (BAN) in Leningrad. The University of Southern California graciously allowed me a leave of absence to spend the time in Moscow (and special thanks to Marshall Cohen, Dean of Humanities, for his consistent and generous support). Reed College, where I taught from 1982–1985, showed

exceptional magnanimity in agreeing to continue as my
Fulbright-Hays sponsor during my transition to USC.

Among individuals my earliest debt of gratitude for this work
is to the Unknown Emigré, who first suggested on a street
corner in Ithaca, New York that I read Platonov's novel
*Chevengur* because it was "incomparable." He was right, and
since then I have been trying merrily to figure out in exactly
what ways. Thomas Langerak and Eric Naiman provided a
fertile exchange of ideas about Platonov, copious bibliographical information, and warm friendship that I hope will
survive the completion of this book. Mariia Andreevna
Platonova lent crucial aid in my dealings with TsGALI.
Special thanks also are due to my editor, Katharina Brett.

As I move into the broader terrain outside *platonovedenie* my
debts of gratitude multiply. One of the largest, for both moral
support and intellectual stimulation, is to my colleagues in the
Slavic Department at USA, especially Alexander Zholkovsky,
Olga Matich, and Sarah Pratt. Caryl Emerson was both
supportive and rewardingly critical at a crucial stage of the
manuscript's progress. George Gibian oversaw the production
of the dissertation on which this book is based, and has been a
much cherished colleague and friend. The same may be said of
Gilbert Holliday, who somehow managed to see something in
me when I was very green. What flaws there are in this study
are my own responsibility, and doubtless result from not
heeding some point of advice offered by those mentioned
above.

In a more personal vein I wish to thank my wife's Moscow
relatives on Fersman Street – Irina Borneman-Starynkevich
(now sadly gone), Asya Starynkevich, Lelia Anokhina – for
their generous warmth, hospitality, and tolerance. If anything
I owe even more to the Leningrad branch of the family – Dii
Starynkevich, Irina Starynkevich, Marina and Boris Smirnov.
My mother, Leah Neuendorf, is responsible for my ever having
pursued this sort of life. The largest debt of all, which really
cannot be repaid, is to my wife Elena, who along the way
provided unflagging love and inspiration.

# Abbreviations

| | |
|---|---|
| ed. khr. | edinitsa khraneniia |
| f. | fond |
| fil. | filologicheskii |
| gos. | gosudarstvennyi |
| im. | imeni |
| izd. | izdatel'stvo |
| kand. | kandidat |
| l., ll. | list, listy |
| L | Leningrad |
| M | Moscow |
| M–L | Moscow–Leningrad |
| op. | opis' |
| V | Voronezh |
| TsGALI | Tsentral'nyi gosudarstvennyi arkhiv literatury i iskusstva (Central State Archive of Literature and Art, Moscow) |
| uch. | uchenyi |
| un-ta | universiteta |

# Introduction
## The problem of reading Platonov

In the current rewriting of Soviet literary history, Andrei Platonov (1899–1951) has come to occupy a central position. Like Mikhail Bulgakov, who together with Platonov first came to the attention of a broad reading public in the 1960s, he is now regarded as one of the buried treasures of the Soviet cultural past whose excavation has been made possible by Stalinism's final dismantling. Eclipsing even some of the hallowed martyrs of Soviet literature, Platonov has been elevated into an emblem of the Stalin era's repressions, a writer of tragic and prophetic vision who "foresaw all that later took place" and in a series of eerily dystopian works wrote about it with unswerving honesty. So abruptly has the "official" Soviet evaluation of Platonov reversed itself that it is not unusual to encounter the claim that Soviet literature (or even world literature) cannot now even be imagined without Platonov as one of its central figures. The traits for which he was once vilified – his works' penchant for the grotesque, their often anarchistic sentiments, and their weird deformations of the Russian language – are now regarded as his most impressive achievements. The stifling of Platonov's unique voice in the second half of his career and the at best grudging admission into print granted his works in the Khrushchev and Brezhnev eras have, since the late 1980s, given way to a flood of once-banned publications, and plans are underway for a scholarly edition of his collected works.

Though part of this recent exaltation can be ascribed to the heady atmosphere of post-Brezhnev liberalization, the restoration of Platonov to the foreground of Soviet literary history is largely justified. What can be claimed for Platonov, but cannot for writers like Bulgakov, Mandelshtam, and Pasternak, is an integral role in the specifically *Soviet* part of twentieth-century Russian culture. An early and enthusiastic supporter of the Revolution, he quickly became involved in the Proletarian Culture movement and immersed himself in the philosophical current of Russian revolutionary prometheanism – the dreams, nurtured already for several years when the 1917 Revolution took place, of an utter transformation of Russian social, political, and even physical existence. Moreover, unlike the majority of his fellow writers, Platonov participated directly in the process of "socialist construction," working up until the late 1920s as a land reclamation engineer and participating in the Party's campaign to bring electricity to the Russian countryside. If anything, this proximity to the mainsprings of Soviet culture may have intensified opposition to Platonov when his works began to voice disillusionment with the Soviet "new world." (As one of his critics rather ominously put it in the 1930s, "more is to be expected from someone of proletarian origin than from a member of the intelligentsia, raised in a bourgeois milieu.")[1]

Platonov's fiction is integral to the Soviet experience in another way as well. Cast, for the most part, in the speech patterns of the Russian lower classes, it presents itself as an embodiment of the voice of the "dark" masses suddenly enfranchised after 1917. What Platonov's works *represent* is the way in which high-flown Marxist–Leninist rhetoric was refracted in the minds of the country's largely unlettered masses. Indeed, it has been suggested that for this reason Platonov's is the one truly proletarian voice among major Soviet authors (which does not, of course, prevent that voice from being one of the principal achievements of Russian modernism).[2] At the same time Platonov has deservedly come to be seen as one of the important early dissenters from Soviet utopianism, whose undermining activities were all the more effective for having been conducted from within that chiliastic world view.

How Platonov's troubled relation to Soviet literary officialdom arose, and how he came to occupy this unique position in the history of Soviet literature, can in part be seen in his biography. Platonov was born in 1899 into the working-class family of Platon Firsovich Klimentov, a metal-worker for the local railroad who lived in a settlement (Iamskaia sloboda) bordering the southeastern Russian city of Voronezh. The settlement abutted Voronezh's industrial section and housed much of its working class, but was separated only by railroad tracks from the open steppe and preserved many features of the traditional Russian village.[3] From this origin on the "margin" between two worlds – rural and industrial, old and new, natural and man-made, traditional and revolutionary – derive many of the contradictions that characterize this writer and his works, and Platonov himself often self-consciously drew attention to the duality of his background. In the preface to his 1922 volume of poems *Golubaia glubina*, for example, he remarks:

Only ten years ago Iamskaia was barely distinguishable from a village ... It had wattle fences, vegetable gardens, vacant, weed-filled lots, huts instead of houses, chickens, boot-makers, and lots of peasants on the high road to Zadonsk. The bell of the "Iron" church was the settlement's only music, and on quiet summer evenings it was listened to with emotion by old women, beggars, and me ... [A]part from the field, the village, my mother, and the tolling of the bell, I loved (and the longer I live, the more I love) locomotives, machines, the moaning of the factory whistle, and sweaty work ... Between the weeds, beggar women, the song of the fields and electricity, the locomotive, and the factory whistle which shakes the earth, there is a link, a native connection; the one and the other bear the same birthmark. What it is, I do not yet know. But I know that the pitiful peasant plowing his field could tomorrow get on a five-axle locomotive and run the controls so well, looking like such a master of the thing, that you wouldn't recognize him. The growth of grass and the swirling of [a locomotive's] steam demand equal mechanics.[4]

What this early and optimistic passage posits as a "native link" between the industrial world and that of the peasant village, the later literary works far more typically register as tension. The contradiction between the desire to remake the world with the help of machines, on the one hand, and to retrieve a sense of oneness with nature, on the other, never fully resolves itself in Platonov's thought.

Platonov's childhood was marked by deprivations and hardship, experiences reflected in his works' many exhausted fathers, emaciated mothers, and children sent off to beg for food. At one point there were ten in the family and Platonov, as the eldest son, was forced to go to work for the "Rossiia" insurance company. Later he became a smelter in a local pipe factory, then an engineer's assistant on the estate of a local landowner named Ia. G. Bek-Marmarchev, who appears to have owned a train (Inozemtseva, "Platonov v Voronezhe," p. 99). His upbringing was not, however, without its own eccentric cultural promptings. Platonov's father was an inventor who held a number of patents, and despite its straitened circumstances the family appears to have cultivated an interest in books. By the age of thirteen Platonov began writing poetry, even, according to one source, sending some of his efforts off to Moscow (where they were politely rejected) and somewhere between the ages of thirteen and fifteen he attempted to construct a *perpetuum mobile*.[5]

Though too young to have served in the war against Germany, Platonov experienced directly the political and military chaos into which Voronezh and the southern front were plunged during the Civil War. He appears from the start to have supported the Bolshevik cause.[6] In 1918 he assisted his father on a locomotive that delivered supplies to the front and cleared snow from the tracks in winter – an experience later to resurface in the opening section of *Chevengur* – then in the summer of 1919 he was sent to the nearby town of Novokhopersk to help repel Denikin. A number of archival documents mention Platonov's service in a "Special Detachment" (*otriad osobogo naznacheniia, chast' osobogo naznacheniia*), identifying his role as that of "rank-and-file rifleman" (*riadovoi strelok*).[7] One scholar suggests Platonov may have participated in the forced requisitions of grain being carried out at the time, though Platonov's reticence on the subject and the paucity of biographical materials available make it difficult to substantiate such conjecture (Shepard, "Origin of a Master," p. 22). However, the several scenes in *Chevengur* portraying revolutionary violence, and those in *Kotlovan* portraying the brutal side of collectivization – in which Platonov certainly did not take part – may nonetheless have their origins here.

Beyond his service in the Red Army, Platonov responded to the Revolution with a surge of activity that was exceptional even by the standards of those hectic years: in this period he participates in the fledgling Soviet state's campaign for the electrification of the Russian countryside (producing a brochure on the topic, *Electrofikatsiia*, in 1921), works prolifically as a journalist for a series of Voronezh newspapers and journals (those allied with either the local Party organs or the Proletarian Culture movement), and assumes a prominent role in the cultural life of post-revolutionary Voronezh. As one of his Soviet biographers puts it, what amazes one about the early Platonov is that "a twenty-year-old who had at one point completed parochial school, a few grades of the local town school, and, just after the Civil War ended, a railway polytechnic institute would, from 1920–1922, write over two hundred articles on the most complex social-philosophical issues, publish a volume of poems, and establish himself as a writer of literary prose."[8]

The year 1920 marked the high point of Platonov's prominence on the Voronezh cultural scene and of his closely related involvement in the local Proletarian Culture movement. Platonov frequented the "Iron Pen," the cafe-club of the local Union of Communist Jouranlists, *Komsozhur* (to which he had been admitted in March of that year), where he contributed readings of his poems and essays to the "literary evenings" held there. At least one such evening was devoted exclusively to a discussion of his poetry and was reported to have gone on long into the night (Inozemtseva, 92–3). In November of that year he read an essay entitled "Sex and Consciousness," in December a report on electrification (taking part as well in the literary-musical program that followed), in February of 1921 an essay on "Consciousness (on the Intellectual Revolution)," and again in September one entitled "On Love." In a review of a collection by local poets, Platonov was singled out as "the most talented of all," and when, following the Moscow Conference of Proletarian Writers, Voronezh organized its own

Union of Proletarian Writers, Platonov was one of three elected
to its provisional directorate (in August 1920). He was also one
of two delegates chosen to attend the All-Russian Congress of
Proletarian Writers in October 1920, an important journey for
him because he there heard Bogdanov and other leaders of the
movement speak and possibly established his first ties with
publishers in the capital (Langerak, "Andrei Platonov v
Voronezhe," p. 449).

Simultaneous with his work for the Voronezh revolutionary
press, from 1918–1921 Platonov studied in the electrical
technology department of the local polytechnical institute, and
in early 1922 left journalism altogether to conduct land
reclamation work for the Voronezh Regional Land Admini-
stration (*Gubzemuprav*).[9] There were probably several reasons
for this departure, but the primary one may have been
ideological (Langerak, "Platonov v Voronezhe," p. 450).
Writing to Voronskii, Platonov later asserted that, "the
drought of 1921 produced an extremely strong impression on
me, and, being a technician, I could no longer be involved in
a contemplative activity like literature" (Inozemtseva, "Platonov v Voronezhe," p. 450). Writing to Voronskii, Platonov
later asserted that, "the drought of 1921 produced an extremely
strong impression on me, and, being a technician, I could no
longer be involved in a contemplative activity like literature"
(Inozemtseva, "Platonov v Voronezhe," p. 100). He may have
been influenced in his decision by the *Proletkul't* poet Gastev's
similar rejection of literature in favor of praxis, and by the
doctrine of "*zhiznestroenie*" ("life-building") championed by
LEF, which placed actual labor above literary creativity and
with which we know Platonov to have sympathized (Langerak,
"Platonov v Voronezhe," p. 454, 456–57). Though Platonov
was eventually to make the reverse transition, abandoning land
reclamation in favor of the "contemplative activity" of
literature, he began with equal intensity the careers of both
writer and engineer, and in the early years the choice between
the two was not a foregone conclusion. The influence of his
technical profession appears in his fiction's enduring concern
with desires to reshape – or, later, the failure of efforts to
reshape – the physical world.

From 1924–1925, then, Platonov produced almost no articles or literary works, but became a central figure in efforts to improve the Voronezh countryside.[10] His accomplishments in this line were considerable – according to a certificate issued him by the Voronezh *Gubzemuprav* he had, by the spring of 1926, managed to dig 763 ponds and 331 wells, in addition to draining 7,600 desiatins (roughly 2,400 acres) of swampland. But his labors were to prove equally important for their contribution to his subsequent literary works, which frequently depict excavation and irrigation projects and elevate such things as water, dams, whirlpools, alluvial silt, and the like into metaphoric symbols.[11]

For reasons which remain unclear, in the spring of 1926 Platonov left his post as land reclamation engineer in Voronezh in order to move to Moscow and undertake what turned out to be a brief tenure at *Vserabotzemles*, the central agency for land reclamation efforts.[12] In a letter written to Voronskii in the summer of that year he claims to be temporarily unemployed, but by autumn we know that he was working for the People's Commissariat for Agriculture (*Narkomat zemledeliia*), which soon dispatched him to oversee projects in Tambov. There, from December 1926 to March 1927 he headed the land reclamation subsection of that city's regional agricultural bureau (*Gubzemuprav*).[13] Following this interlude of work at the national and provincial levels, however, Platonov abandoned his technical vocation altogether and moved in the spring of 1927 to Moscow, where, with the exception of some work for the Chamber of Measures and Weights (*Rosmetroves*), he remained as a professional writer to the end of his life.[14]

This transitional period, in which Platonov finally exchanged his career as engineer for that as writer, has been seen by many as marking a radical realignment in his world view. In this version of his life, Platonov, following his exposure to the realities of Soviet power and the difficulty of transforming the countryside, rejected the *Proletkul't*-inspired utopianism of his Voronezh period in favor of a more complex and skeptical vision of things.[15] This notion of an abrupt *volte-face*, however, oversimplifies our understanding of Platonov's thought in both the early and the later stages of his career. As will be seen, the

ambiguities apparent even in the early articles – their intima-
tions of cosmic catastrophe, of the failure of utopian schemes, of
man's ultimate weakness before the forces of nature – make it
difficult to speak of Platonov as ever having subscribed to an
undiluted utopianism. Nor did the idea of a utopian solution to
the dilemmas of man's existence cease to hold attraction for
Platonov after 1927 – on the contrary, both the lure of utopia
and the conception of it in terms deriving from the immediate
post-revolutionary period persist into his later works, if in more
complicated form.

Nonetheless, it is clear that in the works written during and
after 1926 hesitations regarding the possibilities for utopia's
realization assume a more prominent role, and that these
hesitations were, if not engendered, then at least intensified
during Platonov's difficult sojourn in Tambov. The months he
spent there turned into a nightmare combining intense
loneliness for his family, the need to take on daunting technical
projects with only meager resources at his disposal, and the
petty intrigues of local bureaucrats resentful of the "Moscow
big shot" sent to oversee their affairs.[16] Not surprisingly, in
Platonov's letters to his wife Tambov begins to assume mythic
proportions. It is his "exile," a "nightmare" (Platonova,
"Zhivia glavnoi zhizn'iu," p. 164), and a "Gogolian province"
(167; here one discerns the beginnings of the satire on
provincial life contained in "Gorod Gradov"). Returning from
an expedition to survey land reclamation projects in the region
he writes Mariia Aleksandrovna, "Once again I am overcome
with melancholy (*toska*), once again I am in 'Tambov,' which
in the future will become for me some kind of symbol, like a
difficult dream in a deep Tambov night, dispersed in the
morning by the hope of seeing you." (165)

The letters from Tambov furthermore record Platonov's
struggle with his identity as a writer. In his summer 1926 letter
to Voronskii he was to claim that writing had in fact always
been more important to him than his work as an engineer: "In
terms of quantity I write and think even more [than all he
did in land reclamation], and have done so for an even longer
period of time – it's the essential thing for me, a part of my

body (*osnovnoe i telesnoe*)."[17] But if it is characteristic for Platonov to identify the "most essential" thing with corporeality, it is equally characteristic that he associates it with experiences of tribulation, even of agony. Platonov proclaims his willingness to endure the hardships of Tambov as a kind of martyrdom dictated by the fact that "everything good and priceless (literature, love, a genuine idea) arises on the basis of suffering and loneliness" (165); but at the same time his Tambov experiences appear to be leading him toward an identification of that suffering with art's content. "My trip around the region was very difficult," he writes in one letter. "Life's harder than could be imagined... Wandering these backwaters I've seen such dreary things that it was hard for me to believe that somewhere there exist Moscow, art, and prose. But it seems to me that *genuine art and thought in fact can only appear in such a backwater*" (167; emphasis added).

The letters moreover reveal that Tambov had placed Platonov's urge to write in a complex relation with the role he felt he should play within society. "Sometimes it seems to me I have no social future, only a future meaningful to me alone," he writes at what seems to have been the nadir of his despair, and remarks that when "things are awful" at work he feels left "alone with my soul and my old tormenting thoughts" (165). In one of his most intriguing autocommentaries, he formulates this alienation as the need to adulterate the writing itself.

I will not be a professional writer (*literatorom*) if I expound only my own unchanged ideas. Nobody will read me. I *have to* vulgarize and vary my thoughts in order to produce works that are acceptable... If I were to put into my works the real blood of my brain, nobody would read them... My true self I have never shown to anyone, and probably never will. For this there are many serious reasons, but the chief one is that nobody really needs me (166).

Out of such anxieties, however, were born a remarkable number of works that established Platonov as an emerging writer of national importance. In 1926 alone he wrote "Ivan Zhokh," "Epifanskie shliuzy," "Iamskaia sloboda," and "Gorod Gradov" and began work on "Efirnyi trakt". He published works probably written or begun earlier, such as "O

potukhshei lampe Il'icha" and "Lunnaia bomba"; gathered
together and edited various early and current works for the
collection *Epifanskie shliuzy*; prepared forty of his poems for a
collection which never came out; and wrote but was unable to
publish "Rodina elektrichestva" and "Antiseksus". It was
apparently in this period as well that he began work on
*Chevengur*.[18]

Though Voronskii declined to publish what Platonov had
sent him, Platonov was able on returning to the capital in 1927
to enlist the help of acquaintances from his Voronezh days in
breaking into prestigious "central" journals and publishing
houses.[19] The response to his first volume of stories, *Epifanskie
shliuzy*, was modest (the collection drew only three reviews), but
Gor'kii liked it and in letters of 1927–1928 recommends it to
several correspondents, listing Platonov among the most
promising new writers.[20] To be so recognized by the doyen of
Soviet letters was a mark of having arrived, and together with
Voronskii's eventual sponsorship would seem to explain the
dramatic rise in Platonov's literary fortunes in the late 1920s.
By 1928 he was to add to *Molodaia gvardiia* (which had brought
out *Epifanskie shliuzy*) such prestigious venues as *Krasnaia nov'*
("Proiskhozhdenie mastera"; despite the fact that Voronskii
was effectively no longer the journal's editor, and that
publication of this fragment of *Chevengur* was a compromise
forced on Platonov by the novel's rejection as a whole) and
*Novyi mir* ("Prikliuchenie," another fragment from the novel,
and the satirical sketch "Che-Che-O").

1928 was also the year of Platonov's short-lived but
consequential collaboration with Boris Pil'niak, a writer whose
innovations in matters of form and style affected nearly every
Soviet writer of prose in the 1920s (though Gor'kii certainly
exaggerates when in a letter written in the early thirties he calls
Platonov a "talented writer, but one ruined by the influence of
Pil'niak and by collaboration with him"). Moreover, Pil'niak
himself came under the reciprocal influence of Platonov's works
– especially *Chevengur*, the manuscript for which he almost
certainly would have read during this period.[21] There is
evidence to suggest Platonov lived for a time with Pil'niak in

Iamskoe Pole near Moscow, and on assignment from *Novyi mir* the two of them visited Voronezh and co-authored the satirical sketch "Che-Che-O" (whose title is the local dialectical pronunciation of the acronym for Central Black-Earth Region, of which Voronezh had just been made center).[22] By autumn Platonov and Pil'niak had also completed a satirical play entitled "Duraki na periferii" (which remains unpublished).[23] Their collaborative efforts came to an end, however, and the sordid history of hostility toward Platonov began, when the ultra-left Russian Association of Proletarian Writers (RAPP) mounted its 1929 campaign against Pil'niak and the Leningrad writer Evgenii Zamiatin. Platonov was accused during the campaign of the inevitable sin of "falling under Pil'niak's influence" (*podpil'niachestvo*), most probably for "Che-Che-O," though he claimed that he was the offending piece's true author and that Pil'niak had only supplied editorial advice.[24] Still more ominously, Platonov's only complete novel, *Chevengur*, soon ran into difficulties of its own – either as the direct result of these attacks, or more generally due to the deteriorating political climate of the late 1920s. The novel was to have been published in 1929 by Federatsiia and had already been typeset when in the summer printing was suddenly suspended. Platonov's subsequent efforts to have the novel published proved fruitless.

The truly debilitating blow in this mounting campaign against Platonov, however, came just after the publication, in *Krasnaia nov'* in 1931, of "Vprok," a largely satirical portrayal of efforts to collectivize the Russian countryside (Platonov based the work on his own visit to the Volga region in 1930; see "'...Ia derzhalsia i rabotal'," p. 105). The tale drew vituperative attacks from Fadeev, Averbakh, and other lights of RAPP, who accused Platonov of nothing less than disseminating kulak ideology (critics also used the occasion to condemn the satirical "Usomnivshiisia Makar," which had appeared in *Oktiabr'* in 1929). According to legend "Vprok" drew an expletive even from Stalin himself.[25] The result of these attacks was a three-year period of silence, from 1931 to 1934, in which "Platonov was cut off from publication – abruptly" ("*Plato-*

*nova perestali pechatat' – naotmash'* ").[26] This silence was by no means the result of resignation on Platonov's part. On the contrary he made considerable efforts to see extant manuscripts into print and to produce works more amenable to the political climate of the first Five-Year Plan (perhaps such adaptation appeared inevitable to a writer who already regarded his published works as the products of "vulgarization"). In 1933 he wrote Gor'kii to request a meeting in which they would discuss "whether I can be a Soviet writer or whether this is objectively impossible" and to express his desire to write something about either the White Sea or the Moscow–Volga canal project (Gor'kii had recently complained in print about the lack of writers interested in studying the socialist construction then underway). Gor'kii never wrote back, and the response of Soviet officialdom to Platonov's plight was to search his rooms and remove the manuscripts on which he had been working.[27] As one scholar points out, one of the ironies of Platonov's position in this period was that he sincerely wanted to participate in the culture of the Five-Year Plan, indeed pleaded to be allowed to do so, but was prohibited.[28]

Platonov was finally admitted back into print in 1934 with the story "Takyr," which he wrote as a contribution to a volume commemorating the tenth anniversary of Turkmenia's entry into the Soviet Union (Platonov had traveled there in 1933–1934 as part of a "brigade" sent by the Writers' Union). In aesthetic terms, however, it is questionable whether this was the same Platonov who had written a series of innovative masterpieces only a few years earlier. It is not that Platonov capitulated and began to write conventional Stalinist prose – even in this adaptationist phase he remained something of a marginal figure and his works continued to draw the hostility of orthodox critics – but there is a distinct discontinuity between the pre- and post-1934 oeuvre. Removed from the later works is all trace of satire, grotesquerie, and surrealism, as well as the egregious deformations of the language which had become the hallmark of his literary style. The shape of the oeuvre also changes after 1934. Even after he was readmitted into print Platonov's literary output remained small (in the thirties, a handful of stories and one collection in book form, *Reka Potudan'*), but this was compensated for by a diversion of his talent into subsidiary channels (as a "professional" writer Platonov and his family depended solely on the income derived from such output). From 1937 onwards he contributed critical essays to *Literaturnyi kritik* and other journals (many of which have been collected in *Razmyshleniia chitatelia*) and worked as literary consultant for such periodicals as *Krasnaia nov'*, *Oktiabr'*, and even *Izvestiia* (Chalmaev, *Andrei Platonov* [1984 Voronezh edition], p. 144).

Like many other Soviet writers, Platonov was allowed to publish considerably more during the war (principally in the genre of stories about the bravery of Russian soldiers and the hardy survival of peasants on the home front), and after a brief evacuation he found work as a front-line correspondent for *Krasnaia zvezda*, attaining by 1944 the rank of "Major of Administrative Service" (Vasil'ev, *Andrei Platonov*, p. 225). In the post-war climate of Zhdanovism, however, he again fell into disfavor. "Dve kroshki," a folkloric children's parable published in 1948 and quickly denounced as "cheap pacifism," was the last original literary work published in his lifetime, and he was again forced to turn to other genres (primarily retellings of Russian and Bashkir folktales, the latter work reputedly won for him by Sholokhov). Though he had himself escaped the purges, Platonov's later years were nonetheless marked by personal tragedy stemming from the Terror. In 1938 his son Platon was arrested for alleged leadership of an "anti-soviet youth terrrorist and spy-saboteur organization," and was released from the camps only during the war and through Sholokhov's intercession.[29] He returned infected with tuberculosis, from which he died on 4 January 1943 – having infected his father. Platonov struggled against the disease for the remainder of the 1940s, but died on 5 January 1951.[30] Only in 1958, with the publication of a slim volume of selected works, did the initial, reluctant rehabilitation of his reputation get underway.

The vagaries of Platonov's biography find reflection, in

commentary on his works, in a series of disparate assessments
whose contradictions testify as much to the complexity of the
oeuvre as to the inevitable pluralism of readerly reception. In
effect we have several critical versions of Platonov. Virtually all
of them acknowledge his status as one of the most important
Russian writers of the Soviet era, and among them one finds
many points of agreement about Platonov's principal themes,
the literary and intellectual influences on his works, and the
merits of his "unique" verbal style. Nonetheless Platonov
criticism as a whole has been divided by interpretive
contradictions which extend beyond the expected differences
between, say, orthodox Soviet views of the Brezhnev era and
those offered by westerners and émigrés. The nature of
Platonov's verbal art is itself under contention, with the result
that Platonov is spoken of in an array of critical, intellectual,
and aesthetic contexts which one would be hard put to
reconcile to one another or to attribute to ideological differences
alone.

To begin near one of this field's extremes, Joseph Brodsky,
who has been one of the most articulate encomiasts of
Platonov's significance for Soviet and world literature, places
Platonov fully in a modernist fold of Joyce, Musil, and Kafka;
he claims that one is restrained from saying that Platonov is
greater than this cohort only because "on those heights there is
no hierarchy."[31] For Brodsky Platonov is Providence's singular
gift to Russian prose of this century, the modernist standard
against which other writers must measure themselves, and in
this sense his country's equivalent of Beckett ("...it's still a little
bit more forgiveable for Russian writers to operate the way they
do, with Platonov dead, than for their counterparts in this
country to court banalities, with Beckett alive," "Catastrophes", p. 303).

It is thus symptomatic that Brodsky most closely identifies
Platonov with *Chevengur* and *Kotlovan*, the least conventional
and most formally ambitious of his works, and the ones most
illustrative of the eccentric poetic he had developed by the late
twenties. The oddities of character depiction in these works and
the absurdity of the events they portray allow us to call

Platonov "our [i.e., Russia's] first surrealist writer" (289), but
for Brodsky Platonov's modernist essence is most fully embodied
in his texts' self-conscious preoccupation with the Russian
language. "Reading Platonov," Brodsky asserts, "one gets a
sense of the relentless, implacable absurdity built into the
language and that with each new – anyone's – utterance, that
absurdity deepens. And that there is no way out of that blind
alley but to retreat back into the very language that brought
one in" (287). In the end, this verbal experience supersedes
both the anti-Soviet satire and the surrealist vision with which
one is initially struck in works like *Chevengur* and *Kotlovan*.

For these books are indescribable. The power of devastation they
inflict upon their subject matter exceeds by far any demands of social
criticism and should be measured in units that have very little to do
with literature as such...The whole point about Andrei Platonov is
that he attacks the very carrier of millenarian sensibility in Russian
society: the language itself – or, to put it in more graspable fashion,
the revolutionary eschatology embedded in the language (283).

One gains a very different sense of "the point about Andrei
Platonov" from most Soviet studies of his works, including
many of those produced under the liberal conditions of *glasnost'*.
These studies not surprisingly tend to view him as a particular
kind of realist (indeed, for critics of the Brezhnev era, a Socialist
Realist), and so impute to his works a more or less direct
mimetic concern with social and historical context and a
psychologism of character portrayal that functions as that
context's reflection. A frequent habit of such accounts is to
present Platonov as something of a populist writer who
reproduces the thoughts and feelings of semi-literate workers
and peasants out of a fundamental concern with the Russian
people's response to the Revolution. "The Revolution in his
understanding," asserts L. Shubin, "is a deeply popular
(*narodnyi*), organic, and creative process which introduces
reason and beauty into man's relations with the 'fierce and
beautiful world'."[32] In the more orthodox criticism such
assumptions lead to characterizations of Platonov as a standard
bearer for the values of a certain Soviet "humanism" and
panegyrist of the Soviet worker. Chalmaev, for example, speaks

of Platonov's "enormous humanistic gift" (1984 Voronezh
edition, p. 4), while Zalygin claims that Platonov's heroes are
"before all else inhabitants of this world, its workers, most
typically talented workers inspired by their craft, which appears
uncomplicated and simple but at the same time seriously
transforms the world."[33]

The hermeneutical assumptions of such a reading are not,
however, limited to this type of Soviet critic, whom it is perhaps
pointless to take to task since such statements may have less to
do with actual beliefs than with efforts to rehabilitate Platonov
(specifically, by demonstrating how many of the stock themes
of Soviet literary criticism can be shown to apply to him).
Many western studies of Platonov, and even some that have
appeared in the Soviet Union since the advent of *glasnost'*,
assert the same principle of mimeticism in Platonov. Mikhail
Geller's *Andrei Platonov v poiskakh schast'ia* (Paris, 1982), for
example, treats Platonov in essentially the same manner as its
Soviet counterparts by characterizing his works as both an
autobiographical account of disaffection with Stalinism and a
chronicle of the horrible failure of utopia endured by the Soviet
people. The assumption of "realism" also underlies the
conventional western view of Platonov as a social and political
satirist. One standard study of Soviet literature, for example,
speaks of Platonov as having gotten into trouble for providing
"honest, desolating, and at the same time stunningly beautiful
pictures of peasant [*sic*] life."[34] What is perhaps most
consequential for the way this approach defines Platonov's art
is its tendency to subsume his works' manifest eccentricities –
which it would be impossible for any critical account to ignore
– within a larger mimetic project. Thus Geller claims the
unconventional or "distorting" aspects of Platonov's texts
derive, not from any intrinsic poetic principle, but from the fact
that those works portray a "realistic and for that reason
fantastic world" (270). Yet to shift the strangeness of Platonov's
fiction from the text to the world it "faithfully" portrays is, in
the end, to abdicate the task of analyzing his world view,
particularly in its relation to his poetic, and more importantly
to suggest that Platonov regards the grotesqueries he portrays

as aberrations in what is otherwise, or ought to be, a rational and moral world – a questionable reading of these often philosophically despairing works.

In contrast to this tendency to reduce Platonov to a mere chronicler of his age, a number of recent studies have uncovered a complex, intertextually allusive thematics in Platonov's works that testifies to his sophistication and aesthetic self-consciousness. The émigré scholar Elena Tolstaia-Segal, for example, has excavated a series of intellectual influences on Platonov, ranging from the already well-attested borrowings from Fedorov and Bogdanov to such exotic figures as Gurdzhiev and Uspenskii. Her findings suggest Platonov's works are far more esoteric than a realist or even satirist reading of him might imply, and intriguingly complicate our picture of a writer who in many other respects remained a cultural provincial.[35] The appearance of formal naivety in Platonov's works, which tends to reinforce an impression of him as a literary autodidact, has come under similar attack in other recent studies demonstrating Platonov's intricate, "dialogizing" allusions to and stylizations of other writers (primarily but not exclusively Soviet).[36]

Commentary on Platonov is thus beset with uncertainty over exactly what sort of literary phenomenon his works represent. To a reader impressed with Platonov's odd complexity a definition like Brodsky's has the appeal of designating him a "difficult," esoteric writer, one whose works invite the application of a sophisticated methodology and in the intricacies of whose texts might be discovered the paradigms for a broader set of epistemological concerns (as Brodsky indeed does; a post-structuralist reading would be only the most extreme such example). Yet a uniformly (post-)modernist reading of Platonov immediately begs qualification. There is, for example, the undeniable, "realist" interest of Platonov's major works in the Soviet historical experience, particularly the events of the Revolution, Civil War, and first Five-Year Plan. Nor is the oeuvre itself by any means consistently of an esoteric cast. In addition to the strikingly experimental works of the late twenties and early thirties on which Brodsky focuses (and on

which most of Platonov's reputation rests) there are both the
derivative early stories and poems, and the later, distinctly
conformist, "Socialist Realist" works of the thirties and forties
– so that in celebrating an exclusively "modernist" Platonov
one risks denigrating or even ignoring a significant number of
his works.

Indeed, the nature of even the most "modernist" moments
in Platonov is itself problematic. Platonov's claim to modernist
qualities rests principally on the striking deformations to which
he subjects the Russian language (in works of roughly the mid
1920s to the early 1930s), and on the fact that he does so in the
course of narrating a series of often bizarre events within a
loose, anti-novelistic form. But Platonov hardly qualifies as a
modernist in the effete, aestheticist sense that applies to a Joyce,
a Belyi, or even a Khlebnikov (he was, after all, a writer of
genuinely proletarian origins from an inauspicious cultural
background – a fact of which he was himself keenly aware) and
there is little in his works to suggest that their verbal
peculiarities arise out of a self-conscious, *avant-gardiste* assault on
linguistic and artistic convention. His is rather a kind of *de facto*
modernism developed, at a remove from the centers of Russian
modernist culture, out of the satirical-grotesque tradition of
Gogol', Leskov, and Saltykov-Shchedrin and emphatically
preserving the "crude" perspective of the semi-literate provincial masses (in this he somewhat resembles Zoshchenko,
though there are important differences between the two). If
they resemble anything in the modernist canon, Platonov's
works are closer to the distortions and formal violence of
Picasso's *Les Desmoiselles d'Avignon* or, to draw the parallel
within Platonov's own culture, the primitivism of Larionov's
imitations of peasant woodcuts (like Larionov's paintings,
Platonov's works present themselves as the products of their
own, distortingly portrayed figures).[37] But even here the
divergent aims of Platonov's deformations and those of
modernism as we generally understand it must be taken into
account.

So, too, should the "philosophical" content of Platonov's
works be understood, at least initially, apart from any

abstractly "modern" cast of mind. From the outset of his career Platonov's works display a concern with the nature of man's existence as such which appears to anticipate European existentialism. The sense of alienation from their own existence (especially their corporeal existence) which chronically besets Platonov's heroes thus calls to mind the metaphysical anguishings of Roquentin in Sartre's *La Nausée*, whose being also enjoys only a contingent relation with the body it inhabits; or of Rilke, whose *Duino Elegies* have been described as preoccupied with the question of "how to discover the meaning of the body and of the physical world."[38] Platonov's preoccupation with man's origins in the "base" matter of the world can similarly remind us of the early essays of Georges Bataille (one often thinks of Platonov while reading, say, "The Language of Flowers," "The Solar Anus," or "The Pineal Eye"). In Platonov's works, however, these issues arise out of a very different, Russian tradition conveyed to him primarily through the philosophies of Nikolai Fedorov and Aleksandr Bogdanov, and they are shaped in fundamental ways by his sustained and earnest, if also ultimately parodic, dialogue with Soviet materialism.

To be aware of the above concerns is to realize how difficult it is to write about Platonov's texts (which is not to exculpate the shortcomings of the present study). Those texts lend themselves so fitfully to standard commentary because the elements of their thematic mythology are neither embedded in the psychological and sociological causalities of the conventional realist novel, nor yet suspended in the self-consciously arbitrary practices of a more centrally modernist text. Hence the division of much Platonov criticism into conventionalizing treatments, which diminish his peculiarities but by doing so diminish his innovations as well, and those that take his peculiarities as their starting point, only to be drawn either toward schematizing overview (which risks doing violence to the particularities of the texts) or to lengthy quotation, as though that were the only means for conveying what is there (a practice in which those writing in Russian are at an enviable advantage). In the present study I have attempted to avoid

some of these pitfalls in the course of examining what I consider
the important connections between Platonov's "philosophical"
themes, his relation to Soviet ideology and literature, and his
use of language. Because of my interest in Platonov's verbal
style – which I regard as his major achievement – my account
is admittedly biased toward the longer works of the late
twenties and early thirties (especially *Chevengur* and *Kotlovan*, to
each of which I have devoted a separate chapter). I have also,
however, sought to trace the evolution of Platonov's poetic in
his earliest works and to illuminate some of the important
transformations observable in the later works.

As several scholars have shown, Platonov was receptive to a
wide range of philosophical influences. Two thinkers, however,
influenced him so extensively that a discussion of their ideas is
essential to an understanding of his works. The first is N. F.
Fedorov (1828–1903), an eccentric ascetic who for many years
worked as a cataloguer in the library of the Rumiantsev
museum (now the Lenin Library) and whose blend of positivist
faith in the powers of science with the eschatological yearnings
of Russian religious thought attracted a variety of Russian
writers and thinkers from Dostoevsky and Solov'ev to Bogdanov, Maiakovskii, and Zabolotskii. It is not clear when
Platonov first discovered Fedorov, but by the mid twenties at
the latest his works begin to display characteristic constellations
of Fedorovian ideas and terminology, and his widow later
testified that Fedorov's *Philosophy of the Common Cause* (*Filosofiia
obshchego dela*, 1903, 1913) had for years been Platonov's
favorite book.[39]

Though Fedorov is primarily remembered for his utopian
social philosophy, with its resonances of older Slavophile
notions of *sobornost'*, his influence on Platonov had more to do
with the ontological concepts that accompanied his vision of
social organization. Fedorov begins with the assumption that
the key to understanding man's existence on earth lies in
physical death – for him the one experience common to the
whole of mankind and the sole idea universal to philosophy.
This focus on human mortality then leads him to dualist

conclusions about the nature of the cosmos (a feature of his thought absorbed by Platonov as well). For Fedorov the contradiction between the fact that man possesses physical being and the fact that this being is routinely extinguished by nature itself signals an essential imperfection in the created world. He termed this condition "*nerodstvennost'*," the "un-native" relation of the cosmos to the living beings that inhabit it (a section of his *Philosophy of the Common Cause* is headed by the question, "Why is nature not a mother to us but a step-mother or a wet-nurse who has refused to feed us?"), and traced man's realization of it to the moment when his evolutionary ancestor separated himself from unconscious nature and gained a sense of his own selfhood by standing erect – only to realize his defenselessness before the world around him.

For Fedorov this condition is at once ontological and moral, and visits its principal tragedy upon mankind in the form of social divisions (in his term, "unbrotherly" relations, whose source in a dualistic vision he underscores by citing "the hateful divisiveness of the world and all the sorrows which arise from it"). These divisions ultimately derive from the severance of mankind's links with its ancestral origins, which in Fedorov's thought represent something of an absolute form of ontological security and moral meaning (notions heavily indebted to prechristian Slavic myths of *rod*). All men are brothers, according to Fedorov, because they descend from a single "original father" of the race (*praotets*). But death and entropy have sundered these bonds, leading men to "forget" their ancestors and to live in isolation from one another, each conscious of himself only as a "wanderer in a crowd, oblivious to his native origins" (*nepomniashchii rodstva*, one of the frequent Fedorovian echoes in Platonov's works). In this state man is incapable of undertaking the salvation of the race from the "blind forces" of nature and will be able to do so only when he becomes aware of himself as "the son of all deceased fathers." An important step toward that awareness, and another of Fedorov's prominent influences on Platonov, lies in the rejection of the sexual drive and procreation, which only perpetuate the rule of death and foster an addiction to progress that encourages the younger generation to forget its forebears. Once the procreative cycle has been broken the way will be clear to undertake the "Common Cause" to which Fedorov devotes his *magnum opus*: the unification of men for the purpose of literally resurrecting their ancestors from the dead. "Until men are unified in the common task of transforming the death-bearing force into a life-bearing one," Fedorov warns, "man will remain subordinate to the blind natural force in the manner of cattle, beasts, and soulless matter."

Like his near contemporary Marx, Fedorov was discontented with the proposition that philosophy should merely contemplate rather than change the world, and intended much of his writing as a sort of prospectus for achieving social reunification and the resurrection of the dead. Hence his ethical imperative that men establish "brotherly relations" finds its practical counterpart in a series of projects for remaking the physical world. Extrapolating, often fantastically, from the scientific and technical achievements of his day (and imbued with its positivist spirit), Fedorov suggests that men learn how to control the climate in order to "ventilate and irrigate" the earth. In this he is particularly encouraged by some American experiments that had produced rain by sending explosive devices into the atmosphere. He argues that new sources of energy should be harnessed, particularly that of the sun, and that man is destined to go forth into the cosmos to colonize the planets of the solar system and appropriate their resources (an idea that influenced the father of Soviet rocketry, Konstantin Tsiolkovskii). Fedorov even proposes that men learn how to "steer" the "ship" of earth on which they are passengers in cosmic space.

This program of "practical" feats appears to have exerted a particular attraction on Platonov in the early twenties, when he worked as a land reclamation engineer in the Voronezh countryside and wrote a series of articles calling on Soviet science to learn how to seed clouds and blow open passageways in the Urals (to warm Siberia) and hypothesizing on how light might be harnessed to supply an inexhaustible energy source to Soviet factories. To be sure, there were other influences in this regard, such as the *Proletkul't* movement with which Platonov for a time closely identified himself and the general utopianism of Soviet efforts to electrify and industrialize the country. Yet Fedorov is not irrelevant to these other doctrines of utopian praxis. The *Proletkul't* movement was heavily indebted to Fedorovian ideas, and no less a figure than Gor'kii declared Fedorov's project for the "regulation of nature" to be close in spirit to the "socialist pathos" of Soviet efforts to "subordinate all the energies of nature to the interests of the working class."[40] In prolifically borrowing from Fedorov's ideas, then, Platonov was not merely cultivating an esoteric interest but responding to one of the mainsprings of early Soviet culture.

However, for all the importance to Platonov's thought of Fedorov's utopian themes (brotherhood, father veneration, anti-procreation, the transformation of the physical world), it may be argued that the Russian philosopher's most significant transmission to the Soviet writer was the peculiar set of assumptions underlying his philosophical project as a whole. These assumptions are exemplified in Fedorov's notion of how, exactly, the resurrection of the dead would be accomplished. Fedorov believed the literal resurrection of the body would be possible once science had mastered all the mysteries of man's physical and metaphysical being. Following preparatory work on the creation of a "new" body, in which an encyclopedic knowledge of all the "metamorphoses of matter" would enable man to replace his ailing parts with prosthetic organs, science would master the technique of reviving the recently deceased. It would then work toward the utopian goal of venturing forth into the cosmos to collect all the atoms of the dispersed "dust" of the ancestors, reassemble them in their original form and *in so doing* cause those ancestors to be resurrected.

It is this yoking of positivism to an eschatological vision that defines the peculiar nature of Fedorov's philosophy. Something of a materialist bias is already apparent in Fedorov's preoccupation with mortality, since it is from the physical experiences of the body that all his other insights derive. But the notion of resurrecting "being" by recreating its physical form foregrounds the "vulgar" materialism of Fedorov's thought:

the belief that an act performed on matter can directly cause
the restoration of spirit. The human organism is a "machine,"
he puts it in one passage, and "consciousness is related to it as
bile to the liver; assemble the machine, and consciousness will
return to it!" What makes such a belief contradictory is that it
hopes to derive a distinctly spiritual good from being's
dependence on its material vessel (the overcoming of death is
imagined as the rescuing of spirit from matter's domination,
just as the unification of mankind in a single community is
envisioned as restoring the moral and spiritual values lost to the
workings of entropy). In other words Fedorov paradoxically
seeks assurance for the restoration of spirit in an opposing
doctrine of material determinism. As this study will show, a
similar paradox was to inform Platonov's own understanding of
the aims and means of utopia and to place that understanding
in a complex relation to the professed "materialism" of the
Soviet state. What should be pointed out for now is that the
tensions Platonov inherits from Fedorov's thought inevitably
make his own response to Soviet ideology something more
hybrid and contradictory than a simple idealist critique of
materialism.

Aleksandr Bogdanov (A. A. Malinovskii, 1873–1928), the
second major influence on the formation of Platonov's world
view, belongs to the current of Marxist thought that arose in
Russia in the late nineteenth and early twentieth centuries,
though his attempts to blend Marxism with neopositivism
earned him a reputation as a revisionist and a scathing attack
in Lenin's *Materialism and Empiriocriticism*.[41] Prior to 1909
Bogdanov had been, after Lenin, the second most prominent
figure in the Bolshevik Party, and he became one of the guiding
lights of the *Proletkul't* movement which flourished briefly from
about 1917–1920. Platonov knew him primarily as a theoretician of proletarian culture (he repeatedly paraphrases
Bogdanovian tenets in his articles of the early twenties), and as
the author of the science fiction novel *Red Star*, elements of
which show up in Platonov's own science fiction of the 1920s.
As in the case of Fedorov, however, Bogdanov's influence on

Platonov runs deeper than the series of proclamations about the millenarial future of the proletariat or visions of a utopian society on Mars. What Platonov was to absorb through his exposure to *Proletkul't* ideas was something of Bogdanov's complicated posture, contaminated with idealist leanings, toward a specifically Marxist form of materialism. Though nominally a Marxist, Bogdanov sought to "develop" Marxist theory by providing it with a greater emphasis on epistemology and the problems of being than on the political and economic phenomena central to the philosophy's more orthodox forms. He did so, moreover, in a manner that calls into doubt his allegiance to materialist philosophy in general. What this fertile mélange allowed Platonov to do, with even more specific reference to his culture than that afforded by Fedorov's thought, was to preserve the political and economic vocabulary of Marxism and remain within the context of an at least nominally Marxist vision of history while adhering to a vision of being which was contradictory to, and in the end even seditious of, materialism.

Bogdanov's philosophy originates in an epistemological effort to overcome the dualism of spirit and matter by discovering within human experience the ground for a unitary theory of being. He termed his solution "empiriomonism" and drew many of its basic notions from the "empiriocriticism" of Mach and Avenarius, though he claimed to have transcended that doctrine's lingering dualist assumptions. What philosophical convention regards as the discontinuous realms of matter and idea, he argued, in fact merely represent different aspects of man's experience of the world; their essence is the same. That experience accessible to the individual, and corresponding to the traditional category of idea, he termed "psychical," while "matter" in his definition was merely that "physical" form of experience accessible to the collective and constituted merely the sum of individual "psychical" experiences. The psychical and physical represented only different organizational levels, not different kinds of experience. Matter and idea thus turn out to be, not essences, but attributes of human subjectivity.

These ideas placed Bogdanov in an understandably problematic relation to Marxist thought. On the one hand he praised what he saw as Marx's insistence on the collective efforts of the proletariat to change the world and presented himself as an heir to the philosophical revolution it had begun. But he countered Marx's dictum that "social being determines social consciousness" with the claim that "social existence and social consciousness in the exact meaning of these words are identical." He even went so far along this epistemological line as to deny the existence of a reality independent of the (individual or collective) mind of man. "The objective or physical has no existence apart from man," but is the product of the collective consciousness of mankind, he claimed, and elsewhere stated that the physical world was nothing more than "socially organized experience." Bogdanov pointedly declared that by such "experience" he did not mean merely subjective sense perception alone, and criticized epistemological solipsism for envisioning man in isolation from the realm of nature and passive before it. But the radically subjectivist leanings of his epistemology remain clear, and for Lenin amounted to nothing less than a covert form of idealism that could be traced back through the insidiously agnostic, Humean tendencies of Mach's thought to that lamentable half of Kant which expressed skepticism over the possibility of knowing the thing-in-itself. "To think that philosophical Idealism disappears if the consciousness of the individual is replaced by that of mankind, or the experience of one person by that of socially organized experience," he taunted, "is like thinking that capitalism disappears if one capitalist is replaced by a joint-stock company."[42]

The sources of this paradox lie in Bogdanov's importation of contaminating ethical concerns, which make his philosophy, like that of Fedorov, a peculiar hybrid of epistemological and eschatological goals. The ethical strain may already be discerned in his critique of the "fetishism" with which both materialism and idealism interpret matter and idea as things-in-themselves, in the course of which he shifts to distinctly subjectivist grounds by redefining nature, not as a "kingdom of matter," but as the "field of human labor" (matter is not an essence, he asserts, but the "resistance" presented by the world to human activity, while being is correspondingly defined as "labor" against the world). The ethical concern asserts itself most emphatically, however, in Bodganov's vision of history as the gradual overcoming of "resistance" by "labor," to be culminated in the proletarian attainment of the "organization of living experience" – a fusion of epistemological knowledge and praxis in which the realization that the "psychic" and "physical" levels of reality have a unitary ground will enable that reality's restructuring according to human needs.[43] The struggles and fragmentations Bogdanov ascribes to history are thus but the tragic antecedent to sentient being's triumph over the world, and his anti-dualist epistemology turns out to have been imported essentially as a guarantee that this event will take place. The curious achievement of Bogdanov's philosophy, which was to attract Platonov even as it infuriated Lenin, was that it thus insinuates the aims of an idealist eschatology into a "labor world view" that Bogdanov insisted was but a variant of Marxist historical materialism. More than anything, it was a schooling in this felicitous double sense that Bogdanov imposes on basic Marxist ideas, which was to prepare Platonov to interpret Soviet ideology in light of eschatological concerns.

I have discussed these two philosophies at some length because I wish not only to show that Platonov takes up some of their underlying concerns but also to suggest that the issues to which his oeuvre responds, and the manner in which it responds to them, belong to a larger tradition encompassing some of the most significant developments of fin-de-siècle and early twentieth-century Russian culture (I have in mind a period extending from roughly the 1870s to the 1920s, in which Russian culture underwent its transformation from its principal nineteenth-century forms to the at least nominal materialism of the Stalinist age). Though it would require a separate study to demonstrate this tradition's coherence, one can nonetheless note the frequency with which Russian culture in this period is preoccupied with the problem of dualism, especially that between matter and spirit (or materialist and idealist systems of thought). Moreover, instead of advancing the claims of one side

against the other, Russian thought in this period tends to be
drawn to the boundary terrain between the two, seeking to
elaborate a metaphysics in which the antinomies might be
reconciled without fully erasing the claims of either, but one
whose hybrid nature always remains clear. An impulse toward
imagining this reconciliation in eschatological or apocalyptic
terms is typical as well.

In addition to Fedorov and Bogdanov, for example, one
might cite Vladimir Solov'ev (who was apparently influenced
by Fedorov), who conceived of the present, phenomenal world
as the product of a division in the prime being of the cosmos.
Solov'ev believed the world soul had arisen at some point in the
past in rebellion against God (Absolute Spirit) and, severed
from the Absolute, had been plunged into a state of alienation
and abandonment to the realm of matter, with its law of death
and decay. Redemption from this tragic dualism was to come
about through the eschatological reconciliation of matter and
spirit in a state of "All-Unity," allegorically represented in the
marriage of Sophia (the world) to Christ (the Absolute).
Evidence of the same concerns can be found in lesser figures of
the nineteenth century as well. N. Grot, for example, abandoned his initial adherence to positivism to attempt a synthesis
of monism and dualism in a philosophy he termed "mono-
dualism," whose tenets were that God is the principle
reconciling spirit and matter, the soul of man the principle
reconciling matter and force. The historian Konstantin
Kavelin, otherwise sympathetic to positivism's attack on
metaphysics, nonetheless argued in *The Tasks of Psychology* that
"materialism and dualism are essentially belated heirs of
scholasticism that do not remember their origins and regard the
two sides of Christian dualism as absolutes" and attempted to
transcend their opposition in a doctrine asserting that mental
and physical phenomena, if not reducible to one another, at
least belong to parallel and nonantagonistic orders of man's
being.[44]

In the twentieth century the tradition I am outlining was
sustained, in addition to Bogdanov's dialogue with Marxism,
by the Symbolist redaction of Solov'ev's ideas (for example,

that movement's tragic interpretation of the rift between the immanent and transcendant realms), and in particular by Belyi, for whom the "symbol" in art was the product of that activity of the subject (consciousness) that engages the objective world, and hence represents the fusion of the two. Still closer to Platonov and his involvement with this tradition is the thought of Mikhail Bakhtin, who inhabited the same Soviet (that is, materialist) culture. Much of Bakhtin's thought may be seen as an attempt to restore to the Kantian interpretation of the relation between mind and world (or more precisely, its neo-Kantian reformulation by Cohen, Rickert, and others of the Marburg school) the importance of the immediate world which is not, and cannot, be subsumed within any individual consciousness. Hence his notion that the self/other (or mind/world) dichotomy is overcome in the self's "dialogic" *exchange* with all that is Other (other selves and the world beyond subjectivity). Of equal importance is the fact that Bakhtin elaborated these ideas – that is, restored to Cohen's version of neo-Kantianism the claims of the world beyond mind – in the context of a dialogue with Marxism, articulating his philosophy of "Answerability" midway between the extremes of materialism and idealism.[45] Moreover, as his recent biographers point out, Bakhtin's instinct for "incarnation" was strongly influenced by the kenotic tradition in Russian religious thought – perhaps the ultimate source of this tradition – which had always been fascinated "with the dialogic relationship between spirit and corporeality," and which saw the resolution of the world's ontological antinomies in the transfiguration, rather than the transcendence, of the flesh (Clark and Holquist, *Mikhail Bakhtin*, pp. 84–85).

The twentieth-century participants in this tradition, and here Platonov emphatically belongs, are furthermore joined by their tendency to project their concern with dualism to questions concerning language, and especially into the language of the literary text. If art became for many in the twentieth century the "true metaphysical activity of man" (Nietzsche), it is also the case, as Kenneth Burke has remarked, that "statements that great theologians have made about the nature of 'God' might be adapted *mutatis mutandis* for use as purely secular observations on the nature of words"; this is so, suggest Clark and Holquist, who cite Burke in their explication of Bakhtin's thought, "because the inescapable dualities of theology (man/God, spirit/matter) are at the heart of language in the duality of sign/signified" (Clark and Holquist, p. 83). Of Belyi's *Kotik Letaev*, for example, it has been asserted that "by the blurring of established distinctions between categories such as abstract and concrete, the language of [the novel] recreates a world where such distinctions do not hold."[46] The post-symbolist poetry of Pasternak similarly has as its architheme "a sense of unity induced by the sense of the pervasiveness of cosmic categories...which integrate all the orders of creation," and realizes this theme in a textual structure that "both brings out and cancels certain semantic oppositions, most notably, the opposition 'animate–inanimate'...The boundary between 'I' and 'non-I,' very pronounced within any subjectivist system, is emphatically obliterated in a Pasternak text."[47] Toward the opposite, "materialist" end of the scale one might cite the general preoccupation with "thingness" in Futurism and other representatives of the Russian avant-garde. Pil'niak's *Golyi god*, for example, has been described as an attempt to establish the "thingness" of the text itself (through the incorporation of ready-made linguistic objects, the stripping of substantives of their modifiers and the refusal to let nouns be replaced by pronouns), a project akin to the use of physical ornaments in primitive rituals in which "language is also matter. The forming to which the language is subjected brings out the material properties of the language and the phenomena at one and the same time."[48] To this category also belongs the LEF doctrine of *zhiznestroenie* (to which Platonov appears to have subscribed for a time in the early twenties), which can be interpreted as an effort to transcend art's isolation in the realm of ideas by replacing a passively mimetic art with praxis conducted in the material world.

The tradition I have attempted, however schematically, to outline here was available to Platonov in a variety of its forms: the philosophies of Fedorov and Bogdanov, which he encountered in the competing context of Soviet Marxism; the aesthetic doctrines of LEF and the aesthetic practice of the Symbolists, Futurists, and others such as Pil'niak. The point of my survey is not, however, to suggest a series of "influences" from which Platonov's works derive. Rather it is to argue, before turning to the oeuvre itself, that his works – in which, as I will claim, the prospect of a reconciliation of matter and spirit is in its own way contemplated and undermined in the language of the text, moreover in the context of a half-parodying, half-embracing rendition of Stalinist ideology – are far less "eccentric" or "unique" than is often asserted, and in fact belong to what is perhaps the most significant tendency in the Russian philosophy and art of his era.

# CHAPTER I

# Consciousness and matter: Platonov in Voronezh and Tambov (1917–1926)

The earliest years of Platonov's career (1917–1926) encompass his emergence as a provincial writer of conspicuous, if also idiosyncratic, talent, a "rare, self-made figure" (*"redkii samorodok"*), as the audience declared him following one of several "literary evenings" devoted to his poetry in the Voronezh club of the *Komsozhur* (Inozemtseva, 92). The stream of newspaper articles and essays he produced in these years belongs to the general cultural ferment of the period immediately following the October Revolution.[1] As a result many of the pieces are naively conceived and awkwardly written, and consist mainly of attempts at mixing the *Proletkul't* slogans popular at the time with his own, often quite eccentric views on the changes taking place within Russian society. They are essential, however, to our understanding of the Platonov who wrote *Chevengur*, *Kotlovan*, and "Dzhan," because for all their naive profusion they establish the paradigm of philosophical themes with which his later stories and novels preoccupy themselves. They furthermore reveal habits of thought and expression in which one can recognize the emerging contours of Platonov's literary imagination, providing a portrait *in statu nascendi* of both his world view and the poetic means through which it was expressed.[2]

The bulk of Platonov's journalism suggests that in this period he saw himself primarily as a disseminator of Bogdanov's philosophy and the tenets of the *Proletkul't*: the titles of the articles already reflect this stance (for example, "Kul'tura proletariata," "Proletarskaia poeziia," "K nachinaiushchim proletarskim poetam i pisateliam," "Normalizovannyi rabotnik"), as does his penchant for signing the articles as "rabochii A. Platonov." Perhaps the most pervasive *Proletkul't* theme in the articles is the expected one of the imminence of a genuinely proletarian form of culture, a notion which, in one form or another, exercised much of the utopian left of Soviet culture in the immediate post-revolutionary period. Platonov calls repeatedly for the establishment of a proletarian culture, prophesies its triumphant arrival, and anticipates its significance to science, technology, and the management of industrial labor.[3]

Like the adherents of *Proletkul't*, Platonov assigns to this culture the historical purpose of subordinating the physical world to the human will, treating such "mastery" over the earth even as if it were a precondition for communism. It is in this vein, moreover, that Platonov appropriates Bogdanov's philosophical terminology, with important consequences for the way in which his later fictional worlds were to be conceived. For Platonov as for Bogdanov history becomes the tale of the struggle between the absolutes of "consciousness" and "matter." The articles speak of the former as human intellect, but more particularly as that sentient part of man's being which, distinct from the world, guarantees his eventual transcendence of it (the "world" for Platonov includes both the physical world and those of its attributes, such as the hostility of the elements or the baser instincts within man, that reinforce man's ontological subordination to it). In "Proletarskaia poeziia," for example, Platonov declares history to be the road to man's victory over the cosmos. "We" are marching, he announces, toward release from the prison cell (*kazemat*) of physical laws, away from the disorganization, chance, and horror of the universe; our final stop is the full comprehension (*postizhenie*) of the universe's essence. In the future the human soul will consist of consciousness and intellect, and will bury beneath itself the base instincts and mere sensory impressions that now govern its life.[4]

What sets this mode of thought apart from its more orthodox Marxian contemporaries is its tendency to treat the historical experience of the proletariat as the emanation of something still more fundamental, namely ontology. This tendency, already present in Bogdanov and Fedorov, to ground the social, economic, and political orders of experience in ontology became one of the defining features of Platonov's world view. From this conceptual scheme also derives the almost manichean dualism one finds in the early Platonov, for whom all phenomena are ultimately manifestations of one or the other in a pair of antagonistic principles, though this may also reflect a more general propensity on his part to view existence in terms of radical antinomies.[5]

Platonov's articles further reiterate the Bogdanovian notion that, as the final product of man's evolutionary adaptation to the surrounding world, proletarian culture will generate an ideology enabling the "organization" of man's existence in all its aspects. In "Tvorcheskaia gazeta," for example, he defines newspapers as a form of the "thought" of a society which "organizes its activity," and which will provide communist society with the collective self-consciousness necessary to regulate its social existence.[6] Proletarian culture is uniquely qualified to transcend the individualism and disunity of the preceding, bourgeois era – an important step in the process of Bogdanovian "organization" – by its inherently collectivist nature (hence the insistence, which rapidly degenerated into cliché, on the pronoun "we" rather than "I" in the Smithy poetry Platonov imitates in *Golubaia glubina*). This collective essence is also reflected in proletarian art, which is destined to play a privileged role in the creation of "organization" out of the "chaos" of man's existence. If proletarian art cannot yet undertake the immediate transformation of reality, he writes, it can meanwhile devote itself to the "organization, the adaptation to [man's] inner nature, not of material things or reality, but merely the symbols of these things, for example, words... The organization of words, the symbols of nature, in accordance with [man's] desires – this is what constitutes the poetry of the proletarian epoch." The work of transforming reality itself will begin in the future, when the merging of art and science enables the complete organization of nature by man.

Platonov's reproduction of Bogdanov's arguments at this level of detail shows him to have moved beyond the merely topical theme of proletarian culture to engage the philosophical issues that were central to Bogdanov's thought but often of secondary concern to the *Proletkul't* movement as a whole. Platonov, however, could be an inconsistent pupil of *Proletkul't* philosophy and often indulged in subtle revisions of Bogdanov or departed on eccentric tangents of his own (to the extent, in fact, that his editors would sometimes append disclaimers to his essays). The articles thus supply a record, not only of the set of ideas that influenced Platonov at this early stage, but also of the particular manner in which his mind responded to those ideas, and it is in this moment of appropriation and refraction of *Proletkul't* ideas that one can observe the germination of the themes, plot motifs, characters, and even stylistic idiosyncracies that were later to characterize his poetics. To read the Voronezh articles is to see the features of Platonov's mature works being generated in the engagement, by a precocious, if sometimes intellectually naive, mind, of the social-philosophical notions popular in the revolutionary culture of the time.

The habits of thought and expression that mark Platonov's handling of these ideas as his own, then, initially appear to be the products of intellectual and philosophical naiveté (and they certainly in part were); but they establish patterns he was later to carry over into his literary works, and, indeed, the emphases they introduce in many ways may be seen as inherently novelistic. One such emphasis involves a shift from the social and class phenomena important to Bogdanov to the *subjective experience* of the world's ontological strife, a revision that may be viewed as one of the seminal moments in the derivation of his thematics from *Proletkul't* ideas. This shift may already be discerned in Platonov's inclination toward biological and physiological explanations (the organic function of consciousness, its opposition to "feeling" rather than to matter in general), which concentrate the ontological conflict within man's being, and in his frequent attention to such emotional states as the "torment" man endures because he is unable to grasp life's sense, or, conversely, the "greatest delight" science offers of conquering the dark and frightful aspects of nature.[7] The most telling and idiosyncratic manifestation of this concern, however, can be found in Platonov's preoccupation with the individual physical body as the direct experiencer of ontological conflict and even the primary site on which the struggle between the universe's antinomies is engaged.

A preoccupation with the life of the body, particularly in its unsavory or grotesque aspects, figures prominently in Platonov's thought from the very beginning of his career. In the discussions of consciousness and matter in history, for example, what might be called "the events of the body" are held up as evidence for the larger issues at stake, typically in the course of describing some generalized "man" whose experiences soon acquire a pathetic specificity. Man's ancestors cursed labor, he writes in "Da sviatitsia imia tvoe," and "*the blood flowed feebly in their veins*"; but once man began to work "for the first time *there passed through him* the frightful, destructive, unfettered elements of the world and he came to know their might."[8] In mapping the larger historical "plot" involving consciousness and matter onto the experiences of the body itself, Platonov often draws attention to the boundary between man and the surrounding world, or between inner and outer being, thus suggesting that the lines of ontological conflict run through the very center of man's being. In this manner one article describes the appearance of consciousness during the bourgeois era as its emergence from the confinement of the physical body: "consciousness outgrew the strengths of the individual body (*pereroslo telesnye lichnye sily*)," he comments, and goes on to claim that once "man" became convinced of the impotence of the individual "I", "his heart and mind grew out of his egoistical, bestial, dark body" ("K nachinaiushchim proletar-skim poetam i pisateliam"). The trepidations of Platonov's fictional heroes, who anguish over the condition of their bodies as over evidence for some larger world-sorrow, in part have their origins in these subjective interpretations of Bogdanov's ideas.

The ambivalent nature of this boundary state in which man, in Platonov's subjectivist interpretation, exists, comes vividly to the fore when he addresses the theme of sex (something true of much later works, such as "Reka Potudan'," as well). Platonov echoes Fedorov's suspicion of the existential motivations underlying sexual desire as well as his apprehensions that such desire may sabotage man's quest for utopia (this theme thus providing further evidence for Fedorov's early influence on Platonov's thought). He assigns sex, as a manifestation of the corporeal, to the order of matter that has oppressed man throughout history but whose dominance has now been shaken by the triumphant ascendancy of intellect. Sexual desire thus becomes a vestige of the bourgeois culture that will be overthrown with the establishment of a proletarian "kingdom of consciousness": the "feeling" whose reign has recently come to an end, he says, was "chiefly that of sex (*pol*)" ("U nachala tsarstva soznaniia"), and elsewhere he labels the bourgeoisie "children of sexual lust, children of the body's passions."[9] The warning against the toll physiological demands might exact on man's progress toward utopia is sounded in "O kul'ture zapriazhennogo sveta i poznannogo elektrichestva."[10] Geared toward nothing more than the production of sexual cells, he writes, human culture in the past could not raise man much above the level of vegetable existence. "It's time to put an end to this ancient production" and devote man's efforts to science, he urges; the love line leads only to the culture of the "beautiful lady" (a remark aimed at effete Symbolist culture), while that of "thought" promises to transform the cosmos.

For all the militancy with which they proclaim the ability of consciousness to triumph over corporeal desire, however, Platonov's discussions of sex betray a certain hesitation deriving from the realization that the physiological urges so threatening to man's ascent originate in the very center of his being. Embodied – literally – in man are both the principle of consciousness, whose advent will ultimately enable transcendence of the physical world, and the principle of matter, whose dominance is the root of cosmic suffering. Though he yearns to rise above them, man must suffer his origins in the base, primordial matter of the earth, a circumstance which repeatedly leads Platonov toward apprehension of what might be called the "dilemma of chthonic origin." Several of the articles refer to man as having been produced out of the "dead

rubble" of the earth ("*iz mertvykh glyb*," the epithet "dead"
being one he consistently applies to matter in its opposition to
spirit),[11] or even its "filth." In a letter he wrote to the editors
of the newspaper *Trudovaia armiia* to protest a review critical of
the vulgar physicality in his story "Chul'dik i Epishka,"
Platonov even speaks in these terms of himself and other
proletarian writers: "We grow out of the earth, out of all of its
uncleanliness (*nechistot*), we are steadfastly emerging out of filth
(*griazi*) ... Man is descended from the worm ("*Chelovek vyshel iz
chervia*" – literally, "man came out of the worm") ... We are
rising up from below, help us."[12] Elsewhere he explains the
survival of bourgeois instincts in members of the working class
by lamenting that "we are still covered in a thick layer of filth"
("*Griaz' eshche gusto oblipaet nas*").[13]

A further, intriguing, ambivalence regarding the relation
between consciousness and matter comes to light in those of the
articles that, in an apparent inconsistency, posit *materialization*
as the final outcome of the historical process. "We regard
history as the path from the abstract to the concrete, from
abstractness (*otvlechennosti*) to reality, from metaphysics to
physics," a movement from "idea to matter," as he phrases it
in "Proletarskaia poeziia." In "Revoliutsiia 'dukha'" he
adopts a similar, militantly materialist stance when he dismisses
"spirit" (*dukh*) as nothing more than a "growth" (*narost*) on
matter, a condensation of it that is fully subject to its laws.
"There are no values for us outside of matter," he even
declares.[14] Platonov was hardly a consistent thinker in this
period, and some of this contradictory materialism might stem
from rhetorical demands of the moment (such as his indignation
at the bourgeois suggestion that the proletariat lacks the
"spiritual" properties requisite for establishing its own form of
culture – not to mention the fact that materialism was the
order of the day). But his metaphysical inconsistencies highlight
one of the fundamental paradoxes of his world view, and
consequently one of the major sources of the themes, symbolism,
and even the use of language in his later literary works.

On the one hand the general bent of Platonov's pronouncements in these articles is toward the rejection of the material

world and all it represents (in favor of the proletarian "kingdom of consciousness"). Yet this rejection is complicated by the intimation that for all his efforts to rise above it man cannot escape his dealings with matter (just as sexual desires reveal the cohabitation in man of the principles of both consciousness and matter). What Platonov elsewhere treats as man's complete victory over the world can thus at times assume the subtly compromised form of a rapprochement with matter. The proletariat's progressive instincts, he argues in "Proletarskaia poeziia," express themselves as a striving *toward* the world, a yearning for the thing-in-itself, and the soul of man is presently transforming itself in preparation for its "reconciliation with matter" ("*sblizhenie s materiei*"). There may well be a latent suggestion of carnal intimacy in this phrase, and hence of some of the ambivalence attending Platonov's theme of sexual desire. "Our final stop," he asserts in the same essay, "is the attainment of full knowledge (*postizhenie*) of the world's essence," while elsewhere he speaks of the same experience as an even more suggestive "*poznanie vselennoi*" – the Russian philosophical vocabulary conveniently offering a term denoting either intellectual or carnal "knowledge."

Still more subversive of the doctrine of triumphal consciousness predominant in these articles is their frequent suggestion that entities must be material in order really to exist. The proletarian age is that of "Truth," Platonov declares in "Proletarskaia poeziia," and this truth is not an abstract concept but a *thing*: "Truth (*istina*) is now desired by my whole body [again, a symptomatic grounding of issues in the corporeal – T.S.]; and what the body desires cannot be immaterial, spiritual, abstract. Truth is a genuinely real thing (*Istina – real'naia veshch'*)." In "Svet i sotsializm" he asserts that socialism demands an "equivalent physical force" (in this case, the energy of light, which is to be harnessed for industrial use) if it is ever to become a "tangible thing" ("*tverdoi veshch'iu*," literally, a "hard" thing).[15] The similar claim of "Revoliutsiia 'dukha'" is that there will be a communist art only when communism itself "becomes desire, a tangible, visible thing" ("*stanet zhelaniem, tverdoi vidimoi veshch'iu*"). This insistence on

reification, on envisioning the reconciliation of spirit with
matter in its embodiment *in* matter, may reflect the influence of
Fedorov (together with the whole Russian theological tradition
of incarnation from which his thought descends) and the
attainment of "thingness" discussed in the journalism anticipates the largely Fedorovian contours in which utopia is
imagined in Platonov's later works. It is the burden of those
works, however, to demonstrate the failure of such utopias and
the resulting persistence of man's subordination to matter; and
even in the context of the fulminations against base matter
running throughout the journalism this desire for reification
cannot help but appear a compromise necessitated by fears
over the ephemerity of consciousness (or, more generally,
spirit).

Nor is one forced to turn to Platonov's later works to uncover
evidence of this fear and its attendant abhorrence of matter.
Even some of the most *Proletkul't*-ish passages of Platonov's
Voronezh period betray anxieties that in the end man will
remain weak and subordinate to nature. The many articles on
land reclamation and electrification, for example, speak of
what is taking place in the countryside as "works aimed at
transforming matter." Yet it is equally characteristic of them to
communicate an impression of man's beleaguered existence in
the material world, especially when portraying the central-
Russian countryside ravaged by the drought of 1921. Platonov's
descriptions of the drought's effects turn into a litany of the
woes inflicted on man by a hostile natural order. The very
geographical features of the Voronezh area provide him with
evidence of man's plight: the region suffers from erratic
precipitation patterns, to which current agricultural practices
are ill-suited ("Ocherki bednoi oblasti");[16] it lacks forests and
is far from sources of liquid fuels ("Voronezhskaia gidroelek-
tricheskaia stantsiia");[17] it lies in a transitional zone where "all
three" of nature's destructive forces are at work, swamps,
dessicating winds, and ravines that consume arable land
("Meliorativnaia voina protiv zasukhi");[18] the land in its
present state is exhausted and has been bled of its life-giving
elements ("Remont zemli").[19]

The theme of the pathos of man's circumstance in fact often threatens to overwhelm the very utopian expectations the articles have been written to proclaim. "There has never been real life on earth," Platonov writes in "Zhizn' do kontsa," published in the year of the drought, "*and it will not soon appear. Instead there has been ruin – we dug graves and lowered into them our brother, sister, and bride*" (emphasis added).[20] "Novoe evangelie" similarly speaks of the "senseless arrangement of the world and of the whole universe, which torments and destroys mankind."[21] In much the same vein Platonov can dwell on the proletariat's present exhaustion even as he looks forward to its utopian salvation. In "U nachala tsarstva," for example, he states that there is only enough "vital" force in Russia to maintain the body, with none left over for the strengthening of life, and claims the workers have only enough strength in their muscles to keep them supplied with blood. Even when contemplating the eventual triumph of proletarian science over physical laws he sometimes suggests, in a very characteristic move, that such victory involves, not the actual subordination of nature, but merely a reprieve from it won through the device of turning nature's terrible forces against itself – a tacit admission of man's enduring impotence before a world of which he can be the clever manipulator, but not the master. "Man arms himself against nature by means of nature itself," Platonov writes in "O nauke"; "he hammers at it with the weapons of its own laws. *He does not take it by force (ne nasiluet)*, but adapts himself to it. Having come to know the mortal might of mortal forces [*sic*], man directs them, *lacking the strength to change things directly*, against the other forces hostile to life, and so subdues them, *indirectly* alters and conquers them" (emphases added).[22]

As the reference in the above passage to "adaptation" suggests, what Platonov may be doing here is intensifying the connotation of compromise already present in Bogdanov's concept of man's evolutionary adaptation to the world (that is, if the "organization of reality" is the outcome of a historical process of *adaptation*, the external world subtly retains its dominance).[23] But in the end what makes these uncertainties

regarding man's relationship to matter so important in the
Voronezh articles is that they challenge the standard interpretation of Platonov's oeuvre, in which the early works are
seen as embodying a uniform optimism that gives way to
despair by the time their author attains maturity as a writer in
the late 1920s. The well-known "pessimism" of the later works
would instead appear to derive from the fundamental complexity of Platonov's world view, not merely from disenchantment with developments in Soviet society. Though the
early writings, and the journalism in particular, differ from
those later works by juxtaposing to their expressions of doubt
militant proclamations that the age of "consciousness" will
indeed arrive, their waverings nonetheless prefigure the failure
to which utopian endeavors routinely succumb in works like
"Epifanskie shliuzy," *Chevengur*, and *Kotlovan*.

The prose works that Platonov wrote from 1918–1924, most of
them brief sketches published in the Voronezh newspapers to
which he was also contributing articles and essays, reflect the
eclectic reading of his early years. No literary sophisticate
tutored in the style of an elevated model, Platonov drew
seemingly *ad hoc* on a variety of genres in the minor tradition of
the grotesque or at the fringe of the Russian literary canon –
Gogol's Ukranian tales, the satires of Leskov and Saltykov-
Shchedrin, as well as folktales, the chronicles, science fiction,
and Cosmist poetry – an eclectic tendency that has led some
critics to speak of the "many-sidedness" of his Voronezh period
and the "impressionability" (*vospriimchivost'*) of the author
himself, who was impressed by such disparate sources (for
example, Eidinova, "K tvorcheskoi biografii A. Platonova," p.
215).
    The array of genres to which Platonov was attracted in these
early years is itself of interest to the study of his works, because
it establishes something of a paradigm of informing tendencies.
The list of influences cited above, for example, already reveals
an inclination toward both the ironic and the utopian, strains
that were to merge in his major fiction. The Voronezh works
are most important, however, for their revelation of two

important traits that mark even these eclectic and imitative first attempts as distinctly Platonov's own, and which were to govern the subsequent evolution of his poetic. The first is Platonov's persistence in investing whatever generic form he borrows with the themes already worked out in the journalism: regardless of their ostensible genre, Platonov turns his tales into meditations on the existential dilemma of man's residence in an alienating physical world, frequently couching this theme in the abstract philosophical terms he had derived from his readings of Fedorov, Bogdanov, and the theoreticians of *Proletkul't*. The second, closely related trait involves his penchant for reinterpreting in light of these concerns the stock expressive devices of his borrowed genre. It is these transformations which mark the beginning of his poetic, and the narrative complexities of his later works may be traced back to these eclectic Voronezh experiments. As one scholar remarks, those experiments "combine in unique and unusual alloys depiction of the everyday and literary conceits, the commonplace and the allegorical, psychologism and the folk tale, parable, satire, and homily."[24]

Among Platonov's early stories, the speculative bent of his thought most clearly manifests itself in the several transparently autobiographical tales portraying a child or adolescent hero (at least one of them, "Stranniki," was in fact written specifically for a children's publication). Like Platonov himself, this hero typically lives in a settlement situated between the industrial section of a city and the open steppe, and his feeling of intimacy with his simple, decaying physical surroundings is complicated by inchoate longings to flee across the steppe to some distant land. The tone of these stories is often mawkish, but beneath its surface one can see Platonov formulating what was to become the central dramatic premise of his works: the use of a protagonist preoccupied with the exact nature of his relation to the world around him (a concern leading to alternate senses of empathy with that world and profound alienation from it) and the use of fictional setting (especially landscape) as a tableau to be scrutinized by the hero in his efforts to understand his own existence. In mood and intonation the stories in this group owe

much to the influences of Esenin and Kliuev prominent in
Platonov's verse collection *Golubaia glubina*, as well as to
Symbolist yearnings to cast off the burdens of transitory flesh.

The theme of melancholy longing for escape from a difficult
existence is particularly evident in "Stranniki" ("Wanderers";
1920), a one-page sketch Platonov wrote for the weekly
*Kommunisticheskii voskresnik detiam.*[25] Like many of the child-
characters in Platonov's early fiction, the hero of this story,
Mitia, is a product of straitened circumstances and in the tale
must go beg for credit so his family can buy bread. On this
errand, however, he travels down "a quiet street where the
town already came to an end and the fields began" – that is, he
enters that boundary zone between two worlds so suited to
Platonov's philosophical theme, whose function as an existential observation point is underscored when Mitia climbs
atop a fence to gaze off into the fields. In the searing heat the
steppe seems plunged into a dream-like state (anticipating the
theme of somnambulance in *Chevengur*) and as he watches
pilgrims move down a distant road Mitia's ennui is transformed
into a desire to escape. "Anguish welled up in his heart, and he
wanted to leave for where every day the people with their sacks
depart and never come home" (these pilgrims representing an
early instance of the wanderers in search of utopia who later
traverse the landscapes of *Chevengur* and "Dzhan").

What makes the story so characteristic of Platonov is the
apocalyptic nature of what Mitia expects to find on his journey
and the existential motivations supporting his desire to leave.
He wants to see the "end of the world," and imagines that
place as a refuge from oppressive existence in which universal
brotherhood and sympathy have been restored. The allusion to
Fedorov in this passage is further augmented when Platonov
suggests his hero's wanderlust has been inspired by a kind of
Fedorovian rebellion against mortality – as if Platonov were
using the tale to introduce his young audience to the *Philosophy
of the Common Cause*. Mitia's rejection of his present existence
turns out to have been inspired by a confrontation with the
inevitability of death: his dog Volchok died in the winter ("He
knew that dogs die and get thrown into the ditch"), and Mitia

now longs to journey to that "other land" to join Volchok and the joyous pilgrims, all of whom he imagines seated around the sun as around a giant bonfire.

"Volchek" (1920)[26] still more conspicuously elaborates a set of existential, Fedorovian themes. It has virtually the same hero and setting as "Stranniki" ("There was a yard at the edge of town … when you crawl over the fence you can sit on it for a few seconds and from there see laid out before you the field, the road, and something else far off, dark, like a low quiet fog," 21), and it stars the same dog. The dominant theme here, however, is that of the dangers of sexual/procreative urges. Volchek is troubled by the same pained awareness of existence as the narrator, appearing more human than dog because he "lived and thought like all people … Like me, he couldn't understand and couldn't rest from his thoughts and from life" (21). What troubles Volchek in particular is his timid nature, which causes him to shy away from the kind of gross indulgence of his physical self in sex and procreation vilified in Fedorov's writings as a hindrance to utopia. The local dogs all fight over a bitch named Chaika whenever she comes into heat, but Volchek feels no such desire because he is constitutionally incapable of aggression. As in Platonov's articles on sexuality, this abnegation of the life of the flesh for the sake of a more contemplative attitude toward the world (Volchek is described as having a "contemplative" – *zadumchivaia* – head and eyes that seem fixed in a penetrating gaze at the world) is presented as a nobler response to existence than that of immersion in physicality.

The narrator himself confronts this choice between aggressive indulgence of the body's instincts and passive contemplation of the world when, on an evening walk during which the whole town seems to be on the prowl for love, he sees a friend named Mania with another man. He pronounces Mania and all the other lovers "unthoughtful beings in love" ("*nezadumchivye poliubivshie sushchestva*," 23) and is struck with the sudden realization that "all this" is "base, pitiful, and vile." If everyone were to recognize this fact, he announces in a shift to a declamatory tone taken directly from Platonov's "proletarian" journalism, they would understand that it is not love men need but a hatred for "all this." They would then want to remake the entire earth from scratch. This apocalyptic theme acquires contemporary political resonance when the narrator's father, who despairs of ever finding out why people live, nonetheless tells him that there must be an answer somewhere because the Revolution has demonstrated "how easy it is to make everyone well-fed and content" (22).

A second distinct group among Platonov's early stories consists of a series of anecdotal sketches satirizing various aspects of village life which differ markedly in tone from the portraits of contemplative adolescents just discussed. The newspapers in which they initially appeared were propaganda organs designed to carry the Bolshevik cause to the peasantry, and these sketches thus have the apparent aim of exposing the perennial backwardness of the Russian countryside and instilling revolutionary consciousness in their intended peasant readers. "Pop" ("The Priest"; 1920)[27] and "Istoriia Iereia Prokopiia Zhabrina" ("The Tale of Bishop Prokopii Zhabrin"; 1923),[28] for example, are anticlerical tales satirizing the deceptiveness of priests and their comic efforts to fit into the new Soviet society, while "Voly" ("Oxen"; 1920)[29] portrays ignorant Cossacks who dream of riding off to rid the country of the godless Bolsheviks but are forced, after Denikin's troops ravage their farms, to admit the revolutionaries' humaneness and justness. The grotesque manner many of these stories adopt thus seems calculated specifically to lampoon traditional village ways, and in them Platonov relies heavily on the expected satirical models of Gogol, Saltykov-Shchedrin, and Leskov.

However, as part of an effort to render their political message more appealing to peasant readers, these sketches make a visible attempt at affecting a kind of folk "earthiness," and the provisional sympathy for the work's satirical target which this device generates was to have a determining influence on the uses of the grotesque throughout Platonov's later works. Its chief result here is to cause those elements of the works originally intended as objects of derision to be reconceived in a very different key. "Originally" intended to invite ridicule, the tales' grotesque distortions come to represent the world's tragic aspect, while the ludicrous figures of the heroes, the anecdotal predicaments they are made to endure as either the comic victims of village depravity or eccentric embodiments of its baseness, now become available as examples of the vicissitudes of existence itself (much as Platonov reads the theme of man's relation to the world into the children's stories discussed above). Indeed, although the effect almost certainly owes more to coincidence than to conscious imitation, the combination in these "village" tales of burlesque tone with an underlying seriousness of theme causes their protagonists to resemble some of the tragicomic heroes of modernism – the "mock" but ultimately genuine and representative sufferings of Stravinsky's puppet-hero Petrushka come readily to mind – and when the *skaz* narrative manner Platonov adopts in them undergoes a similar transformation in the mid 1920s, the result is the similarly "grotesque but profound" style of his mature period.

"Pop" offers a good example of this tendency to turn comic predicament into a representative instance of suffering from the world's disorders. Published in *Krasnaia derevnia*, in the context of that paper's campaign to disabuse the peasants of their religious faith, it recounts a satirical anecdote about a priest who exploits a simple-minded peasant by demanding a series of ever-larger gifts in exchange for marrying off the peasant's son. The tale is conveyed in humorously typifying dialogue ("– *Kak by mne, batiushka, syna, k primeru, ozhenit'? – A, tebe syna zhenit', tebe vot syna zhenit'! Aga, tebe syna zhenit'!...*"; 113) and motivates its anecdotal plot in the baudy theme of the son's irrepressible lust for a certain Mashka Bezrukina ("all he does is go around bellowing," the peasant complains).

This sexual theme already recalls the views on physiological drives Platonov had derived from Fedorov; but it is in the second half of the tale that the slapstick confrontation of the poor and timid peasant with the scheming and arrogant priest is transformed into a tragicomic plight. To the peasant's diffident and contemplative nature is contrasted the priest's callous indulgence of the flesh, while the peasant's awkward remarks turn out to contain an unexpected insight into the

nature of man's existence. When the priest threatens him with
the wrath of heaven the peasant's mumbled response, in
illiterate rural dialect, unwittingly voices the materialist
"truth" about the world that Platonov in other contexts cites
as a justification for the building of utopia. The priest points
menacingly to the sky, but the peasant answers that "it's the
daytime sky, just the regular stuff up there" (*dennoe nebo,
obnakovennyi verkh'*, 114). If the antireligious intent of this
episode is clear, Platonov sustains its philosophic connotations
at the end by portraying his hero as a contemplative soul,
anguished by his awareness of the human predicament. Driven
with curses from the priest's house, he wanders, "along the
wattle fence and thinks about the whole world," and when his
son comes out of Mashka Bezrukina's house, the peasant looks
on him "with grieving eyes," then goes off into the weeds "to
think" (115).

The physical descriptions in these tales are the direct
descendants of Gogol's vision of the Russian village as the realm
of the uncouth, and Platonov uses them to much the same end.
"Detskie vospominaniia" ("Childhood Recollections"; 1922),
for example, graphically describes an old man near death (a
theme perhaps borrowed from Pil'niak's 1917 "Smerti") who
sleeps oblivious to the saliva bubbles forming at his mouth and
to the snot which "forgotten, wets his beard."[30] One of the
characters in "Chul'dik i Epishka" ("Chul'dik and Epishka";
1920)[31] is similarly described as snivelling and reeking, while
the hero of "Starye liudi" ("Old People"; 1921)[32] has a dream
in which he urinates so copiously that the Don river overflows
its banks and he drowns. In these stories, however, the satirical
emphasis on the uncouth tends to acquire an additional
function as a symbol of the base physicality Platonov regarded
as evidence of man's origins in, and subordination to, the world
of matter. The eccentric, beggar-like existence of Ivan Mitrych
("Starye liudi"), for example, echoes the pathos Platonov
elsewhere associates with man's chthonic origins. Ivan Mitrych
abases himself through an attraction to "filth" – sent by his
daughter to the bazaar, he buys up all sorts of leftovers, "the
filthiest stuff, cheap and unclean" (*samuiu griaz', deshevku i*

*nechistotu*) – and in the uncouth dream just mentioned he completes his return to chthonic filth by drowning in his own urine. One of the heroes of "Chul'dik i Epishka" similarly ends up buried in the "fouled corner" of the cemetery where village boys smoke and defecate.

The underlying problem of "matter" signalled in this preoccupation with human physicality comes to the surface in "Erik" (1921). A rather bizarre tale published in the peasant-oriented paper *Krasnaia derevnia*, it also reveals Platonov's early attraction to mythic plots.[33] In this particular example the devil appears to an eccentric peasant named Erik and offers to teach him how to make men out of clay. After the two turn their *homunculi* loose on the world rumors start that the "devil's children" have been turning the earth inside out and showing everyone the "filth" it contains (" *Vsiu pakost' nutrenniuiu budto darom pokazyvaiut vsem na potekhu i uteshenie*," 29). Though the devil's progeny, it turns out they have sworn off both the devil and God, and are preaching the message that people themselves ought to make another world from scratch. Erik and the peasants decide the *homunculi* are not demonic, and that anyway God and the devil have always been in cahoots against man. Five days later Erik's own creatures show up, break open the sky, and turn the earth inside out so that "filth and uncleanliness" pour out of it (29). This feat proves to the peasants that there is no God, and they suddenly find themselves united with one another as brothers.

The grotesqueries of this tale are probably meant to contribute to a materialist parable capable of weaning peasant readers from their religious beliefs and convincing them that the apparently "demonic" Bolsheviks will in fact bring about a reign of universal brotherhood. Thus the "devil's children" go about desacralizing the world, demonstrating that it consists of nothing other than matter and citing this fact in their call for man to remake the earth. Likewise Erik, whose name perhaps suggests " *eretik*" ("heretic"), is said to have once dreamed of cutting a hole in the sky to see if God is really up there. But when a bald head finally peers out through the hole in the sky the peasants just laugh at it (cf. Maiakovskii's 1914

"Eshche Peterburg": "A s neba smotrit kakaia-to drian'/ velichestvenno, kak Lev Tolstoi"). In a manner characteristic of these early works in general, however, the very elements of this "myth" intended to make a "scientific" materialist world view comprehensible to peasants (the opening up of the world to see what is inside it, sticking one's head through the clouds to see what is there, all functioning as proof that there is no God) simultaneously convey an allegory of the world's ontological nature. Erik's intention to break a hole (*prolomit'*) through the sky embodies one of Platonov's fundamental philosophical obsessions – the desire to see whether there is anything beyond the visible, material world – and the tale reflects Platonov's ambivalent attitude toward "matter" in general. On the one hand the ostensible point is that man can, once he realizes there is nothing to the world but matter, remake that world to suit his needs; but what "Erik" more subtly thematizes is the disappointment of expectations that there might indeed exist something beyond the physical realm. The stuff of which the earth turns out solely to consist is "filth" (*pakost'*), while what pours down from the sky when it finally breaks open is nothing but "filth and uncleanliness" (*pakost' i nechistotu*).

Of the genres at which Platonov tried his hand from 1918–1924, a third group consisting of science fiction stories probably bears the closest topical relation to his journalism. Like the other early works, they serve primarily as vehicles for ideas Platonov had absorbed from Bogdanov and other theoreticians of *Proletkul't*, if anything more directly than the others because their plots are self-consciously conceived as illustrations of the victory of proletarian "consciousness" over the cosmos. In this Platonov was undoubtedly influenced by the precedent of Bogdanov himself, who had written two science fiction novels (*Krasnaia zvezda*, 1908, and *Inzhiner Menni*, 1913) to popularize his views, as well, perhaps, as that of Tsiolkovskii (the father of Soviet rocketry who also wrote science fiction). These tales are furthermore extrapolations from Platonov's own technical background, and often imitate the kind of quasi-utopian scientific discourse he deploys in some of the articles on technological themes (for example, "Novaia mekhanika," where he attempts to found a new branch of mechanics and prove the feasibility of a *perpetuum mobile*; or "Svet i sotsializm," where he discusses how light might be harnessed to power Soviet factories).

As a result of this close link, however, the science fiction stories also incorporate some of the abiding ambiguities of Platonov's world view. Far from depicting the kind of unqualified victory over the universe foreseen in some of the articles, they tend to portray science as failing, or at least attaining only partial success against the cosmos, and their protagonists are often endowed with a loneliness and melancholy that contradict the supposed utopianism of their plots. That they do not fully resolve the ontological dilemmas on which their plots are based may, in fact, further testify to how appropriate this literary form was to Platonov's themes. As Mark Rose suggests, the science fiction genre arises out of the attempt, prompted by the technological revolutions of the nineteenth and twentieth centuries, to mediate between materialistic and spiritualistic views of man's place in the universe.[34] Nor was such an affinity to prove irrelevant to Platonov's Soviet context. The devices of the "production" novel that Platonov parodies in his later works incorporate their own millenarial faith in technological and social utopia and may, indeed, partly derive from the science fiction genre (moreover, a cosmic-ontological theme had already been joined to that of social utopia in Bogdanov's *Krasnaia zvezda* – and parodied in Zamiatin's *My*).

One of the more programmatic, and perhaps for that reason optimistic, examples of Platonov's early science fiction is "Potomki solntsa" ("Descendants of the Sun"; 1922), which appeared on the fifth anniversary of the Revolution.[35] Narrated by an old man left behind on earth after the rest of mankind has departed for other worlds, the story recounts in retrospect humanity's struggle against the forces of matter. In "1923–1924," we learn, the earth was wracked by cosmic catastrophe (perhaps a comet) that swept away the entire culture of the past; this was countered, however, by the world's communists,

who soon brought about social revolution and forged in the
process a collective of men who believe "in the brain and in
their machines" and are ready for the final showdown with
nature (38). This new humanity sets machines to work building
a "home" for it "out of the formless earth" and redirects its
own erotic energies toward the more vital demands of subduing
matter (38). Eventually an interplanetary craft is invented, and
mankind takes off to investigate the solar system.

The same stock elements appear in more fictionally involved,
and hence more ambivalent, form in "Markun" (1921) and
"Satana mysli" ("A Satan of Thought"; 1922), both of which
exemplify the kinds of ambiguities attending Platonov's outlook
even in this early period. The former is less science fiction *per se*
than the tale of an adolescent's fantasies about transforming the
world.[36] Set in an atmosphere of poverty and squalor borrowed
directly from Chekhov's "Spat' khochet'sia" (the story opens
with Markun keeping watch over his sleeping brothers, whose
stomachs are distended from hunger and who are infested with
bedbugs, while cockroaches run over the floor), it uses this
dreary portrait of existence as motivation for its protagonist's
utopian desires. Markun has been working on blueprints for a
machine that will rescue man from his sordid physical condition
by harnessing the "infinite" energy of the cosmos. Platonov
uses his hero's technical deliberations to paraphrase the notion
advanced in some of the articles of man's clever use of the laws
of nature against nature itself, the design of the machine itself
serving as a kind of metaphor for the utopian potential
available to scientific consciousness but as yet locked within the
cosmos. Nature, Markun reasons, is energy; it is also infinite,
and hence must hold infinite reserves of energy available to
man. His plan is to harness that energy by connecting one
water-powered turbine to another, larger one, whose energy
output would then be resupplied to the first, thus yielding a
geometrical increase in power with which he finally could
remake the world.

Markun eventually constructs his machine out of whatever
materials he can find (as will be seen, this becomes a cherished
theme in Platonov) and sets it to work. However, although the

story concludes with Markun declaring that the "entire world has opened up before him" (31), Platonov's description of the experiment makes it less an epiphany of "consciousness" than an ambivalent mixture of ecstasy and terror: the machine works so well that it reaches a furious velocity and explodes, sending parts through the wall of the barn in which Markun has kept it. Platonov may have meant this violence to symbolize the tremendous might of consciousness waiting to be unleashed by science, but there is a self-destructive note to it that recalls if anything the industrial accident used in his very first story, "Ocherednoi," to illustrate the horrors of factory work under the bourgeoisie. In the case of Markun's engine, "the lower spiral burst, a chunk of the pipe tore off with a shriek and, spinning, hit the wooden wall of the barn, broke through it, and flew out into the yard" (30). In the earlier work a motor also overheats (because the bourgeois bosses have skimped on oil), then a "white-hot beam tore away from the furnace and flew high over our heads... the fallen beams of white-hot metal lay in a circle around the furnace, still hissing, slowly cooling, releasing their terrible might."[37]

Thus even in this most *Proletkul't*-ish phase of Platonov's career, alarms go off as one approaches utopia. A similar apprehension of the potential terrors attending the victory of consciousness over matter informs "Satana mysli" (1922).[38] The hero in this case is an engineer named Vogulov, who, having grown up in "the great epoch of electricity and the transformation of the globe," has been selected by the "World Congress of Workers' Masses" to supervise humanity's efforts to transform the earth (32). As in "Potomki solntsa," the proletariat is already hard at work attacking matter and creating out of the earth a "home for mankind," but it still suffers at the hands of the elements (33). Vogulov decides to solve this dilemma by blowing up mountain chains and letting warm air currents flow in to transform the earth's cold areas into tropical gardens (the solution Fedorov had suggested in *Philosophy of the Common Cause*).

Like Markun, Vogulov derives his explosive from an application of the violence of the universe against the universe itself: after great effort he discovers a means to compress light into "ultralight," which in the process of disintegrating back into its ordinary form releases fantastic amounts of energy. The "satanic" theme appears when Vogulov plunges himself into the fierce labors required to oversee the several detonation projects he has set up around the globe. Platonov uses his character's frantic state to illustrate the heroic paradoxes that must be endured in wrestling with the cosmos. Vogulov's duties force him to grapple with the very essence of the world, but he does not shrink from engaging "the horrifying resistance of matter, the whole monstrous, self-consuming universe"; in the violence with which he performs his duties he comes, in fact, to personify that antithesis of matter that alone can subdue it, the "violent, screeching, fire-tempered thought that is harder and more material than matter itself"; he is "the embodiment of that consciousness, harder and more resistant than matter, which alone is capable of blowing the universe to chaos and creating out of that chaos a different universe" (36).

Ambivalence already enters into this picture in the form of Vogulov's ruminations on the nature of the universe. He discovers that the cosmic essence fluctuates between two poles of energy that between them encompass all the forms of matter (his model of this cosmos is the geometric figure of an ellipse, perhaps symbolically related to the spiral tubing in Markun's invention). Ostensibly this discovery of the finite, and hence assailable, nature of the universe guarantees man's eventual liberation from the burden of matter (the argument having been made in Platonov's articles that final knowledge of the cosmos would provide the key to its overthrow). This very *finitude*, however, begins to suggest itself as a metaphor for the universe's tragic entrapment within itself. When Vogulov constructs a laboratory model to test his theory he suddenly sees "how that which is called the universe rushes around this closed circle...Thus, around the ring, up the right side and down the left the universe fluctuates and knocks in the *prison cell* of its own self" (37); emphasis added; cf. the articles' frequent reference to the "prison cell of the universe's laws" from which proletarian consciousness will free man).[39] The suggestion of an eternally circling universe, closed in on itself, from which there is no escape short of absolute destruction has pathetic, even absurdist overtones. As in "Erik," there is no escaping matter. Nor is the ambivalence dispersed by any final triumph: the story ends only with Vogulov's plans for detonating the cosmos, not his actual accomplishment of the feat.

Moreover, there is a distinctly masochistic or even suicidal streak to Vogulov himself (repeated in such later heroes as Perri in "Epifanskie shliuzy" and Likhtenberg in "Musornyi veter") that leaves unresolved the question of whether Platonov intends the violence his hero endures to be seen as necessary self-sacrifice, or whether he means it as a warning of the self-destruction awaiting anyone who dares to take on the cosmos. Vogulov has become the antithesis of "weak-willed poets, who resemble women and crying children" (36), but the story begins by describing him as someone who "once was a tender, sad child, who loved his mother, his home's wattle fences, the field, and the sky above all of them" (32), the tonal dissonance between the two parts recalling the tension in Platonov's poems between melancholic verse in the spirit of Esenin and brash proclamations of proletarian victory. In the end Vogulov goes mad and, prior to blowing up the universe, wanders the earth in mourning for a former love who died soon after they met. Hence the story's final sentence qualifies its promise that Vogulov will eventually "sweep away the universe without fear or regret" with the remark that he will do so "with pain for that which is irretrievable and lost, which man needs not in some countless ages, but right now" (40). The tension introduced in the closure of this early tale between the immediate needs of subjectivity and the process of building utopia was to resurface in many of Platonov's later works. Indeed, in many ways it was to define them, just as it more broadly did Platonov's own relation to the "official" culture of the "construction of socialism." The ways in which this dilemma was affected by Platonov's decision to become a writer by profession, and in which the vision of existence from which it derived began to shape the very language of his texts, will be the subject of the following chapter.

# CHAPTER 2

# Learning the language of being (1926–1927)

The innovative configuration of themes, imagery, and verbal devices for which Platonov is best known emerged with striking rapidity over the course of just two years, 1926 and 1927. However, at least two works of this "transitional" phase between Voronezh and Moscow, between careers as an engineer and a writer, directly continue the concerns of Platonov's early literary and publicistic prose. These are the two science fiction tales published in 1926. Both illustrate how the science fiction genre continued to serve Platonov as a forum in which to inject ambivalence into the theme of utopian transcendence of the material world. "Lunnaia bomba" (".The Lunar Bomb"; 1926)[1] dramatizes the notion, probably borrowed from Tsiolkovskii but common to a wide array of Russian utopian thinkers, that man is destined to venture beyond the bounds of earth and colonize outer space.[2] On the level of this ostensible meaning the story may in fact be read as an allegory of transcendence: an engineer named Kreitskopf builds a lunar projectile and has himself flung into space, from whence he transmits back to earth his sometimes ecstatic impressions of what he sees ("Tell everyone I'm near the source of earthly poetry," he radios at one point; 57).

In its utopian redaction, the scenario Platonov reproduces here is associated with expectations that such an emergence into the cosmos would constitute a literal escape from the bonds of earthly "matter," as well as the culmination of man's striving for knowledge about the universe (the *poznanie* repeatedly spoken of in the Voronezh articles). Having predicated its central episode in these terms, however,

Platonov's story proceeds to undermine any suggestion that being can attain a final epiphany. Kreitskopf's first revelation is that the cosmic space he had presumed to consist of immaterial "ether" is in fact some kind of physical substance, a discovery that subtly deflates the story's premise of transcending material bonds. He notes feeling the projectile inexplicably "rubbing against" something, then reports that "strange forces twist its path, sending it over bumps and making it heat up tremendously, although surrounding it should be nothing but the ether" (57). Once out of matter's realm, Kreitskopf finds only more matter, and as he approaches the moon he discovers that its surface is nothing but "desert, dead mineral, and platinum twilight" (58).

Kreitskopf at the same time discovers a universe consisting of pure "consciousness" (the moon strikes him as a "monstrous brain" which feeds him with "white-hot intellect," 58), but the contradiction introduced by this theme is less important than its contribution to the story's underlying mood of intimidation before the cosmos. Kreitskopf's final gesture is an ironic reprise of the story's main plot: he decides to exit his craft, thus attaining a final release from earthly bonds that is at the same time clearly suicidal ("ia otkryvaiu liuk, *chtoby naiti iskhod sebe*," [59], he reports; emphasis added).

"Efirnyi trakt" ("The Ethereal Tract"; 1926) provides a philosophically more involved version of the ambiguities present in Platonov's other science fiction tales.[3] His last contribution to the genre, it was also his first work of any length (it is a *povest'*, some three times longer than anything he had written before) and in this regard looks forward to the (mock-) epic plots of later works like *Chevengur* and "Dzhan."

The gnoseological preoccupations that had by now become typical of Platonov – his stories' concern with scrutinizing the extant world in an effort to discern its essence, already the reflection of a certain estrangement from that world – here find expression in a series of attempts by Russian scientists to prove the essential unity of living and non-living matter and to harness that unity to utopian ends. (This notion of discovering an underlying unity, of course, stems directly from Bogdano-

vian and Fedorovian strivings toward monism.) The hero of
the story, an engineer named Faddei Popov, theorizes that this
unity lies not in abstract physical laws but in a principle of
shared organicity: electrons (the "basic units of matter")
possess biological as well as physical essence; they are in reality
a form of microbe and thus, as living bodies, share man's
essence even if a "whole gulf" separates their life cycle from
his.[4] Popov then extends this notion from matter to the "ether"
that surrounds it, thus enlarging the hypothesis to incorporate
the whole of what exists. If the electron is a biological entity, he
reasons, then the ether must be but a "cemetery of electrons,"
the "mechanical mass" of their deceased forms (157). What
had made the inorganic world appear inert in man's eyes was
the enormous discrepancy between the life span of an electron
and that of man, which prevented even the most sensitive of
instruments from detecting matter's vital processes. As kindred
forms of being, however, the two are in essence the same.

Popov's hypothesis would thus appear to recuperate nature
as a wholly organic domain, reconciling man with the cosmos
by retrieving the cosmos from its apparent status of "otherness"
and reincorporating it within the domain of "life." What
follows from this, on one level, is hopes for a utopian remaking
of man's existence on earth. Science will now transform what
had been the "tragedy of nature" into "lyric" by reconciling
man and electron "in brotherhood" and the essential unity of
life (158). The chronic scarcity of earth's resources will be
redressed by setting up an "electromagnetic channel" to
"feed" the expired electrons of the ether to the "living" ones
in a chunk of metal, which will then reproduce itself and make
it possible for man to cultivate iron, gold, and coal "as easily as
farmers raise pigs" (153).

The paradoxes of "Efirnyi trakt," however, can make its plot
seem more a *parody* of the utopian pronouncements of Platonov's
journalism than their simple dramatization. The telling
moment in this regard is that in which the ether is identified as
the "general body" of the world, since that involvement in
corporeality leads Platonov to assert that the ether is a
"cemetery" filled with the corpses of deceased electrons.

Platonov thus allows the rapprochement between organic and inorganic forms, but the cosmos has been recuperated as organic only to qualify, as it were, for mortality. Whatever Fedorovian hopes for resurrection are raised by the mention of all those electron corpses are, moreover, subverted in the tale's vision of a necrophagic universe bent on consuming itself (cf. Vogulov's "*sama sebia pozhiraiushchaia vselennaia*" in "Satana mysli"): "Electrons eat the corpses of their ancestors," is how Popov describes the workings of this newly organicized matter, and the scientist must "kill" electrons and "feed" their corpses to the electrons in the chunk of metal in order to make them multiply (158).

Platonov's hesitation between epiphanic and horrific visions of matter is in turn reflected in his tale's fitful shuttling between utopian and anti-utopian versions of its plot. Each of the subplots devoted to one of the scientist-heroes begins heroically, with some important insight into the nature of matter inspiring that hero to pursue the utopian project of constructing the "ethereal tract," only to end in abnegation of the task and the hero's lurid demise (often by suicide). There are, to be sure, optimistic vignettes of a socialist landscape already transformed by machines and electricity, and these interpolations represent an important foreshadowing of some of the accommodations Platonov was to undertake in his "transitional" period. But on the whole it is as though he began each episode with utopian intentions, only to succumb to pessimism and apprehensions of catastrophe, then beginning the process again – the tale's relative length and the difficulty he had completing it resulting from this vacillation between desire for utopia's success and anticipation of its demise.[5]

Platonov's growing dissatisfaction in this period with the utopianism of his early years found still more important reflection in a series of stories that forgo the fantastic elements of the science fiction genre to portray small-scale projects in land reclamation or electrification – the two principal activities in Platonov's other career as a technician. It is the reduction in both narrative and ideological scale in these tales, in fact, which is characteristically cited as evidence for an evolutionary change in Platonov's views in 1926–1927. For one scholar they represent an exchange of utopian heroes for "little Prometheans" whose smaller accomplishments reflect the belief that the revolution must now be accomplished "from below" rather than "from above"; for another they parody the cosmic scale of Platonov's earlier works by opposing to it acts of a humble and "organic" service to mankind (Shepard, p. 203; Tolstaia-Segal, "Naturfilosofskie temy," p. 223).

These stories' shift of focus is important in another way as well. Preserving the science fiction tales' concern with the earth's transformation by human "consciousness" while translating it into more diminutive and plausible terms, Platonov's tales of reclamation engage contemporary Soviet reality more directly (that is, less fantastically or anecdotally) than any of the fiction he had written before them. (Hence the reading of these works predominant in Soviet studies of Platonov as a salutary turn toward a more "realistic" manner and the theme of the "construction of socialism" need not be dismissed out of hand as tendentious). Or to put it in other, possibly more relevant terms, they moved him from the fringe nearer to the center of Soviet literature as it was evolving in the twenties, annexing, without fully joining, his writing to the nascent literary and cultural myths of "socialist construction" that were shortly to become the staple of Soviet literature. In this regard, in fact, the reclamation tales anticipate the accommodations to socialist realism undertaken in his works of the later thirties and forties.

As their titles already suggest ("Rodina elektrichestva," 1926; "Kak zazhglas' lampa Il'icha," 1926, originally assigned the more despairing "O potukhshei lampe Il'icha"; "Peschanaia uchitel'nitsa," 1927; and "Lugovye mastera," 1927) these stories are conceived at least provisionally as contributions to that body of Soviet literature devoted to the themes of "reconstruction of the national economy," "socialist industrialization," and the "struggle for the socialist transformation of the countryside" that had appeared after the civil war in response to the Party's campaign for electrification and industrialization.[6] This intent is borne out in their central episodes of land reclamation and electrification, which are presented as synecdoches for the larger efforts by the Soviet Union to transform the countryside and industrialize itself (though the diminutive scale of their deeds may at the same time already represent a subtle detraction from the kind of large-scale triumphs portrayed in works like Gladkov's *Tsement*). Thus the hero of "Kak zazhglas'" constructs an electrical generator for a village, that of "Rodina elektrichestva" ameliorates the lot of some peasants by converting their makeshift generator into an irrigation pump, the heroine of "Peschanaia uchitel'nitsa" begins to teach villagers in the central Asian desert how to build wind breaks and grow crops, and the peasants in "Lugovye mastera" drain and cultivate a former swamp.

Similar echoes of the literature of socialist (re)construction may be detected in the stories' frequent reference to that genre's favored theme of the need to bridge the gap between worker and peasant (Lenin's famous *smychka*). The projects all take place in more or less remote villages, with the heroes who execute them clearly embodying the idea of "linkage" between village and city. Thus, the narrator in "Rodina elektrichestva" is an electrician sent from the city to assist the village of Verchovka, Mariia Nikiforovna in "Peschanaia uchitel'nitsa" is a city-educated teacher sent to transform a remote desert village, and so forth. The narrator of "Kak zazhglas'" merely renders this topicality explicit when he remarks that he wants to set up the generator not only for the use of the thing, but also for "the construction of socialism," and later declares in a speech that by building a power station the villagers are fulfilling "Il'ich's bidding" ("*zavet Il'icha*") and laying "the basis of socialism."[7]

The very ideology of the Soviet drive toward electrification and industrialization, with its program for the physical transformation of the Soviet countryside and accompanying vision of an electrified Russia imposing "order, progress, knowledge, and technology"[8] on dark, chaotic nature, undoubtedly appealed to Platonov's own, rather manichean, view

of the world as the site of conflict between "consciousness" and
"matter" (indeed, the two visions share some philosophical
sources). But in these tales of reclamation what is typical of
Platonov's relation to the Soviet literary mainstream in general
is that even as he appears to participate in the literature of
socialist (re)construction he alters both the focus and the tenor
of the genre by insinuating into its stock terms his own tragic
vision of existence.

The strategies of this ultimately ironic participation are
perhaps best seen in the stories' adaptation of the theme of
Russia's backwardness that figured prominently (as part of the
"pathos" of socialist construction) in the literature of the mid
1920s, but was later all but eliminated under the more
voluntarist emphases of its Stalinist successor.[9] What Platonov
does is to distort the place allotted in the myth to these trials of
the present, exploiting the possibilities they present for
investigating the hardships of physical existence and postponing
any vision of the radiant future that might supplant them. With
the present thus magnified and the future deferred, the kinds of
suffering he had witnessed during the central-Russian drought
of the early twenties are allowed to stand as a definitive portrait
of man's existential lot.[10]

The characters of these stories thus inhabit a realm of dire
scarcity, in which physical sustenance, if present at all, is locked
away beneath the surface of the earth and living beings tend to
be desiccated, enfeebled, and tragically subject to decay (as
"Dzhan" would later, "Peschanaia uchitel'nitsa" literalizes
this condition by situating its tale at the edge of the "dead
Central Asian desert"). In "Rodina elektrichestva," for
example, the whole of nature is said to smell of "decay and
dust" and the effects of the drought are brought home to the
narrator as he watches a religious procession move across the
"dry, naked earth" (60), conducted by a priest who chants
into the "hot silence of nature" and waves his censer at the
"wild, sullen plants" along the path (62). The villagers in
"Rodina" are starving, as are the peasants among whom
Mariia Nikiforovna is sent to live in "Peschanaia uchitel'nitsa."
Even the inanimate objects contiguous with human life bear

the imprint of the world's hostility, such as the huts in Verchovka, which "had already decayed, the beams of their foundations rotting in the earth" (64).

More important to the evolution of Platonov's prose than such cameos of desolation, however, is the manner in which these tales begin to translate the abstract philosophical notions at the center of Platonov's world view into a more particularized, and hence "realistic," vision of the self in its relation to the physical world. One salient reflection of this process is the emphasis the stories place on their characters' physicality. References to the body occur frequently, its condition at any given moment serving as a kind of barometer of how being is faring in the world (even gulleys in the parched fields of "Rodina" are said to have formed in the "body of the earth," like "the sunken spaces between the ribs of an emaciated skeleton," 60). Platonov is particularly concerned with the evidence left on the body by the world's frictive opposition, the corporeal traces of the "difficult existence" being must endure. Just as the decaying huts in Verchovka stand in yards overgrown with weeds, the aging priest who heads the procession in "Rodina" is said to be "overgrown" with "gray wool" ("*obrosshii sedoi sherst'iu*," 62), and appears "tormented and blackened" ("*izmuchennyi i pochernevshii*"), as though a decaying object. The icon of the Virgin borne by the procession is similarly desacralized into a portrait of a weary, working-class woman, whose lifetime of hardships manifests itself in the appearance of her hand ("huge and covered with veins") and the wrinkles around her mouth, which reveal her familiarity with the vicissitudes ("*zlost'iu*") of everyday existence (63).[11]

The moment in which the ontological vision of Platonov's major works begins to take shape, however, is that in which he turns from simple "physicality" to the more specific theme of the relation between the body and the being that resides within it. It is to this theme and its associated imagery that Platonov would repeatedly turn in his (ultimately unsuccessful) efforts to reconcile the idealist and materialist impulses underlying his world view. Its clearest expression among the works of his "transitional" period may be found in the description of the religious procession in "Rodina" (62–64) – a passage more anticipatory, in both theme and style, of his mature manner than perhaps anything he wrote before *Chevengur*.

Among the procession's members the narrator meets an old woman who announces that even though she crosses herself she knows the gesture to be in vain, since despite her prayers her entire family has died and she herself now lives purely "by habit." The narrator tells her that "nature" fears "reason" rather than prayers, and it is her response to this *Proletkul't* slogan which foregrounds the passage's ontological theme. She has lived so long, she claims, that all that remains of her is "reason and bones," her flesh having long ago been "poured into" work and cares, so that "there is little left in me to die; everything has died little by little." What is characteristic in her remark is not only its pessimistic account of life as perpetual struggle, but also its depiction of that life as a *physical* process of depletion, in which being appears as a finite entity gradually depleted of its vital force and converted bit by bit into its opposite (matter, death). This implied reduction of being to its physical vessel is further underscored when the old woman removes her kerchief and tells the narrator to look at her head (a common episode in a Platonov work, presenting the protagonist with an opportunity for examining a specimen of "being").

What the narrator sees is a decaying vessel, marked with traces of the world's frictive opposition, which moreover physically constitutes the extent of the "life" contained within it. He looks on her "skull grown bald," "the bones of which have become decrepit, decayed," ("*obvetshali*," the same verb used to describe the desuetous huts), and which are already prepared "to surrender to the irreversible dust (*bezvozvratnomu prakhu*) of the earth her painstakingly accumulated (*skupo skoplennyi*) and longsuffering mind, which had come to know the world through labor and hardships." That which is living (being, mind) turns out to be something carefully gathered within – but for that very reason wholly circumscribed by – the body; the possibility of its existence outside of or transcending this "skull" is cancelled by the promise of its conversion to matter when the body's own disintegration is complete. Not only does the physical vessel return to "dust," as it does in conventional Christian metaphysics, but the "life" accumulated within it does so as well.

This disintegration of being together with the corpus it fails to transcend essentially defines Platonov's existential theme as it had evolved by the mid twenties, and the mention in the passage of "dust" that cannot be gathered together again (*bezvozvratnyi prakh*) points up that theme's now dissentious relation to the philosophical doctrine from which it derives. The notion of collecting the "dust" of the deceased body is central to Fedorov's philosophy of the "common task," with its imperative that mankind unite in order to return the souls of the deceased to their redeemed and re-collected material vessels. The negation of this idea in Platonov's passage may thus be read as a dismissal of Fedorov's faith in resurrection and a return of being to the "dead" matter it had hoped to transcend.

Somewhere between the plausible endeavors of these tales of reclamation and the fantastic schemes of the earlier science fiction stories stands "Epifanskie shliuzy" (1927),[12] a relatively long work (*povest'*) often said to have inaugurated Platonov's career as a serious writer. "Epifanskie shliuzy" realizes the central theme of Platonov's works of the twenties – man's efforts to "take on" (conquer, manipulate, "*poznat'*") the world in which he lives – in the tale of an engineer's doomed attempt to complete a land reclamation project of gargantuan proportions. An English engineer named Bertran Perri (i.e., Bertrand Perry) arrives in Russia in the early eighteenth century to oversee a grand Petrine scheme for constructing a series of locks between the Don and Oka rivers. The project is undertaken on a vast scale, but, after the expenditure of enormous labors and the deaths of countless peasant laborers, fails because the supply of water in the steppes is so meager that not even a raft can float through the canal, let alone a ship.

What has become characteristic of Platonov by this point in his evolution as a writer is that "reason" ("consciousness") enters this struggle to impose itself on the physical world

already enfeebled.[13] Perri arrives in Russia already weary,
lonely, and apprehensive about the labors before him, troubled
by the premonition that he has come to a land where "difficult
labor, loneliness, perhaps even an early death, awaited him."
The construction scheme that had intrigued him in far-off
Newcastle and appeared eminently feasible ("*iasno i spodru-
chno*," 232) on the charts he studied in Petersburg now provokes
in him the kind of apprehension of immoderateness that
underlies the catastrophic dénouements of Platonov's science
fiction works and is implicit in the reclamation tales' rejection
of grand endeavors. The very enormity of the steppes, which
seem to present no aspect of themselves on a scale manipulable
by man, begins to make the canal scheme appear the whim of
a "mad tsar." Exceeding the scope of reason, Perri's undertaking crosses over into the absurd, and he begins to be haunted
by the "frightening height of the sky over this continent,"
which one never sees over the "narrow" British isle on which
he was raised (231).

The focus of "Epifanskie shliuzy" thus becomes the process
of disintegration to which Perri's endeavor succumbs, the tale
amounting to a dystopian parable on the inevitable failure
awaiting any such attempt to transform the recalcitrant world.
Perri's regrets at having taken on the task "by storm" ("*takim
shturmom*," 234) soon prove justified as the steppe begins
sinisterly to disappoint his efforts to excavate the canal.
Earthen walls built to house the locks threaten to be washed
away in spring floods; the clerks and technicians assigned to a
second work site begin to die from fever, while the peasants
under their charge begin to abscond. Perri's fear that his
earthworks will be washed away prove groundless, but this is
the ironic result of his discovery, with horror, that he has
grossly overestimated the area's average rainfall. It turns out
that there will not be enough water in the locks for even a
rowboat to pass: the earth, which Perri earlier believed to
harbor fertility beneath its meager surface, refuses to release its
riches to man. Brief hopes are raised when an assistant discovers
a spring beneath a nearby lake that might be diverted to fill the
canal (another example of the fantasy of "passive harnessing"

of nature found in Platonov's earlier works), but the attempt to do so only perversely makes matters worse. Instead of tapping a supply of water, the hole the engineers drill begins to drain the lake. Their frantic efforts to stop the hole prove futile as the various objects lowered into it disappear into the "depths beneath the earth" ("*podzemniuiu glubinu*") and the water continues to drain into the "dry greedy sands" below ("*sukhie zhadnye peski*," 244).

I have paraphrased the dénouement of Perri's scheme at some length because its motifs reveal some of the ways in which Platonov's dramatization of his experience as a hydrologist, which already begins in the Voronezh articles and continues in both his science fiction and the tales of reclamation, was beginning to coalesce into a coherent symbolism of the natural world informed by ontological themes. The motif of drawing riches *from beneath* the surface of the earth (here represented by the hope that water can be brought up from beneath Lake Ivan), for example, appears in several stories as an embodiment of the proposition that the material poverty of man's existence is illusory, that he is not, after all, alienated from the earth – the routine disappointment of such hopes then doubling the pathos of man's lot by cancelling a foreshadowed redemption. Thus, in "Efirnyi trakt" the technological advances are supposed to enable man to draw buried minerals to the earth's surface, while in both "Rodina elektrichestva" and "Epifanskie shliuzy" reference is made to the fertile soil underlying the withered vegetation on the surface. That *water* is often the element chosen to symbolize the earth's redemptive riches is not surprising, given Platonov's profession and his experience with drought (not to mention the general mythological associations of water with life). But Platonov's use of it in this regard may also carry more specific ontological overtones: in its fluidity as well as its ability to sustain life water may have suggested itself to Platonov as a fitting antithesis, representative of "spirit," to the "dead matter" typically represented in his works by immobile and inorganic rocks, minerals, and sand.

Another hydrological motif important in Platonov's works of the 1920s involves episodes of sinister "rupture" or "puncturing" (sometimes a related "seepage"), which almost always serve as the proximate cause of their story's disaster. In "Epifanskie shliuzy" the "rupture" of the lake bottom signals the final collapse of Perri's scheme and concretizes the very theme of failure central to that tale: the draining of human effort by indifferent nature. A similar puncturing occurs in "Erik," when the troop of demons pierces a hole in the sky and out of it flows the "filth" of creation, and again in Erik's desire to stick his head through a hole in the sky to see if God is there – his absence proving that the world is just matter. The motif of ominous "draining" also figures in "Lugovye mastera," in which the river is called "*Lesnaia skvazhenka*" because at its center lies a large hole into which objects as large as trees have been known to disappear, while the title of "Buchilo" is a specialist term for this very phenomenon (a "sink"). The *spiral motion* of *whirlpools* further links this motif with that of endless circling, which in Platonov's earlier works is often tied to disaster (Markun's *perpetuum mobile*, which explodes, consists of a series of spiral tubes) or to the meaninglessness of existence. "Buchilo" deploys such a motif to represent the deadening ennui of village life; Vogulov's model of the universe is an ellipse symbolizing the universe's "imprisonment" within its own physical laws; while in "Peschanaia uchitel'nitsa" the desert condemns its nomadic inhabitants to a perpetual, cyclical journey in search of grass.

What is interesting about this symbolism is that, in addition to supplying an allegorical resonance to the elements of Platonov's landscapes, it suggests an emerging analogy with his vision of ontology. The analogy pivots on the image of *continence* central to both its orders.[14] Platonov's characters are forever struggling to erect some sort of barrier to hold at bay the invading forces of nature. In "Epifanskie shliuzy" Perry must build earthen walls along the canal route but worries that they will cave in during the spring floods; Mariia Nikiforovna's goal is to plant pine trees to serve as a windbreak against the intruding desert's sands ("Peschanaia uchitel'nitsa"), the flood waters must be kept out of the meadows in "Lugovye mastera," and so forth. These efforts to secure "continence" moreover routinely invoke an opposition between "inner" and "outer," in which what is "inner" is valorized positively and presented as vulnerable, in need of a sheltering wall, while what is "without" is in some way associated with the hostility of nature, the elements, or matter. This is precisely the task "Rodina elektrichestva," in its description of the old woman, portrays as the lamentable result of man's existence within a body: the painstaking hoarding of "being" (her "*skupo skoplennyi um*") within a corpus that is itself subject to decay. What resonates in these episodes of sinister rupture (of which "Epifanskie shliuzy" is merely the most protracted example), then, is the ultimate form of tragedy in Platonov's world: the yielding to relentless pressure from without of the vessel in which being is housed, and the resulting surrender of that being to the dominance of the physical world.

In addition to its ontological symbolism, "Epifanskie shliuzy" further accomplishes an important transition to Platonov's works of the late 1920s and early 1930s by paying more elaborate attention to social and political themes, particularly that of the state (*gosudarstvo*).[15] Perri must contend not only with the elements and the daunting topography of the steppes, but with an obstinate peasantry and the Russian bureaucracy as well. The Epifan' peasants are constantly either running off in droves or threatening to rise up, and are "wild and gloomy in their ignorance," as Perri's brother William warns in a letter (221).[16] The theme of "bureaucracy" appears when these same peasants enmesh Perri in a web of gothic intrigue by sending the tsar a denunciation of their "evil" overseers, even though it turns out they have been getting out of work by bribing the military commander in charge of them. Perri also develops a specific fear of *the state's* retribution for his failure to build the locks, and when a messenger from the tsar at last knocks on the door he trembles at "the sharp rap of an official hand" ("*ot rezkogo stuka kazennoi ruki*," 228).

A response to the all too genuine bureaucratization of Soviet society in the mid 1920s, the bureaucratic theme formed an important topos of early Soviet literature and culture. In Platonov's case it also had specific autobiographical impli-

cations as the literary reflection of that disappointment with his
role as *Proletkul'tertrager* for the Soviet state so evident in the
Tambov letters to his wife. The theme is equally important,
however, as an early example of the specific type of historical
irony informing such later works as *Chevengur* and *Kotlovan*.

Both the historical setting of "Epifanskie shliuzy" and its
self-conscious imitation of "Petrine" forms of speech may be
attributed directly to the tale's underlying theme of the conflict
between mind and the material world. The Russian historical
consciousness traditionally views Peter's reign as having
brought about a fateful confrontation between the scientific
culture of rationalism, imported from the West, and a
benighted, primitive Russia.[17] It was in fact for this very reason
that Petrine historical themes enjoyed a revival in Soviet
literature of the mid twenties, which looked to the eighteenth
century as a paradigm for the new regime's efforts to build
socialism (this partly in reaction to a somewhat earlier
infatuation with "Eurasianism," with its interpretation of
Peter's reign as the calamitous truncation of Russia's true
historical self).[18] As in the reclamation tales, however,
Platonov's participation in this aspect of his literary context
turns out to be largely ironic. The pessimism underlying
"Epifanskie shliuzy" is such that in the end neither nature, the
peasants, nor the scheme of the mad tsar serves as the final
cause of Perri's disaster, which instead stands as the product of
a pathetic inevitability. Nonetheless, what is signalled in the
tale's adaptation of the dual Petrine legend of a tsar bent on a
voluntarist reshaping of the world and the "dark," recalcitrant
peasants who resist his will is Platonov's rejection of the entire
phenomenon of state sponsorship as an agency capable of
mounting an assault on nature. In this the very geographic
setting of "Epifanskie shliuzy" may have played an important
role. The locks Perri attempts to build have their authentic
prototype in the abandoned remains, dating from the Petrine
era, of some locks Platonov had seen on the Voronezh river.[19]
What their presence must have communicated to him was the
inevitable failure of state-sponsored projects for subduing
nature, the ready-made fatalism of the local landmark

deepened by its ironic proximity to a settlement named "Epifan'" ("Epiphany"). Nor, the tale's eighteenth-century mask notwithstanding, were critics slow to perceive an allusion to the Soviet present. V. Strel'nikova, for example, accused Platonov of writing "Epifanskie shliuzy" explicitly to cast doubts on the progress of socialist construction.[20]

In "Epifanskie shliuzy" the consequences of this historical irony extend to the very poetics of the text. Like several of the protagonists who precede him (Vogulov in "Satana mysli," Kreitskopf in "Lunnaia bomba," for example), Perri is torn between his public role as engineer and his own rather morbid private life. The latter typically provides Platonov with the vantage point from which to derive insights into man's corporeality and the alienating disharmonies of the world. But it also, paradoxically, often threatens to subvert the very public utopian activities that have been undertaken to alleviate the sufferings of the private self. This rearrangement of priorities can be sensed when Perri turns out to have enlisted in Peter's attempt to civilize Russia *so that* his fiancée Mary will want him as a husband, or when both Vogulov and the heroes of "Efirnyi trakt" abandon their projects out of personal grief. One can even detect a consistent pattern in these works, in which the plot begins in the intimate sphere (the lonely and troubled life of the hero), then moves outward into narration of the utopian project (which the hero directs), only to revert to, and close with, the hero's personal demise (typically following the failure of his utopian project).

At the root of this tension lies a hesitation between genres, which itself derives from one of the deeper ambivalences of Platonov's world view. On the one hand, the kind of intense consciousness these works display of the self in its troubled relation to the world naturally inclined Platonov toward narrative forms that accept an anxious subjectivity as the only tenable perspective on life (for example, late romanticism, or some of the varieties of Russian modernism that almost certainly influenced him). But on the other hand Platonov had long been drawn to systems of belief promising the resolution of man's existential dilemma within the larger framework of human history (Fedorov's insistence on uniting humanity before resurrecting the dead, Bogdanov's on the historical evolution of "consciousness"), and this interest impelled him in the direction of literary forms embracing, rather than negating, the significance of social and historical experience. This second narrative tendency may be regarded as a kind of "realism" capable of drawing Platonov into the Soviet literary mainstream; but it was the tension *between* these two narrative tendencies which was to define the peculiarly hybrid "genre" of Platonov's major works, in which the hero's intimate sufferings enter into uneasy involvement with utopian attempts to bring about history's end. Those works' tendency to entertain, then abandon, historical solutions to the problems of being in turn reflects a hesitation between the desire for ontological redemption and pessimism over whether the sorrows of subjective existence can ever be overcome.

Platonov's doubts concerning the utopian perspective he had embraced in his Voronezh period found further expression in "Gorod Gradov" ("The City of Gradov"; 1927, 1928), which inaugurates the cycle of satirical, antibureaucratic tales he wrote in the late 1920s and early 1930s (the others are "Che-Che-O," "Usomnivshiisia Makar," "Gosudarstvennyi zhitel'," "Vprok"). The story has received much attention for its attack on the Soviet bureaucracy, but it is considerably more complex and incomplete than its apparent satire might suggest. There are, in fact, two competing versions of "Gorod Gradov" reflecting different thematic emphases.[21]

In one version (or, since the delineations are not entirely clear in either version, in one of the tale's evident motivations) "Gorod Gradov" is a denunciation of the backwardness of provincial Russia in the tradition of Saltykov-Shchedrin (with whose "Istoriia odnogo goroda" it is often compared). To this motivation belongs the tale of Shmakov's journey to Gradov in order to introduce reason into its benighted affairs. The town has acquired a reputation for squandering state funds on pointless but elaborate schemes, and has evolved into a nest of Soviet civil servants, one of whom is lavishly feted in the story's central scene. To this Shchedrinian context Platonov adds the theme of bureaucracy as an abnegation of the task of transforming nature – a typical method of recontextualization for him. As Shmakov rides the train to Gradov, he hears in the distance how "weak locomotives" wail mournfully as they "prepare to overcome the melancholy autumnal spaces filled with sparse and impoverished life," while the sound of children crying in the third-class section intensifies a general air of "agitation and helpless pity" (301). Gradov's bureaucrats, however, believe that nature can be conquered on paper. They sit "in safety from the wild elements of the world, multiplying written documents, conscious that they were multiplying order and harmony in an absurd and uncertified world" (312).

Competing with this Shchedrinian line, however, is a different narrative whose representation in the text was enhanced by the changes Platonov made for the version published in *Krasnaia panorama* (1928). Here Shmakov emerges not as an agent of common sense but as a utopian theoretician of bureaucratism whose "*Zapiski gosudarstvennogo cheloveka*" praise the "clerk" as the "most valuable agent of Soviet history" and bureaucracy itself as the force unifying the otherwise chaotic Soviet state. Whereas the Shchedrinian satire exalts reason, this second line recalls Zamiatin's *My* (1920) in its rejection of empty, bureaucratic order and implicit elevation of things natural and irrational. Shmakov, for example, is ironically presented as disliking nature because it resists bureaucratic manipulation ("in it something is always going on," 306), though even he begins to recognize that "laws and other official directives" may in fact represent a "violation of the living body of the universe" (323).

What is striking is that the desire for a utopian organization of the cosmos here derided is identical to that espoused *unironically* in so many of the Voronezh articles. Bogdanov's "organizational science" is clearly parodied in one of the titles Shmakov invents for his paean to bureaucracy ("Sovietization as the Basis for the Harmonization of the Universe"), while that of a manuscript discovered after Shmakov's death satirizes the proletarian poet A. Gastev's *Normalizovannyi rabochii*: "The Principles of the Depersonalization of Man, with the Goal of his

Rebirth as an Absolute Citizen with Properly Regularized Acts at Every Moment of his Existence" (327). "Gorod Gradov," then, makes explicit the access of dystopian doubt that Platonov had been experiencing since the mid 1920s. But it also, in a manner very characteristic of him, *simultaneously* laments the failure of "organizational" schemes (the bureaucracy will only tackle nature on paper) and rejects them as overweening and artificial.

Even more than Perri's involvement with the state and the satire of bureaucracy in "Gorod Gradov," two of the most significant works Platonov wrote in this transitional period show how his fiction was becoming increasingly responsive to Soviet historical experience, at the same time that he continued to interpret that experience in the idiosyncratic terms of his vision of being. "Iamskaia sloboda" ("Iamskaia settlement"; 1927) is instructive precisely because it reads like an experimental piece in which Platonov has not yet fully worked out the relationship between competing historicist and subjectivist impulses. The tale is clearly intended as a realistic examination of the Revolution's social effects – arguably Platonov's first serious treatment of this theme – and it is informed, moreover, by a Marxist–Leninist understanding of class relationships. In this sense it appears to be an attempt to merge with or at least parallel the literary mainstream of the late 1920s.

Following an ironic account of the settlement's origins in the reign of Catherine the Great (reminiscent at once of the tsarist theme in "Epifanskie shliuzy" and the history of the provincial town provided in Pil'niak's *Golyi god*), "Iamskaia sloboda" chronicles the existence of a meek, impoverished peasant named Filat on the eve of the Revolution. The particular concern of this "realist" chronicle is the workings of the provincial bourgeois economy that is about to be overthrown, especially the fringes of that economy where people like Filat eke out their sorry existence. The local landowners collect easy rent and exploit their peasant tenants to the hilt, while the peasants themselves live in destitution virtually outside the money economy (though Filat eventually joins in a scheme to manufacture hats out of discarded felt boots). In the end, however, soldiers returning from war report the region to be in the hands of the soviets and Filat begins to understand what the Revolution means.

Insinuated into this realist tale of a poor peasant's emergence from provincial poverty into an awareness of his place in history, however, is another which prompts a reinterpretation of the ostensible narrative's themes. The burden of this second narrative line is to recount, in ontological terms deriving from Platonov's Voronezh period, the genesis of "consciousness" within a life wholly ruled by the forces of matter.[22] One indication of this interpolated concern is the tale's attention to the theme of physicality, which, as in the earlier "village" sketches, tends to move beyond its anecdotal function in order to convey the burdensome nature of existence. Filat, for example, at one point feels "his body, which brought him constant misfortune from the desire to live," while inanimate objects inspire envy because they appear to escape an alienated consciousness of their lot: "Svat envied dead, immobile things... they lived in some kind of peace and complete self-absorption (*v kakom-to pokoe i polnom otdanii sebia*)."

More interesting in "Iamskaia sloboda," however, is the manner in which Platonov discovers a pretext for his ontological theme within the tale's "realist" concern with the settlement's economy – testimony to that theme's persistence even as he moved away from the formulaic means of expressing it contained in his early articles and fiction. "Iamskaia sloboda" turns out to be as much about the "economy" of physical existence as it is about that of wage and labor relations. Perpetual hunger has reduced Filat to a state in which the presence or absence of a single meal influences the level of vital energy within him, this severe arithmetic of survival underscoring the immediacy of his "being's" dependence on the body. His employer will give him only vegetables to eat, and though he has grown used to this condition it is because (again, with a consciousness of life's energy equation), "you don't have to eat much just in order to breathe" ("*na odno dykhanie mnogo*

*est' ne nado,"* 278). The *wearing out* of his clothing over which
Filat agonizes becomes emblematic of the general fate of
physical things in this Platonovian world (*"nikakaia ushivka
bol'she ne derzhalos' na prozrachnykh, sgorevshikh ot pota shtanakh, a
pidzhak istersia v kholodnyi lepestok,"* 291). Even the local
merchants' greed takes the form of stinginess rather than
acquisitiveness: Iamskaia so scrupulously guards its possessions
that even drinking glasses are willed to future generations, and
children are beaten exclusively for breaking things.[23]

This same "subversive" reinterpretation of realist themes
extends to the tale's central episode of Filat's emergence from
benighted oppression into historical "consciousness." Before
the Revolution Filat is portrayed as dim-witted and only barely
capable of self-reflection, and Platonov supplies this condition
with a direct political-economic cause (the endless need to work
has prevented Filat from ever having time to "come to his
senses and think with his head about extraneous matters,"
278). Platonov's descriptions of the process by which "consciousness" stirs within Filat, however, reveal a more fundamental concern with the theme of "mind's" epiphanic
generation within the material substratum of existence. Filat's
efforts to "think" are presented as the laborious struggle of
"consciousness" to manifest itself physically. His mind is
variously described as overlaid by "fat" and capable of only
the most ponderous of movements (at one point, for example,
he is on the verge of entertaining a thought; "his mind,
overgrown with the complacent fat of inactivity, imagined and
recollected darkly, hugely, and frighteningly – like the first
movement of mountains frozen into crystals by pressure," 282);
or to it is ascribed a kind of literal "thickness" and viscosity (at
night Filat hears the far-off barking of some dogs "through the
thickness of his darkened slow consciousness," 270). There is an
important paradox in these descriptions, however, because
even as they provide vivid literalizations of the advent of
"consciousness" within the physical body they also (subtly)
imply its *reduction* to that body. This reduction of consciousness,
at the very moment of its ascendance, to the matter of the body
becomes explicit when Filat's soul is said to reside, palpably, in

his throat ("Filat felt his soul like a lump in his throat, and sometimes stroked his throat when he felt miserable from loneliness," 283). The generation of thoughts inside Filat is ultimately portrayed as the literal ascent through the body of something physical, which then emerges in a crude verbal form suggestive of Platonov's own "deformed" literary style:

"Like everyone who has worked a lot, Filat was unable to think right away...he first felt something, then his feeling made its way up into his head, rattling and changing its tender construction. And this feeling at first so roughly shook his thought that the thought came out monstrous and he couldn't pronounce it smoothly" ("*ona rozhdalas' chudovishchem i ee nel'zia bylo gladko vygovorit'*," 286–7).

"Iamskaia sloboda" thus invests the tale of a poor peasant's awakening to historical awareness with an account of the burden of physicality that existence cannot escape. "Sokrovennyi chelovek" ("The Innermost Man"; 1927) places these concerns in a still more explicit confrontation with the events of the October Revolution. Its hero is a semi-literate mechanic of peasant origin named Pukhov who fights in the civil war on the side of the Red Army but as the hostilities come to a close has difficulty finding a place for himself within the new Soviet society. After some peripatetic wanderings he accommodates himself to the new order by signing on to work among the oil rigs of Baku; but the tentativeness with which he does so suspends rather than resolves the story's underlying tensions. Pukhov remains, as the officials in his native Prokharinsk put it, "not an enemy, but some kind of wind blowing past the sail of the revolution" (393).

The factors complicating Pukhov's acceptance of the new regime in part suggest that "Sokrovennyi chelovek" is a response to the general preoccupation of Soviet literature of the mid to late 1920s with the problem of individualism versus collectivity (itself a facet of the "spontaneity-consciousness dialectic" discussed by Clark).[24] Pukhov grows wary of the bureaucratism in which he sees the Party entrenching itself (former friends of his become officials with pretentious titles and desk jobs), and takes offence at the Bolsheviks' attack on religion – not because he himself is a believer, but because "people are used to placing their heart in religion and they haven't found such a place in the revolution" (366). It is the "preoccupation with one's own life" ("*obol'shchenie sobstvennoi zhizn'iu*") which keeps people going, he declares, and wonders how one can institute an "International" among people when "the native land is a matter of the heart, and not the entire earth" (364). Both the story's title and its picaresque genre (Voronskii on reading it declared its hero "a regular Russian Eulenspiegel") point to this theme, which is in turn but a variant of the tension between "intimate" and "historical" perspectives informing many of Platonov's works of the 1920s.[25]

In this assertion of the priority of the intimate self over the collectivism of the new regime "Sokrovennyi chelovek" differs markedly from such encomia to subordination as Furmanov's *Chapaev* or Gladkov's *Tsement*, and in its ambivalent accommodation recalls the scene of capitulation to the collective with which Olesha's *Zavist'*, published in the same year, ends. But the essential difference between Platonov and other Soviet contributors to this theme lies in the ontological context within which his notion of "individualism" is asserted, and from which Pukhov's reservations about the new regime ultimately derive.

Pukhov has other doubts about the new order that apprehend a failure more fundamental than its bureaucratism, conformism, or lack of respect for machines. The story opens just after his wife has died, and it is "abstract thoughts" having "nothing to do with his qualification or social origins" about her death and what it reveals of the "workings of the worldwide laws of matter" that most complicate his acquiescence to Soviet rule. Pukhov is tentatively willing to admit the "justness" of such laws (a mirror of his tentative accommodation on another level to the Soviet order), but his sorrow over the loss of someone close to him makes him realize his alienation from nature ("*otlichie ot prirody*"). He wants to "complain to the whole collective of mankind about [man's] general defenselessness" (364).

Pukhov's picaresque journey across the landscape of Russia's civil war in fact comprises a series of revelations of nature's relentless opposition to man. Pukhov experiences the world's malevolence in the form of both natural catastrophes (the blizzard that thwarts efforts to clear snow from the tracks and, later, the violent storm that turns back a naval assault on Vrangel's forces in the Crimea) and the human devastation brought about by the civil war, which is here treated, like nature itself, as another of the destructive forces at large in the world.

The literalness with which this myth translates its philosophical sources into narrative may be seen from Platonov's repeated characterization of the natural obstacles Pukhov encounters as an obdurate substance whose impeding mass must be "overcome" or "plowed through" (cf. Bogdanov's notion of matter's "resistance" to human labor). The locomotive on which Pukhov goes to clear the tracks, for example, struggles through snow "heavier than sand," until finally, in one of Platonov's favorite versions of catastrophe, it crashes into an enormous drift, spinning its wheels and "trembling from the fierce penned up force inside it, its breast violently pressing the mountains of snow in front of it" (336). Even the sea ventured into during the naval assault takes on the features of a viscous and impeding materiality (cf. Kreitskopf's experience of the material cosmos in "Lunnaia bomba"). One of the boats becomes lost in the "nocturnal thickness" ("*nochnaia gushcha*"), the ships make their way through the thick gruel of darkness ("*prodiralis' v sploshnoi kashe t'my*") with their propellors churning "they could see not what, some kind of thick wetness (*kakuiu-to tiaguchuiu vlagu*)," while the waves "rub against one another from so many of them being pressed together," their "brimstone" foam "hissing like some poisonous substance" and drops of water strike the sailors' faces "like gravel" (352–53).

Correspondingly, the plight of living beings in "Sokrovennyi chelovek" tends to express itself in terms of the fragile body's exposure (usually literal) to some frictive force at large in the world. One of the ships struggling to cross the Straits of Kerch, for example, is flung about the sea "like a dry leaf," its "fragile

body creaking mournfully" (353), while Pukhov, riding a
train, is said to have "lowered himself into the wind together
with the others, drawn along and helpless as an inert body"
(368). Moreover the impingement of such forces on the body is
often literalized as the body's erosion or wearing away (*iznos*,
an important motif in Platonov). The naked trees and dead
grass Pukhov sees from the train are frail from "climatic erosion
(*ot klimaticheskogo iznosa*) and trampling by the war's campaigns" (365), and Pukhov attributes his wife's death directly
to her "having *worn out* prematurely" ("*ot prezhdevremennogo
iznosa*," 396; in both examples the Russian conflates mechanical
and natural processes of decay).

The suggestion accruing from all these juxtapositions of frail
beings to the world's corrosive forces is that the story's title
alludes, not so much to the theme of the individual versus the
collective, as to the vulnerable, inner being-within-the-body
whose existence is perpetually under assault from the forces of
matter. The link between ontological themes and revolutionary
events comes to the fore, however, when we are told that it is
specifically the death of Pukhov's wife which makes him realize
"in what direction and to what end were aimed all revolutions
and every kind of human agitation." The Fedorovian note in
this passage is confirmed when Pukhov hopes the new order
will bring about the "scientific resurrection of the dead," and
when he feels that resurrection to be guaranteed by the
mechnical calm with which death operates ("death acted with
such calmness that it seemed the belief in the scientific
resurrection of the dead was not mistaken," 385; cf. Fedorov's
belief that if man is essentially a physical object, then
resurrection must follow from the simple reassembly of that
object's parts).

The eccentric, individualistic Pukhov's relation to the new
regime is thus made to turn on the question of whether it will
tackle the dilemmas of physical existence, and this dependency
amounts to an assertion of ontology's priority over history.
Even his capitulation preserves this hierarchy: when Pukhov
agrees to settle down, his decision is motivated by the
opportunity he has found to work on machines, which provide

him with a feeling of empathy with all the "people who had labored alone against the matter of the entire world" (396). At the same time the topical theme of the individual's relation to the regime need not be viewed as extraneous to the tale's deeper concerns. A progression from *resistance to* some larger order or force, to reluctant *submission* to it all the same, is precisely what characterizes Platonov's vision of ontology.

## THE EVOLUTION OF PLATONOV'S LITERARY STYLE, 1919–1928

This study has concerned itself until now primarily with the thematics of Platonov's prose, in particular with the process through which his interest in the utopian philosophies of Fedorov and Bogdanov translated itself, in a variety of generic and episodic contexts, into a series of examinations of man's ontological condition. Yet Platonov's reputation as one of the major figures in Soviet literature rests more than anything on his verbal style, on his creation of a linguistic medium widely held to be both "strange" and somehow highly apposite to the world view expressed in his works. In fact, an investigation into the poetic principles motivating this "unique" Platonovian style forms the necessary culmination of any discussion of his themes. This is so because, far from serving as mere embellishment, the semantics of literary style in Platonov's mature works comes to serve as the iconic embodiment of his ontological theme. Platonov resembles the modernists in that it is ultimately to language, especially to its odd but idealogically motivated permutations in the Soviet era, that he looks for evidence of the ontological fate of the world.

How, then, did this in many ways untutored, provincial writer of working-class origins, an adherent of a rather eccentric set of utopian beliefs, come to produce some of the most sophisticated literary prose his country has known – in a style, moreover, which is interpretable in either a modernist or a populist vein, and which perhaps shares features of both? Platonov's works of the Voronezh period do not obviously anticipate what was to come. They imitate a plurality of styles, but the eclectic nature of the imitation suggests the awkward searchings of an autodidact as much as it does any urge toward verbal experimentation.

This eclecticism presents itself as early as the verse collection *Golubaia glubina* (1922), whose obvious borrowings range from Nadson, Bal'mont, and the symbolism of the "peasant" poets, to the sharply contrasting declamatory manner and utopian themes of the Smithy group.[26] A similar magpie quality characterizes the manner of Platonov's first attempts at literary prose. The fact that a significant portion of the works completed in the Voronezh years (including several first published in the 1927 *Epifanskie shliuzy* collection) are written in a form of comic *skaz* suggests that Platonov was infected with some of the era's infatuation with egregious stylistic effect (that is, the early Soviet vogue for "ornamental prose," whose roots lie in the preceding decades' modernist experimentation). "Chul'dik i Epishka" (1920), for example, deploys markedly vulgar lexicon and syntactic patterns typical of oral speech to create the impression of a peasant narrator, while the verbal grotesqueries and onomastic play of "Buchilo" (1924) point toward a specifically Gogolian influence.[27] The childhood stories, on the other hand, are written in an emotive style closely related to the sentimental and folk intonations of *Golubaia glubina*. Typically these works blend intentionally simple, "childish" phrasing with "village" lexicon and rhythmic patterns reminiscent of Russian folk songs, often interweaving a kind of philosophical diction deriving from Platonov's immersion in the writings of Bogdanov and Fedorov.[28]

That the motley array of styles affected in Platonov's early works was preparing the ground for a stylistic manner defined by its very heterogeneity perhaps first becomes apparent in the science fiction tales, which typically depict some confrontation between childhood/rural and adult/urban milieux, and in which a sort of generalized village-sentimental diction runs up against passages couched in either *Proletkul't* slogans or the technical manner of "scientific" description (the latter especially in passages describing the heroes' utopian inventions). "Satana mysli" (1922), for example, opens with a nostalgic glance at the hero's childhood that is saturated with sentimental folk lexicon, only to shift rapidly to a series of utopian slogans masquerading as descriptive sentences.[29] "V zvezdnoi pustyne" (1921) similarly begins with a sentimental-philosophical meditation on clouds passing overhead, then switches abruptly to what are best described as barely mediated Smithy refrains.[30]

To this array of verbal manners the *Epifanskie shliuzy* collection (1927) adds the conspicuous, if short-lived, influence of Pil'niak, in whose brand of literary modernism attention is drawn to the language of the text through the device of stylistic heterogeneity ("montage"). In this regard the collection anticipates the brief interlude of collaboration between the two authors in the second half of 1928. The most pronounced signs of Pil'niak's influence in these texts is their frequent incorporation of complete "documents" and their use of differing typefaces and typographic devices to delineate such linguistic realia as signs, labels, letters, and the frontispieces of books (all reminiscent of *Golyi god*; Langerak, "Kommentarii k sborniku A. P. Platonova 'Epifanskie shliuzy'," pp. 143–44). A Pil'niakian inspiration would also seem to underly some of the stories' interest in pre-Petrine Russia (especially that of provincial towns, as in "Ivan Zhokh" and the opening section of "Gorod Gradov"), while "Epifanskie shliuzy" itself embarks on one of the most radical of Platonov's early stylistic experiments by affecting an elaborate, quasi-eighteenth-century diction reminiscent at once of Pil'niak and Remizov (the latter influence may be inferred from Platonov's allusion, in a letter to his wife, to the tale's style as "*slavianskaia viaz'*," or "slavonic word-weaving").[31]

For all the awkwardness, derivativeness, and conventionality that these stories reveal in comparison with Platonov's later masterpieces, their verbal manner nonetheless anticipates some of the fundamental stylistic principles of the mature prose. Though it clearly arises out of a desire to participate, via imitation, in the 1920s vogue for "ornamental" prose, Platonov's willingness to experiment with a variety of literary styles signals an important preoccupation with the verbal surface of the text and an urge to assign it a poetic weight rivalling that of themes, imagery, and plot. Over time, that urge was to place linguistic phenomena at the center of his works' structure of meaning. The stylistic *clashes* this urge engendered also point toward one of the hallmarks of Platonov's later style. It would be overstating the case to claim that the stylistic "lapses" of even Platonov's earliest works represent a conscious effort at disharmony – the "unexpected tonal shifts" ("*perepady tonov*"; Eidinova, "K tvorcheskoi biografii A. Platonova," p. 221) of those works suggest rather an un-premeditated, "sincere" correspondence with the contradictions of Platonov's world view.[32] But the stories of 1920–1927 display a positive tolerance for stylistic dissonance that, even as it appears the product of Platonov's literary provincialism, paves the way toward an aesthetic of the grotesque and establishes affinities with the verbal "deformations" cultivated by the avant-garde.[33] Nor should one overlook the importance of the very principle of *stylization* Platonov derived from ornamental prose. Be it through *skaz* imitation of peasant speech, the incorporation of bureaucratic documents, or the affectation of Petrine Russian, Platonov's works demonstrate from the outset a tendency to identify a specific set of verbal traits with an underlying and motivating world view, and it was the eventual use of this principle to designate certain forms of discourse as a "language of utopia" that prepared the ground for the complex ironization of Soviet rhetoric in *Chevengur* and *Kotlovan*.[34]

The "peculiar" literary style for which Platonov is known begins to emerge from the eclectic experiments of his early prose in the works of 1926–1927, that is, in the "transitional" period between Voronezh and Moscow during which he had decided to leave his technical career in order to devote himself to writing, and, significantly, had begun work on *Chevengur*. The matrix of the literary style that began to appear in these works may be said to lie in a reinterpretation of certain principles of *skaz* narration – though Platonov was to transcend that genre's traditional emphases and, indeed, the tale of that transcendance in many ways defines the evolution of his verbal art.

As the examples cited above demonstrate, *skaz* initially appears in Platonov's stories in its conventional pairing of oral performance with Leskovian sociolect, the "uncouth" speech of both characters and narrator typically deployed as part of a satirical-propagandistic effort to expose village backwardness and peasant resistance to the Soviet regime.[35] When this "substandard," provincial speech comes into contact with the literate culture of the Revolution – specifically as Platonov begins increasingly to portray his semi-literate characters' encounters with the new, Soviet world and the bookish rhetoric of *agitprop* and Marxist–Leninist theory in which it expresses itself – the predictable outcome is a grotesque hybrid of elevated and base speech reminiscent of Zoshchenko's Soviet philistines. The peasants in "Kak zazhglas' lampa Il'icha" (1926) garble *agitprop* and technical phraseology, the village official in "Rodina elektrichestva" (1926) ludicrously describes everyday affairs in Smithy verse, and Pukhov in "Sokrovennyi chelovek" (1927), epitomizing the tendency and laying it bare, comically misreads *agitprop* posters and supplies confused answers to an examination in political and technical literacy. Indeed, a number of passages so resemble Zoshchenko as to suggest his direct influence (the importance of which at this stage is not diminished by the fact that Platonov was later to feel a certain antipathy for the kind of literature Zoshchenko embodied).[36]

This collision of literate with illiterate speech forms, as well as the parallel it establishes with Zoshchenko, sheds light on the moment in Soviet culture from which Platonov's prose, in general, derives: that of the linguistic turmoil generated by the sudden enfranchisement of Russia's largely unlettered masses and their exposure (through indoctrination, mass education, and the endless meetings of a plethora of newly-formed organizations) to a radically new form of public discourse saturated with the abstract concepts of Marxist–Leninist political theory and the bookish forms of their expression, and characterized by an unprecedented rhetoricity and penchant for figural speech.[37]

For all its reflection of Russia's post-revolutionary babel, however, the "vulgarized" language of Platonov's prose departs fairly early from the social-mimetic intentions predominant in the 1920s vogue for *skaz*. The crucial shift takes place in various of the works written in 1926–1927, when the popularity of *skaz* in Soviet literature was itself receding in favor of a more neutral narrative manner (*"priamoe slovo"*; Chudakova, *Poetika Mikhaila Zoshchenko*, p. 87). In these works verbal patterns clearly originating in an imitation of substandard speech begin to be deployed in a significantly altered relation to authorial voice. If "Buchilo" (1924) is still written in the conventional manner of *skaz*-as-oral-performance, its dialecticisms and stylistic lapses imposing a fictive narrative mask between author and text, by "Rodina elektrichestva" (1926) the narrative status of this mask deteriorates and the text becomes lingistically more complex. The types of solecism characteristic of *skaz* reproductions of "substandard" speech now begin to be disseminated alongside a variety of unironically literate and even elevated forms, all of which are subordinated to a narrative voice for whom such locutions represent but one among several possible modes of expression. From its opening paragraph the story offers up linguistic oddities (*"ia...snial s sebia rabochii pidzhak i lapti, chtoby na mne ostavalos' malo odezhdy,"* 60; here and elsewhere in this section, emphasis added), and it establishes the presence of a first-person narrator to whom they might be attributed. But that voice is, uncharacteristically, *not* attached to a figure of lower social origins (if anything, as a city-educated engineer dispatched to help bring light to the village, the narrator occupies a high, rather than low, position in the cultural hierarchy), and in later passages its role diminishes to that of a mere frame, within which *skaz*-like solecisms appear on strangely equal terms with neutral, descriptive forms (*"Shestvie naroda ostanovilos' okolo toi iamy, ikony byli postavleny likami sviatykh k solntsu,"* 62; *"tut zhe nakhodilsia vysokii stolb, i na nem gorela elektricheskaia lampa, osveshchaia den',"* 65). In works like "Peschanaia uchitel'nitsa" and "Iamskaia sloboda," written something on the order of a year later (1927), similar violations of syntax and style appear in the course of narratives making no attempt to supply a motivating, first-person mask whatsoever (for example, "...ee soznanie rastsvelo v epokhu, kogda sotsializm uzhe *zatverdel*," 75; "Zakhar Vasil'evich, *ne oslabliaia svoei raboty nad obedom*, dal cheloveku podoiti k stolu," 259).[38]

This reordering of the conventional *skaz* narrative configuration entails an important redefinition of the function Platonov's texts assign to "substandard" speech. No longer displayed as features of an eccentric narrative mask, the solecisms appearing within his texts lose their discrediting stamp of social estrangement and are elevated to the level of authorial speech, where they are legitimized as authentic, and unmediated, means for expressing authorial world view. In the terms of Bakhtin's redaction of the *skaz* concept, what had been the speech of the Other is fully appropriated as the author's own. At the same time in this transitional period Platonov's style sheds the sundry verbal embellishments used in the earlier works to create an impression of specifically oral speech – the egregious vulgarisms and dialecticisms, important in his early sketches as markers of peripheral social origin, as well as various deictic gestures used to sustain an atmosphere of performance (such as apostrophes to the audience and parenthetical remarks like "*mol*" or "*tak skazat'*"). What is retained from a *skaz* imitation of "substandard" speech is its principle of linguistic deformation alone (be it syntactic, semantic, or lexical), and what Platonov accomplishes in the course of legitimizing such speech as authorial is the redeployment of this deformation, not as an emblem of social origin, but as trope.

It is the emergence of this trope of deformation in his works of the mid twenties which justifies a comparison of Platonov's prose with that of modernism.[39] The deformations to which a Platonov text subjects standard literary Russian are conspicuous even to non-native readers, and have unsettled reviewers from his first appearances in print (in one early review, for example, N. Zamoshkin groused that "A. Platonov can drive the reader mad, so difficult is his language sometimes – he wags his tongue like a trunk – and so overloaded with all sorts of semantic difficulties.")[40] In purely linguistic terms Platonovian deformations comprise such devices as unexpected

concatenation, awkward tautology, the contamination of one
set expression by another, and the retrieval of "folk"
etymologies, all of which strikingly recall the pre-Karamzinian
language of the eighteenth century, that other age of Russian
linguistic turmoil.[41] Such a catalogue of specific devices,
however, is less important than the attention Platonov's texts
draw to themselves, once free from the social etiology of *skaz*, as
occasions for using the word "outside the boundaries of its
standard set of combinatory possibilities" and in such a way as
to "expand [its] combinatory valence" (Tsvetkov, "Iazyk A.
P. Platonova," p. 97), practices essentially related to literary
modernism's infatuation with "difficult form" (*zatrudnennaia
forma*) and "indirect usage" (*nepriamoe slovoupotreblenie*) as a
means for rendering the verbal surface of the text palpable and
revitalizing poetic speech. The analogy with an avant-garde
poetic appears all the more compelling in light of the works of
the late 1920s and early 1930s, in which deformations supply
the basis for a parody of Soviet political clichés.[42]

Yet for all these tendencies toward something resembling a
modernist aesthetic – whose importance in distinguishing Platonov from the neo-romantic *narodnichestvo* with which he is
sometimes identified should not be underestimated – the
"destruction of syntax" (Marinetti) in his prose ultimately
proceeds under different poetic auspices than that in the works
of such writers as Belyi, Kriuchenykh, and Khlebnikov. Despite
their fostering of new meanings in unexpected contexts, the
solecisms in his works remain alien to modernism's cult of
aestheticism, its exuberant setting free of the "word as such"
and reveling in the "freedom of language and its inexhaustible
resources." In this regard Platonov's adaptation of *skaz* differs
especially from that of Remizov.[43] Instead, at the same time
that it achieves many of the same effects as the literature of the
avant-garde, Platonov's prose retains from its *skaz* origins an air
of inadvertancy that makes it appear naive, innocent of its
deformations, anything but the premeditated product of artistic
virtuosity. In other words, while the kind of prose Platonov was
beginning to write in the mid twenties distinctly represents a
form of "distorted speech" (*kosnoiazychie*), it is not that lofty

form of it (*vysokoe kosnoiazychie*) prescribed by Gumilev and aspired to in one form or another by the exemplars of Russian and European modernism. It is instead a form of speech making claims for itself similar to that of a *iurodivyi*.[44] In Tolstaia-Segal's description:

> From the point of view of literary evolution, the case of Platonov presents itself, in the light of *opoiaz* conceptions, as the elevation of that prose line that had been junior to the postsymbolist ornamental prose of Remizov, Pil'niak, and Zamiatin. It represents the resurrection of the line of "poor," "sincere," "home-grown" prose – the line of Gor'kii's *Znanie* group. In Platonov's works this line is freed from the description of everyday life and overcomes its provincialism. The accent shifts to expression, and the instances of deformed speech that had appeared already in his poems become a conscious device. The traditional hero of *pochvennik* literature – the holy fool – rises from the level of theme to become the means for speaking about the world. ("'Stikhiinye sily'," 106)

Or, to put it in somewhat different terms, Platonov represents the paradoxical conjunction of certain features that separate *skaz* and ornamental modernism in their otherwise shared emphasis on the aesthetically self-valuable word: the orientation in *skaz* toward forms of speech *outside* the literary norm (particularly oral and dialectical) and the effort in ornamental prose to elevate the language of prose to the level of poetic speech.[45]

Platonov was not entirely alone in exploiting this paradoxical terrain between *skaz* and modernism, but even the poetry of Zabolotskii, who among contemporaries perhaps comes closest to Platonov's poetic (especially in *Torzhestvo zemledeliia*, with its portrayal of the yearnings of dumb, mute animals for consciousness and speech) betrays an allegience to aesthetic sophistication uncharacteristic of Platonov. As Bocharov points out, Zabolotskii's poetry is ultimately that of a sophisticated author discovering and celebrating lower forms of consciousness that are essentially alien to him; the striving of Platonov's prose is instead to establish authorial identification with such forms (Bocharov, "'Veshchestvo sushchestvovaniia'," p. 332). An ideological rationale for this urge might be found in Fedorov, who exalts the "unlearned" manual laborers (*duraki*) over the coterie of the "learned" (*umnye*); nor should a more general link be overlooked with Soviet literature's interest, in 1920s explorations of the social upheavals occasioned by the Revolution, in the "crude" thinking of the lower masses.[46] What is important to the evolution of Platonov's prose, however, is not any ideological message as such, but the way in which this persistent adherence to the perspective of "incorrect," "lower" forms of speech provides the impetus for developing *skaz* in the direction of modernism. One of the principal contributions of that adherence is to Platonov's preoccupation with questions of ontology: the perspective of "crude" speech generates in Platonov's prose a certain chthonic quality that enables the language of his texts to appear closely bound to the root issues of existence. "Lower" forms of speech furthermore provide the basis for that ambivalent combination of naive faith in, and ironic undermining of, Soviet utopian rhetoric that is his central contribution to Russian literature in the Soviet period.

### THE EMERGING SEMANTICS OF PLATONOV'S STYLE

The relation between these various strands of Platonov's poetic defines itself fully in his works of the late 1920s to the early 1930s, but some of the specific semantic effects of his style can be detected earlier. Already in the village sketches the "naturalistic" aspect of peasant speech foregrounded in the texts' burlesque form of *skaz* can be seen introducing into the language of the text an orientation toward physicality as such – much as the works themselves transcend their ostensible social emphases by reinterpreting social conditions as ontological states. "Peasant" speech does so by creating a general atmosphere of "crudity," but also by constantly turning to the body and its physical processes as a means for describing the world. Thus in a descriptive passage of "Rasskaz o mnogikh interesnykh veshchakh" (1923), to cite just one example, the narrator's "naive" recourse to the vocabulary of the physical body underscores the materiality of nature: "Osennee solntse *nagnetalo silu v zemliu* – i zemlia *shevelilas'*, i *shevelilos'* vse, chto *zhivet na kozhe u nei*: seleniia i goroda vsiakie" ("The autumn sun drove its force into the earth, and the earth rustled, and everything that lives on the earth's skin also rustled: villages and all sorts of towns"; *Starik i starucha*, p. 81).

In the works of the transitional period, when Platonov had already begun to abandon the more obvious accoutrements of *skaz*, this orientation toward the physical refines itself into a device of syntax. The ascription of materiality now derives not from the use of conspicuous, "naturalistic" lexicon but from unexpected confrontations between the semantics of the abstract and the concrete: incorporated within the text's framework of "awkward" speech, words denoting abstract phenomena suddenly find themselves the objects of verbs or prepositions referring to the concrete, the result of which is that their denotata appear crudely interjected into the realm of things. "Confusion" over participial reference in Platonov's texts, for example, can cause the literal, concrete sense of a verb to assert itself where its figurative sense had been expected: "*i Pukhov shagal, nalivaias' kakoi-to prelest'iu*" ("and Pukhov strode, filling with some kind of delight"; "Sokrovennyi chelovek," 396). The use of the verb *nalivat'sia* in conjunction with the noun *serdtse* generally denotes a figurative "swelling," an access of emotion (for example, "*Serdtse nalilos' [radost'iu, zloboiu]*"; Dal'), but in Platonov's phrase its odd governance suggests the literal filling of Pukhov's body, as if with some liquid.[47] As the apparent misprisions of a verbally unsophisticated narrator, such expressions retain their link with the "baseness" of Platonov's earlier experiments in *skaz*. In them, however, the *skaz* principle of assuming a "low" manner of speech increasingly survives only as a set of referential presuppositions: as the narrative's tendency to appear the product of a mentality inclined to regard the world as consisting solely of *things*.

That this "materializing" tendency of Platonov's prose may have been associated with a certain conscious attitude toward language – a situation underscoring the interdependence of style and philosophical themes in his oeuvre – is suggested by some of the metalinguistic remarks appearing in the early journalism. In the essay "Proletarskaia poeziia" (1922), for example, Platonov reiterates some of the tenets of the LEF aesthetic of *zhiznestroenie*, which privileges real world praxis over "detached" aestheticism and assigns it the ultimate function of hastening the arrival of proletarian utopia.[48] Where LEF theorization had emphasized movement outward from art into the world, however, Platonov returns the "life-organizing" activities of proletarian poetry to the domain of language: man is as yet unable to attain his final goal of "organizing" the matter of the world, he argues in a Bogdanovian vein, and so must for the time being take up the "organization" of words in poetry. But he overcomes the paradox of this apparent retreat from reality into art by insisting that words are not abstract symbols, but extensions of realia, of matter itself (echoing, incidentally, arguments Lenin had used in his *Materializm i empiriokrititsizm* to deride Berkeleyen epistemological skepticism – that is, the notion that words provide no access to the thing-in-itself). It is because the essential relation between words and their real-world referents makes language contiguous with the realm of matter, Platonov argues, that the "organization of the symbols of things, words" will initiate that process by which the proletariat will eventually master the "organization" of those things-in-themselves.[49]

This tendency toward a semantic of materialization, however, proceeds only incompletely and ambivalently in Platonov's literary style. It is undermined in the first place by the lingering aura of misprision that attends his deformations of standard literary usage and syntax, and which was to provide an important source of irony in later works. But it is also threatened by an opposing tendency toward abstraction that, though it likewise enters Platonov's prose under the sign of a confused confrontation with literacy, has the effect of projecting, not a world reduced to physicality, but one underlaid by absolutes. Thus in "Iamskaia sloboda," in the passage that reads, "Davno umershee derevo *ot vremeni i zabveniia* stalo kak by pochvoi i zanialias' tikhim mkhom" ("The tree, which had long ago died from time and oblivion became as it were soil and devoted itself to quiet moss," 252), the "failure" fully to articulate causal process (e.g., to say, "*ot togo, chto* derevo davno stoialo"; "*ot togo, chto* zabyli pro nego") renders "time" and "oblivion" themselves the immediate agents of the tree's decay (cf. the theme of entropy's "wearing away" of being in the story). A similar introduction of absolutes and accompanying investment of an episode with existential overtones results in "Rodina elektrichestva" from the substitution of the generic for a particular term: "...ia uzhinal i odnovremenno snimal s sebia rabochii pidzhak i lapti, *chtoby posle uzhina na mne ostavalos' malo odezhdy*" ("I ate my supper and at the same time removed my worker's jacket and bast shoes, so that after supper there remained on me little clothing," 60). The substitution of the generic *odezhda* here foregrounds the notion of the self in relation to its cloaking, which in turn ironically invokes Platonov's theme of being's desire to be shed of its physical vessel.[50] It is this complementary tendency toward abstraction which serves as the basis for the often-remarked "philosophism" of Platonov's prose: its penchant for abstract vocabulary and phraseology, whose origins undoubtedly lie in his extensive readings in philosophy and whose presence contributes to the impression that his works somehow deal in "ultimate" questions of being and are organized around abstract ideational schemes.

What arises at the intersection of these two, equally "deforming" semantic tendencies in Platonov's prose (which are in fact aspects of the same phenomenon and often co-inhabit the same device) is a trope that was to become central to his most characteristic uses of style. One might label that trope *ironic materialization*, and define it as the persistent urge within the language of Platonov's prose toward a fusion of abstract and concrete levels of reference, the "deforming" character of which, however, continually subverts such a fusion and causes it to appear at best tentative or incomplete.[51] This trope was to provide the basis for that iconic relation between the language of Platonov's texts and their ontological themes that in the end defines his verbal art. The vacillation in his prose between establishing and undermining an identity between the abstract and the concrete becomes invested with the complex interrelation between materialist and idealist impulses defining his view of being.

That iconic relation was, again, to establish itself most fully in his masterpieces of the late 1920s and early 1930s, and its particulars will be dealt with in subsequent chapters. For now it is important to note the further parallel with the literature of modernism suggested by this trope of "ironic materialization." An effort to bridge the opposition between spirit and matter, or, in its linguistic surrogate, the abstract and the concrete, plays a significant role in the poetics of a number of Platonov's immediate predecessors and contemporaries. In her discussion of the devices through which "ornamental" prose strove to approximate the language of verse, N. A. Kozhevnikova devotes particular attention to the semantic of "materialization" arising out of such characteristic ornamentalist concerns as the effort to heighten the tropic nature of prose and to present the object of narration through striking visual imagery:

The general tendency of ornamental prose – its effort to present the object via a visual image of it – expresses itself in the "thingness" or materialization of what is portrayed, this process extending to both material and immaterial phenomena. The trope is so constructed as to lend materiality to the abstract and to underscore still more clearly the materiality of the concrete.[52]

Nor does one have to search very far for parallels in the twentieth-century literary canon. The linguistic experimentation of Belyi's *Kotik Letaev*, for example, has been described as accomplishing a "blurring [of the] established distinctions between categories such as abstract and concrete" in an effort to "[recreate] a world where such distinctions do not hold" (moreover, through the adoption of a child's perspective and speech, a device not unrelated to Platonov's posture of *iurodstvo*).[53] A certain rapprochement between the material and spiritual worlds may also be seen to lie at the heart of the celebrated Pasternakian metonymy, which characteristically manifests itself in episodes of "*contact* between the small-scale, everyday manifestations of man and the large-scale manifestations of life and the universe" and is capable of giving rise in Pasternak's verse to locutions convergent with those in Platonov's prose.[54] Still closer to Platonov's poetic of materialization are Futurism's cult of the self-valuable word, or the texts of Boris Pil'niak, where the technique of montage is directed toward supplanting the principle of verbal *representation* with an indexical one enabling a gesture toward verbal "things as such."[55]

These parallels represent more than mere instances of convergence, since, as discussed in the introduction to this study, the modernists and Platonov may ultimately be seen as deriving from the same post-positivist movement in Russian thought for which the spirit/matter antinomy was of central concern, and for which the pathos of disjuncture figured just as importantly as longings for reconciliation or strivings for philosophical monism. More specifically, Platonov, Belyi, Pasternak, and Pil'niak, may all be regarded as heirs to Symbolism's desire to assign language a privileged role in the antinomy's working out, to see the opposition of spirit to matter played out or potentially even resolved within language itself (the culmination of which is arrived at in Bakhtin's philosophy of language).

Platonov's particular contribution to this philosophical-poetic current, however, was to expose the persistence of its concerns within the rhetoric of the *Soviet* era, especially that associated with Stalinist utopianism.[56] Platonov had himself received a schooling in some of the peculiarly Soviet forms of speech in his early career as a journalist. His articles for the Voronezh press abound in the very sort of metaphoric figures (*obraznaia rech'*) Selishchev identifies as a distinguishing characteristic of post-revolutionary Russian usage, especially of the speech of the revolutionary leaders: all those "avengers of the downtrodden, images of iron and blood, predatory beasts, hydras, hydras with millions of tentacles, images of the enormous flame sweeping over the world like a whirlwind" (Selishchev, *Iazyk revoliutsionnoi epokhi*, p. 133). What seems to have characterized Platonov's rendition of this rhetoric from the outset, however, was a tendency to extend these "agitational" metaphors to the point of near-literalization – a habit in which the seeds for his later *parodies* of this type of speech can be discerned. In Platonov's articles metaphoric figures are extended to the point where they acquire miniature plots of

their own and their focus threatens to shift from the realm of
tenor to that of vehicle (one result of which is the implication
of a certain concreteness, particularly when, as it often does in
Platonov, that vehicle involves some reference to corporeality).
In "Zhivaia ekhidna" (1920), for example, the use of "viper"
(*ekhidna*) as a metaphor for the Whites unfolds into a tableau in
which the viper is graphically hacked to pieces, the pieces
multiply, and the proletariat tramples and burns them ("My
poka tol'ko drobim i rvem telo beloi ekhidny, *i chasti ee
mnozhatsia i kazhdaia iz nikh zhiva. No skoro my nachnem toptat' ee i
zhech'*.") The metaphoric bayoneting of the bourgeoisie in
"Mir na krasnom shtyke" (1920) is similarly elaborated into a
concretized episode of stabbing ("Vgonim shtyk v telo
burzhuazii *do rukoiatki, do krika ee smerti*, vo imia nashei zhizni,
vo imia nashei pravdy..."), while in "K nachinaiushchim
proletarskim poetam i pisateliam" (1919) the metaphor of
building a universal temple of human creativity unfolds into a
"construction" plot anticipatory in many ways of the events in
*Kotlovan*:

Чтобы начать на земле строить единый храм общечело-
веческого творчества, единое жилище духа человеческого,
*начнем пока с малого, начнем укладывать фундамент для этого
будущего солнечного храма, где будет жить небесная радость
мира, начнем с маленьких кирпичиков.*
[In order to begin building on earth a universal temple of human
creativity, a universal residence for the human spirit, let us begin with
small things; let us begin to lay the foundation of this future sunny
temple, where the heavenly joy of the world will reside; let us begin
with the smallest of bricks.]

Yet for all their oddity, Platonov's literalizations of metaphoric
figures should be viewed as responses to a kindred urge already
present in the language of Soviet *agitprop*. In their function as
propaganda the type of metaphoric identifications established
in *agitprop* between the particular events and personae of the
"real world" Soviet context and their correspondents on the
figural plane of revolution's idealized allegory (where there
rage various fires of revolutionary battle, the bloated bourgeoisie leers, the proletariat thrusts with the bayonet of
historically justified indignation, and so forth) characteristically

serve as exhortations to a given audience to initiate some version of that action depicted in the metaphor's "plot." In effect *agitprop* represents the imposition on metaphor of a synecdochal reading, in which a relation of morally binding contiguity is posited between the actual and figural realms. Gladkov's *Tsement* is merely continuing this rhetorical practice when it portrays the construction of a particular cement factory as the realization of that "cement" between the working class and the peasantry essential to the country's emergence from the civil war, and derives this reading of its plot from an identical use of the metaphor in *Pravda* (Clark, *The Soviet Novel*, pp. 70–77). As for Platonov, his awareness of this verbal logic finds explicit expression in a letter he wrote Mariia Alekseevna from Tambov, which Soviet sources often quote to demonstrate his positive response to the Revolution. Recounting how at the start of the civil war he was assigned to work on a train he writes, "The phrase about the revolution being the locomotive of history was transformed in me into a strange and wonderful feeling: *recalling the phrase I would work as hard as I could on the locomotive*" ("Fraza o tom, chto revoliutsiia – parovoz istorii prevratilas' vo mne v strannoe i khoroshee chuvstvo: *vspominaia ee, ia ochen' userdno rabotal na parovoze*").[57] The idealized locomotive of history that is the Revolution and the actual locomotive on which Platonov works are here treated as coextensive, as though Platonov's increased efforts on the latter might contribute to the former's historical realization.

The initial impression produced by Platonov's early prose, then, is that of an awkward jumble of verbal styles in which literate, even elevated diction collides, often within a single phrase, with a linguistic crudity whose deformations of syntax and sense border on the comic. Such a melange inevitably appears the product of linguistic naiveté; but the texts increasingly suspend their insistence on mediating oral performance in favor of what amounts to the stylization of certain principles of semi-literate speech. On the one hand, the world projected within these texts appears everywhere contiguous with absolutes; but on the other hand, the texts appear to follow the dictates of a linguistic consciousness bent on regarding the world as consisting solely of things. The prose that results reverberates with the pathos of mixed referential intentions and reads as if poised ambivalently between interpretations of life as spiritual and as physical event. In some utopian context these two impulses might prove adequate to the description of a kind of allegorical reality, in which the distinction between the material and the spiritual has been erased, and at times Platonov's early linguistic consciousness seems prepared to embrace just such a utopia.[58]

Any such gesture toward identity, however, breaks down in Platonov's works in the prevailing atmosphere of verbal grotesquery and dislocation that he had derived from *skaz*. This particular form of irony first manifests itself in connection with *agitprop* in the "Zoshchenko-like" episodes of literalizing misprision in "Sokrovennyi chelovek" (as when Pukhov reads on the wall of a train station the "agitational" message, "Every day we live through is a nail in the head of the bourgeoisie," and likes it because it contains "firm words" – "*tverdye slova*"). It was to assume its definitive shape, however, only in the masterpieces of the late 1920s and early 1930s, where the peculiarly Soviet forms of political rhetoric find themselves suspended between the realization of their intention toward metaphoric identification and that intention's ironic dissolution. It was in those works, as well, that Platonov was fully to realize the implications such language held for his vision of being.

# CHAPTER 3

# Chevengur *and the utopian genre*

Platonov appears to have begun working on *Chevengur*, his only novel, as early as 1926 when he was still in Tambov. A letter of that year to him from Litvin-Molotov discusses an unnamed work closely resembling what we know as *Chevengur*, and one of Platonov's 1927 letters to his wife mentions plans for writing a "fantastic story" on "the theme of how history begins and when it will end."[1] Platonov completed his text, which at this point he was calling *Stroiteli strany : Puteshestvie s otkrytym serdtsem*, in 1928–1929.[2] By this time he had already established himself as a writer in Moscow with the publication of several shorter works in *Novyi mir* (two of them fragments of *Chevengur*), and two books under the impress of Molodaia gvardiia publishers (*Sokrovennyi chelovek* and *Lugovye mastera*).

Platonov's novel, however, soon ran into difficulties, perhaps in connection with RAPP's attacks on him in the late 1920s. It was to have been published in 1929 by Federatsiia and had already been typeset but the printing was suspended.[3] Platonov's subsequent appeals to Gor'kii, and the latter's response, have become fixtures of commentary on the novel: Platonov pleads that the novel is not "counterrevolutionary" and asks for Gor'kii's help; Gor'kii pens an equivocal response that praises Platonov's style but laments the plotless nature of his novel and, worse, suggests that no editor would touch a manuscript such as Platonov's, in which revolutionaries are portrayed as "cranks" and "half-wits."[4] Indeed, *Chevengur* did not appear in full in Russian until its 1988 publication by *Khudozhestvennaia literatura*.[5] This absence of nearly six decades was undoubtedly one of the major losses incurred by Russian

literature under Stalinism and its heirs. Yet in many ways the
novel's lengthy history of non-publication, together with the
question of Platonov's political and aesthetic intentions that
stands at its core, reflects the ambivalent properties of the text
itself, rather than merely the whims of conservative Soviet
editors. In this sense, in fact, Gor'kii's hesitant, equivocating
comments may be said to inaugurate the history of the novel's
reading.

The ambivalences in *Chevengur* are exacerbated by the
convoluted and often opaque quality of its narrative, which
frustrates any attempt at straightforward interpretation
(Gor'kii was not the only reader to complain of its "laxness"
and the "obscuring of action" in it).[6] It is not that nothing
recognizable takes place within the work. In simplest terms the
novel could be summarized as the tale of how one Sasha
Dvanov, an orphan from a drought-stricken provincial Russian
town, comes of age during the Revolution and sets off for the
heartland in search of "true socialism." On his journey he
meets up with another revolutionary named Kopenkin (who
rides a horse called "Proletarian Strength"), and, after a series
of adventures during the civil war, the two find their way to the
isolated town of Chevengur. They have been told that
communism has already arrived in the town. Once there they
discover a band of eccentrics that has installed its soviet in a
former church, slaughters the bourgeoisie, and declares the end
of history. The members of this would-be utopia then suspend
labor, believing that nature will provide for them. It does not,
autumn approaches, and the town is invaded by a detachment
of cossacks. Kopenkin is killed in the ensuing battle, while
Dvanov rides off to commit suicide.

Though it is possible to summarize the novel in this fashion,
the emplotment of events in it is often maddeningly diffuse, and
*Chevengur* can appear as much an extended exercise in
Platonov's odd verbal style as any kind of novelistic narrative.
Moreover, opacity in its text often inhabits the level of
individual episodes, with the result that a brief summary such
as that offered above courts inaccuracy by imputing a greater
degree of coherence than actually obtains in this concatenation

of loosely connected and often intentionally bizarre episodes. Or, to put it another way, even at the episodic level the narrative complexities of *Chevengur* are such that any attempt at producing a synopsis of the text begins to resemble a theory *about* that text (à la Chomsky).

If no uncomplicated reading of *Chevengur* is then possible, the novel may nonetheless be seen as cohering around certain key oppositions of attitude and theme. These are most readily approached through the political themes in whose terms the novel tends to be read, though as will be argued below the place of political ideas in Platonov's poetic mythology is ultimately a subordinate one.[7]

In one light *Chevengur*'s tale of the rise and fall of a communist utopia in the steppes suggests itself as an anarchistic lament over the surrender of revolutionary "spontaneity" to the encroaching forces of the Soviet bureaucratic state.[8] (Gor'kii, after all, commented on Platonov's "anarchistic frame of mind," and an antipathy toward bureaucratic order figures prominently in Platonov's satires of the late 1920s and early 1930s.) The Party official who dispatches Dvanov on his journey tells him to search for that form of socialism that "self-generates" among the rural masses, and the series of acts Dvanov witnesses in Chevengur are the essence of spontaneity: the Chevengurians declare that they have instantaneously "demobilized" society and released even the cattle from their former bondage (*Chevengur* (Moscow: Sovetskii pisatel', 1989), p. 174), and weekly move the town's houses and gardens from one spot to another in a literal campaign against settledness (as one character puts it, communism is "eternal motion"). This nostalgia for spontaneity is moreover heightened by the fact that their experiment unfolds against the backdrop of the NEP period, which they perceive as a retreat from earlier, more radical ideals.[9]

From this perspective the catastrophe with which the novel ends signals the tragic surrender of spontaneity to an iron will toward order that assails it from both without (the machine-like detachment of soldiers, whom the novel identifies as cossacks and cadets but who are perhaps meant to be seen as the Red Army dispatched from the "center" to restore order)[10] and within (through Prokofii, Dvanov's greedy half-brother, who wants to "organize" everything and whose pronouncements on the topic make overt allusion to Dostoevsky's Grand Inquisitor).[11] Geller's view of Dvanov and Kopenkin as "apostles" of the communist faith who witness the tragic incursion of the "ecclesiastical" authority of a bureaucratic "church" is representative of this approach to the novel. Still more compelling evidence for this reading may be found in the novel's implicit allusions to its own political context. *Chevengur* was completed in 1928–1929, during yet another episode of imposition from above of the Party's iron will to organization – that of collectivization and the cataclysmic first Five-Year Plan. The novel implicitly protests these events through its anachronistic return to a civil war setting and consequent evocation, in the face of those years' RAPP hegemony, of the literature of "revolutionary romanticism" (particularly Pil'niak's *Golyi god*).

For all the evidence one can summon in support of this "anarchistic" interpretation, however, other, equally prominent elements of *Chevengur* suggest the presence of a contrary point of view from which both the Chevengurians' activities and the utopianism motivating them are condemned as provincial folly (cf. the play Platonov co-authored with Pil'niak, "Duraki na periferii," and Pil'niak's version of the theme, his response to *Chevengur*, in *Krasnoe derevo*). This contradictory line of meaning derives primarily from the extremism (to them, anarchistic "spontaneity") of the Chevengurians' behavior which encourages the reader to assign everything that takes place in Chevengur to the category of the bizarre (as Gor'kii essentially does). The particular bearers of this attitude are the characters who arrive in provincial Chevengur from the more sober "center." Dvanov and Kopenkin never quite shed the skepticism with which they arrive in the town and remain throughout essentially outsiders to its experiment. So, too, does the cynical Muscovite Simon Serbinov declare on his arrival, "I've seen your actions, and they're in vain" (an echo of Lincoln Steffen's famous remark about seeing the future that works?). Without necessarily endorsing the forces that crush Chevengur, this skeptical or "conservative" side of the novel projects that dénouement as the predictable outcome of utopian excess. Read in this second light Platonov's novel emerges as a *parody* of revolutionary romanticism whose political statement would seem to involve the *equation* of the excesses of the civil war with those of Stalinism just getting underway in 1928–1929, its depiction of the attempt to build "socialism in one town" amounting to an implicit condemnation of the Stalinist intent to do the same "in one country."[12] It is this apparent antipathy toward communist utopianism in general that has fueled the novel's dissident/émigré reputation as an attack on the Soviet system as a whole – and which, indeed, may have provoked its rejection by Federatsiia as "counterrevolutionary."

That such hermeneutic ambivalence characterizes *Chevengur* should not, however, be taken as signalling that one is left with a work that makes the impossibility of meaning its central theme.[13] In terms of Platonov's political biography one can, for example, describe the novel as a record of the uncertainties generated during his roughly ten-year experience of Soviet power. If in the years immediately following the Revolution Platonov had professed his faith in *Proletkul't* dreams of "organizing" nature and society, by 1928 he had succumbed to doubts over whether to reject those aspirations for having given rise to the bureaucratic Soviet state, or to regard them as having been betrayed by that state's evolution (this indecision giving rise, among other things, to the array of character types present at Chevengur's utopian experiment, from "anarchists" like Chepurnyi to the malevolent "organizer" Prokofii and the ambivalent fellow-travelers Dvanov and Kopenkin).[14]

That ambivalence nonetheless *is* the theme of *Chevengur* becomes clear if one shifts the ground of inquiry from the political themes that have so preoccupied the novel's readers (or similar attempts to isolate some undivided "message") to that of literary genre. Closely related to its political uncertainties, but residing at a deeper level of textual meaning, is the conflict of generic impulses observable in *Chevengur*, which are important because they raise the issue of authorial posture toward what is narrated in the novel. Certain of the novel's elements place it in the context of pilgrimage literature (or literature of quest) and suggest its intention as a kind of philosophical "road to Calvary" (*khozhdenie po mukam*). This narrative is concentrated in the figure of Sasha Dvanov and his plot line. It originates in the *Bildungsroman* opening of the novel (where Dvanov is shown awakening to consciousness of his own existence and the world around him) and unfolds in the novel's middle section into the hero's melancholic transit through a series of trials in search of some absolute form of truth about existence (Geller's label for this is "*ispytanie idei*"), only to close tragically when the protagonist, in despair over Chevengur's rout, drowns himself in Lake Mutevo.

Parallel to this tragic line, however, runs its comic-grotesque obverse. This narrative twin is elaborated around the same search for socialism in the steppes (not only intersecting, but often joining in a single episode with the pathetic tale of Dvanov's pilgrimage). Its generic affinities, however, lie with the mock-epic and the picaresque and its intentions correspondingly tend toward the satirization of the quest and its motivations rather than toward pathos ("Sokrovennyi chelovek" is similar in this regard, but belongs more unambiguously to the picaresque genre). If Dvanov is the protagonist of the novel's tragic quest, this satirical line is headed by Kopenkin, a combination of Quixote and a Russian *bogatyr'* who rides a horse named "Proletarian Strength" and devotes himself to preserving the memory of the German revolutionary Rosa Luxemburg. To it belong the host of the novel's eccentric characters and situations, whose exaggerated, anecdotal nature suggests their descent from Platonov's early burlesques on village life and whose presence lends the novel something of the air of a *lubok* (for example, Pashintsev, another mock-allegorical "knight of the revolution," who literally walks around in medieval armor; the man Dvanov and Kopenkin encounter on their journey who rolls on the ground periodically in order to rest his legs; the peasant who calls himself "Dostoevsky," and so forth).[15]

*Chevengur* thus combines quest with mock-quest, angst ending in suicide with anecdotal farce: Gor'kii summarized well the disparate poetic terms in which the work is executed when he labelled its mood "lyrico-satirical" (*Gor'kii i sovetskie pisateli*, p. 313). But there is an epistemological issue here as well. Implicit in the tale of Dvanov's pilgrimage into the world in search of the Answer is the desire for a certain involvement of the self in that world, the optimistic belief that the domain "out there" contains that which might complete what the self lacks; this side of the novel thus endorses the notion of the quest. The opposing line, on the other hand, is defined by its skepticism toward such involvement and its retreat *from* the world into a posture of aloof contemplation, from which it regards the unfolding peripeties as folly (cf. the works of the philosopher "N. Arsakov" cited by one of the characters on Dvanov's journey, which recommend that man withdraw from history and spend years passively contemplating the world before beginning to act). The root issue in *Chevengur*, then, has to do with man's relation to the world; and the fact that the generic opposition in Platonov's novel can be described in these terms points once again toward questions of ontology, which form the core of the novel's meanings. Before attempting to show how ontology unites the novel's disparate levels, however, it is necessary to examine in some detail how that theme is itself represented in *Chevengur*.

PLATONOV'S ONTOLOGICAL MYTH IN "*CHEVENGUR*"

*Chevengur*, then, is an expansive and complex text, the product of more than one conceptual point of genesis (Shubin remarks that it "grew like a tree, in rings").[16] It addresses itself, variously with and without irony, to multiple literary, philosophical, and political antecedents, and so suggests that it might be read in a variety of contexts. I believe nonetheless that one can identify the immanent principle lending coherence to this heterogeneity, and that it lies in the ontological myth Platonov had been elaborating throughout the 1920s. Or, to borrow Hans Günther's terms, the ontological myth is precisely that "secondary semantic level" whose recovery is invited by the impression of intricate allusiveness that is the hallmark of this text.[17]

Indeed, it is in *Chevengur*, Platonov's first truly major work, that this myth completes its transition from being "read into" some pre-existing generic form to serving as the organizing center of textual meaning. In *Chevengur* also Platonov's ontological myth begins most visibly to infiltrate even the syntax of his prose. Thus not only do the novel's characters themselves appear at every moment to be exercised by the fundamental problems of existence (they are in fact less psychological types than a series of typified existential postures), but a broader atmosphere of gnoseological uncertainty is generated, in which the authorial language itself seems preoccupied with assessing being's status in the world.

Like "Iamskaia sloboda," with which it was probably composed simultaneously, the novel begins with an ostensibly realist survey of social types on the eve of revolution (in the very same setting of a *sloboda* situated at the boundary between city and nature); but even more quickly than its predecessor it completes its transition from *byt* to *bytie*. Dvanov and Kopenkin journey through a countryside ravaged by the horrors of war communism and only fitfully beginning to accommodate itself to bolshevik authority, but these civil war motifs are translated in Platonov's novel into a Fedorovian vision of the world's hostility toward man (a process begun in "Sokrovennyi chelovek").[18] The novel opens on scenes of severe drought and its accompanying famine (itself a Fedorovian preoccupation, and a theme already important in "Rodina elektrichestva," "Peschanaia uchitel'nitsa," and "Epifanskie shliuzy"). It proceeds to elaborate the miseries endured during a time of mass starvation, when many die and those who survive are driven far afield in search of food, while their central Russian town (the description of which abounds in Platonov's cherished motifs of desiccation and decay) is abandoned to the encroaching weeds. So, too, does Platonov derive from this portrait of nature's hostility a warning against human procreation, which only perpetuates the cycle of mortality. The women of the settlement are terrorized by a lustful hunchback named Kondaev, while Dvanov, an orphan expelled for the malthusian reason that his adoptive family cannot support him, feels revulsion on seeing his stepmother pregnant yet again.[19]

As in the earlier works, however, in *Chevengur* Platonov departs significantly from Fedorov by emphasizing the subjective experience of being over its social–ethical implications, thus inverting the relation these issues enjoy in Fedorov's thought. The focus of that experience is once again man's corporeality: the novel abounds in the kind of graphic, "naturalistic" details that had first appeared in Platonov's early sketches of village life, and its characters are perpetually scratching, sweating, vomiting, hunting for lice, or spitting. What sets *Chevengur* apart, however, is the degree of self-consciousness with which its characters recognize this problem of possessing a body, and the acuteness with which they experience that possession as a burden. When the ill Iakov Titych is being looked after by the other Chevengurians, for example, he "feels sorry for his body and for the people who were located around him [it] – he saw how at this moment, when he felt so depressed and ill, his torso lay alone on the floor and people stood near him [it], each with his own torso and nobody knowing where to direct his body at this time of Iakov Titych's grief."[20] Elsewhere Serbinov similarly "compressed his body under the blanket, feeling his legs and his breast to be another, equally pitiful, man, whom he was warming and caressing" (343). This theme of alienation from one's own body even gives rise in the novel to a peculiar language of description, which treats the body as if it were a mere appendage, nonidentical to the "being" lodged within. Thus some Red Army soldiers riding with Dvanov on the train "snored and scratched their *bodies* in their sleep" (61; that is, not "scratched themselves"), while the wind is said to cool not Dvanov but "Dvanov's *body*" (60).

One of *Chevengur*'s most important contributions to this theme is its elaboration of a particularly literalized spatial imagery of being's enclosure, even imprisonment, within the

body – what one scholar has called Platonov's "semantics of
bodily space."[21] When Dvanov, for example, struggles in the
agonies of typhoid fever he is described as feeling heat and noise
"within the closed space of his body" (68), and the same motif
of enclosure within a dark space recurs in the description of the
child whose death signals Chevengur's demise: his heart
"*isolated in the darkness of his body* beat with such insistence,
ferocity, and hope, that it was as if it were a separate being from
the child" (270; emphasis added). In this latter passage the
theme of corporeal alienation is in fact subtly doubled, since
being is portrayed as distinct from the body in which it is
contained, but the boy's "life" is also ironically reduced to the
physical organ of the heart. Indeed, Platonov's spatial literalism
may itself be viewed as the natural extension of his preoccupation with physicality.

   If Platonov's interest in the flesh as the focus of existential
concerns joins him to a host of contemporary figures and their
antecedents (from Rozanov and Zabolotskii among his fellow
Russians to Nietzsche, Freud, Sartre, and Georges Bataille), he
nonetheless differs in the important respect that for him the
body or the flesh turns out to be, not a reservoir of fecund (if
threatening) vital force, but a constituent of alien and "dead"
matter and as such the very essence of ontological alterity (cf.
the old man who explains the presence of skin and nails on the
human body by asserting that nails are "dead" and grow out
from within man so that nothing "dead" remains at the center
of his being; 252–53). In Platonov what makes this distribution
of ontological values so tragic is the belief that the alien matter
of the body is itself but a frail substance subject to the
destructive "laws of matter." In essence his vision ironically
conflates the Christian-idealist notion of perishable flesh, which
is usually held up as evidence for the soul's transcendence (the
flesh passes away, but the soul does not), with the materialist
conviction that spirit is subordinate to matter. And the
corollary of that belief for Platonov is that the soul finds itself
condemned to inhabit a vessel which is itself subject to decay.

   As always in Platonov, primary evidence for this decay as a
symptom of the world's hostility is to be found in the almost

universally decrepit condition of physical objects. Hence the
novel's opening descriptions of the settlement's houses and
wattle fences, which threaten to disintegrate in the drought,
and its similar lamentations over the propensity of machines to
break down and rust. As with things, so with the body.
Translated into Platonov's semantics of bodily space, the
entropy that is the general tendency of the physical world
manifests itself as the persistent erosion of the corpus to which
being is confined (a kind of literalization of Bogdanovian
"opposition"), as a result of which man ends up, after an
arduous existence, with nothing better than "wasted flesh."
Hence the many emaciated characters in the novel, such as
Gopner, who strikes Dvanov as having been so consumed by
years of work that only "bones and hair" are left of him, "that
which remains in the grave" (158); or the vagabond women
rounded up to marry Chevengur's proletarians, who are said to
look more like girls and old hags than brides because their
"bodies had been wasted prior to death and long before it"
(346). Gurvich's sardonic comment on all this was that in
Platonov's works even the living characters appear "dead."[22]

Given this subjection of the body to relentless erosion, and
the resulting imperilment of the being within, the human
condition for Platonov becomes one of literal exposure to, or
"shelterlessness" before, a hostile world. (Zakhar Pavlovich at
one point has a vision of "the *defenseless* existence of people
living *naked*, without any deception of themselves with faith in
the assistance of machines"; emphasis added, 41.) This theme
of "shelterlessness" in fact supplies the very premise of the
novel's plot: Dvanov's fateful journey begins when he is
expelled from his adoptive home into the threateningly open
world of the steppes, and the condition of "shelterlessness"
figures prominently among the sorrows he witnesses en route to
the communist utopia of Chevengur.[23] The characters' longing
for some form of "shelter" is particularly evident in their
repeated performances of a gesture that typifies the Platonovian
response to this condition, that of providing a sheltering
embrace, or "huddling" (in Russian most often "*prizhimanie
sebia k chemu/komu-nibud'*," literally "pressing oneself to

something"). Dvanov, for example, survives a cold night in the open by lying in the embrace of a total stranger, finds refuge in a hut filled with railway passengers, and is later given "shelter" by, and accepted into the nocturnal embraces of, a peasant woman named Fekla (a reprise of a similar episode in "Buchilo"). The children of Urochev likewise escape a wind that has "chilled the entire town" by "warming themselves near the hot bodies of their typhus-stricken mothers" (70). The theme even appears with ironic ideological overtones, as when one old man's conversion to bolshevism is described as his "*pressing himself* in spirit to Soviet power" (emphasis added, 177).

If Platonov thus portrays man's existence as a tragic subordination to corporeality, experienced as a paradoxically direct, physical exposure to the corrosive forces abroad in the world, then the ultimate fear troubling this vision is that, for all being's apparent separateness from matter, nothing but matter truly exists.[24] This apprehension regarding what one might call the *ephemerity of spirit* is the dominant paradox of Platonov's ontological myth, if not the dominant theme of his oeuvre as a whole. It is as though for him the soul, which initially appeared to have substance, somehow threatened to evaporate, leaving behind only its material substratum. At the same time, this fear marks the extremity of his pessimistic redaction of Bogdanov and Fedorov. Seizing, as it were, on the two thinkers' shared "materialist" premise that man's *present* existence constitutes slavery to physicality (particularly Fedorov, with his discussion of the tragedy of physical death and of man's subordination to the elements), Platonov proceeds to cancel both their utopian visions of spirit's redemption (be it in resurrection via "supramoralism" or in tectology's final "organization of matter"). Indeed, what Platonov accomplishes might be thought of as the ironic inversion of Bogdanov's philosophical project for unifying spirit and matter, in which what is elaborated is a monism of matter rather than consciousness. Moreover, as will be seen below, it is this very uncertainty that defines the peculiar form of utopianism presented in the novel and serves as the focal point for its response to Soviet materialist efforts to "construct socialism in one country."

Apprehensions regarding their possible reduction to matter form one of the perennial preoccupations of the characters in *Chevengur*. Zakhar Pavlovich, for example, is troubled by the thought that man may have descended from the worm, because the worm is "just a horrible little tube with nothing inside it but empty, stinking darkness" (15; perhaps an allusion to Darwinism's supposed threat to man's spiritual origins). The horror contemplated here is that of the corporeal vessel alone, devoid of its spiritual content, and one should note again the spatial literalism of Zakhar Pavlovich's thought, with its reductive image of the soul actually residing inside a physical vessel. This fear assumes still more visceral form in the thoughts of the gloomy, cynical Serbinov, who decides that "man is not sense, but a body full of passionate sinews, crevices filled with blood, hills, openings, gratification and oblivion" and identifies the ontological degradation this implies when he thinks of himself as nothing more than "the by-product of my mother, on a par with her menstruation" (324; see the notion in some of Platonov's earliest works of man's origins in, or reduction to, the "filth" of matter).[25]

As in earlier works such as "Rodina elektrichestva" and "Sokrovennyi chelovek," in *Chevengur* this theme of man's reduction to matter finds its fullest expression in scenes of death, with whose ontology Platonov shows man's existence as a whole to be coextensive. What the novel's several episodes of extinction dramatize is a final surrender to the physical realm, typically showing this through the ironic device of first suggesting, then negating, the opposition of inner being to its fleshly container (a device which in effect recapitulates the succession of attitudes informing Platonov's own ambivalence).[26] Hence a central motif in these descriptions is that of blood or other bodily fluids, which potentially represent the coursing of "life" within the body, but whose copious issue at the moment of death reveals what had been contained within to be purely physical substance.[27] Just after Dvanov wanders away from the train wreck early in the novel he discovers the swollen corpse of a soldier. At first he fears the body will burst and "spatter him with its life-fluids" ("*bryznut' svoei zhidkost'iu zhizni*"), but it turns out that the soldier has been dead for some time and the swelling is only due to the fact that "inside him were stirring *dead substances*" (emphasis added; 65).[28] Dvanov's encounter shortly thereafter with another soldier dying from a wound to the groin similarly presents the gushing of blood as a horrific image of "life's" departure from the body. The soldier pitifully curses the blood and pleads with it to stop – his life essence already ironically reduced to physical substance – but keels over, and Dvanov watches as the "matter" of the world reclaims the body from the being which had fleetingly occupied it. The reduction is completed as the soldier's eyes transform themselves into "round minerals" (that is, inorganic matter) and, at the moment of death, reflect the sky overhead, "as if nature were returning into man after the life that had opposed and blocked it" (65).[29]

Where Pukhov ("Sokrovennyi chelovek") was still able to discern in the "mechanical calm" of very similar deaths the promise of a Fedorovian "scientific resurrection of the dead," the characters of *Chevengur* perceive only the irremediable tragedy of being's final surrender to entropy. Thus Iakov Titych in one scene examines the "little corpses" of some spiders that had fallen to earth and there "made themselves into unrecognizable dust." In yet another ironic allusion to Fedorov he then goes around Chevengur picking up all sorts of "particles" ("*chastichki*") of things he finds in the road, wondering what "they used to be," whether they are "pieces of people" or of the same dead spiders (cf. Voshchev's similar activities in *Kotlovan*). If for Fedorov resurrection was to be accomplished by literally reassembling the molecules of the deceased, a feat to be preceded by the collection in "museum-shrines" of ancestral artefacts, Iakov Titych's collection of detritus signals to him only that nothing "remains whole, all creatures who once lived…are destroyed into parts that don't resemble them" (288–89).

The ontological themes in Platonov's novel find their summary expression in the figure of the so-called *prochie*, the destitute vagabonds rounded up from the steppes and installed as the "proletariat" of Chevengur (the word that becomes their ironic label throughout the novel means roughly "the others" or "the rest").[30] The *prochie* first of all epitomize the spatial literalism with which the novel treats its theme of man's exposure to the forces of matter. Abandoned by their mothers at birth, they are said to have expended their lives in the effort to preserve *within their bodies* a remnant of maternal bodily warmth, which they struggle to guard against the "uprooting, opposing wind of alien and hostile life" (255). The emblem of entropy's effects in the novel, they already look like "decaying skeletons" without flesh, and are first sighted on the outskirts of Chevengur *huddling* together for warmth on an *exposed* and *eroded* ancient burial mound (a hypallage that ironically transfers their features to their setting).[31]

The psychological or mental condition resulting in the *prochie* from this exposure to the world typifies the pessimistic materialism of Platonov's novel. The *prochie* (and some of the other characters as well) are often described as wandering the earth in a somnambulant state in which they have sentience but no higher consciousness of either themselves or their relation to the world around them. This condition is sometimes motivated by illness, as when Dvanov, sick with typhus, is said to lie "in forgetfulness of his life" (68); but more often it receives more explicit ontological motivation as the result of being's extreme dependency on the physical economy of the body (cf. anticipations of this theme in the "economic" motifs of "Iamskaia sloboda" and some of the sketches contained in *Epifanskie shliuzy*). Mind, one passage tells us, is a luxury enjoyed only by those possessing "*spare reserves of the body* and the warmth of a room over their heads" (emphasis added). The hapless *prochie*, however, were born to physical scarcity, by parents who were themselves but the "remnants" of a body worn out in labors, and from which, in the absence of "rest and tenderly-nourishing substances," the "higher trait" of mind had long since disappeared (253).[32]

One critic has conjectured that the source for this theme lies in the theosophical writings of Gurdzhiev, for whom the recovery of "memory of oneself" enables mastery of the separate levels of divided consciousness.[33] The more apparent source, however, is once again Fedorov, who assigns memory a redemptive role as an agency capable of countering the effects of entropy and, through the preservation of artefacts from the past, initiating the process of resurrecting those lost to death. The point of *Chevengur*, however, is to deny its characters this function of higher consciousness. Instead, their processes of thought are shown to be inextricably bound up in events of the purely material world. Like their forerunner Filat in "Iamskaia sloboda," they are in thrall to a process of "slow thinking" that underscores their tragic inhabitance of the border between organic life and inorganic matter (and in so doing supplies an important philosophical subtext to the "eccentricity" and "half-wittedness" prominent in the novel's utopian theme).[34] Unable to think except in crudely physical terms – no "idea" can exist for them except as the appendage of some material object – their cognition takes the form of a primitive translation of sensual promptings into "palpable" mental phenomena. As Dvanov tries to explain socialism to the peasant calling himself "Dostoevsky," for example, the latter "slowly absorbed Dvanov's words and translated them into visible conditions" (108), while Chepurnyi "mumbles" his thoughts because he does not know how to "comprehend" in silence (160). In the absence of the higher functions of consciousness, then, what the mind contains amounts to nothing more than fragments of immediate, sensual experience, or at its parodic extreme is reduced to matter altogether, as if thoughts were nothing but some kind of excretion of the brain. When Chepurnyi announces to Chevengur's bolsheviks that they will henceforth have to think up solutions to the town's problems on their own, they undertake the struggle to "think." Kirei, in particular, begins "to listen to the noise in his head and await thoughts from out of there," but he is finally forced to tell Chepurnyi that "from thinking pus comes out of my ears, but no thoughts" (235). Here the comicality of the episode characteristically intermingles with the suggestion of ontological tragedy (inside one's head instead of "mind" there is only "pus").

Platonov's portrait of the *prochie* is further important in that it makes explicit yet another form of "shelterlessness" that may be thought of as the metaphysical counterpart to the physical condition of exposure: that of orphanhood or "fatherlessness" (*bezottsovshchina*), which establishes one of the novel's most patent links to Fedorov. The nomads are described as never having seen their fathers and so having lived their lives "on the empty earth" without that "first comrade who might have led them to contacts with other people" (254). Chepurnyi even refers to them directly as "the fatherless." The theme of "fatherlessness" figures prominently in Dvanov's tale as well. Orphaned by his father's suicide, Dvanov frequents his father's grave (which he later dreams of lying down next to, remembering the stick he planted in it as a sign of how dreary it is for him to walk the earth alone, 214). However, where the principal emphases in Fedorov fall on the social–moral implications of orphanhood, the need to resurrect the deceased "fathers" of the human race serving as the imperative for establishing a relationship of true brotherhood among men,[35] *Chevengur* returns the theme to the domain of ontology, where it comes closer to the Freudian precedent sometimes discerned in it.[36] The absence of the father in Platonov ultimately represents the loss of a kind of fundamental ontological security, the severance of a link with origins that might justify one's existence on earth. In a definitive passage the novel identifies ancestors as the only entity capable of providing an antidote to entropy and exposure – though the endowment is at best tenuous, and the novel ultimately marks its distance from Fedorov by narrating the *failure* to rejoin the "fathers" (or the ironic reunification with them in death, as when Dvanov rides into Lake Mutevo):

Perhaps the very reason why the heart beats is that it is afraid of being left alone in this wide-open and monotonous world. In its beating the heart is linked with the depths of the human race, which gave it an initial charge of life and sense; but its sense cannot be something far-off and incomprehensible, it must be right here, near to the breast so that the heart can beat. Otherwise it will lose its ability to feel things and will die (304).

## "*CHEVENGUR*" AND THE UTOPIAN GENRE

That the pathetic creatures rounded up from the steppe are imported as the "proletariat" of a spontaneously generated communist society points to the ways in which existential and utopian themes are linked in *Chevengur*. On one level the work's utopian orientation is obvious. Its portrayal of how the "end of world history" arrives in the provinces (the great "out there" of the Russian cultural tradition) culminates a series of earlier works by Platonov preoccupied with either legends of ideal societies or myths of how society began (cf. Platonov's claim to Gor'kii that the novel was a sincere attempt to depict the "beginnings of communist society").[37]

That Platonov's novel asks to be read in the context of utopian thought in general is furthermore underscored by the variety of utopian doctrines on which it reflects. The most prominent is of course Fedorov's project for uniting mankind in order to overcome nature's hostility and resurrect the ancestors of the race ("supramoralism"). Fedorovian themes are particularly apparent in the Chevengurians' obsessive discussions of "comradeship,"[38] in the novel's infatuation with rural half-wits (who echo the philosopher's privileging of *duraki* over *umniki*), and in the Chevengurians' rejection of procreation (at one point sexual relations with women are declared to be "an alien and natural activity, not a human and communistic one," 233).[39] But Fedorov is far from the only presence in this richly allusive meditation on utopian activity in the context of bolshevism. The novel's remote steppe location, anarchistic overtones, and peasant characters all point to the Russian peasant tradition of utopias set in a "distant land" (as in the earlier "Ivan Zhokh"). At the same time these elements suggest the influence of the "scythian" resurgence such myths enjoyed in early Soviet literature (such as in Pil'niak's *Golyi god*, or, to name a more obscure example that Platonov nonetheless almost certainly had in mind, Ivan Kremnev's 1920 *Puteshestvie moego brata Alekseia v stranu krestian'skoi utopii*).[40] So, too, may the eccentric apocalyptic broodings of Platonov's characters allude (perhaps under the influence of Belyi's *Serebriannyi golub'* or

Rozanov's *Liudi lunnogo sveta*) to the sectarian religious movements that persisted in Russia into the twentieth century, many of which were active in the Voronezh region during Platonov's youth.[41] In a more esoteric vein it has been suggested that the radical egalitarianism of Chevengur and the ruthlessness with which its communists exterminate non-members reiterate the social program of the medieval chiliasts (such as Münster's 1534–1535 commune), and that the novel alludes, through its characters' belief that the sun will labor on their behalf, to Campanella's *City of the Sun*.[42] Nor should we overlook the obvious fact that the Chevengurians couch their utopian aspirations in the Marxist–Leninist terminology of class struggle and attempt, if dim-wittedly, to derive from Marx's writings a blueprint for their utopian society. It is, after all, "communism" they have established by declaring the "end of world history," the victims of their executions are labelled the "bourgeoisie," and the vagabonds whom they import are supposed to become a "proletariat."

If the theme of a utopian organization of society is thus prolifically represented in *Chevengur*, any attempt at dealing with the novel in terms of some specific version of utopia is nonetheless rendered problematic by the very plurality of utopian doctrines the novel has absorbed. On closer reading, no one of these turns out to enjoy distinct authority. This polyphony has much to do with the fact that the novel's theme is as much *utopianism* itself, the logic of and motives for utopian action, as it is any specific utopian doctrine, and the novel's omnivorous incorporation of just about every millenarial notion Platonov could have been exposed to is the direct outgrowth of this metageneric character. Utopian doctrines instead enter into the novel primarily in what might be thought of as an ideological pun: whatever their social, ethical, and historical tenets, these are reinterpreted as potential formulae for reshaping the conditions of being (even those of Fedorov, whom Platonov in this sense outdoes in his emphasis on ontology). Nowhere is this truer than in the case of bolshevism itself, which had its own millenarian record and which in Platonov's rendition of it bears some resemblance to the

*Proletkul't*. The examination of bolshevism's fitness in this regard, in fact, forms the crux of Platonov's dialogue with his ideological milieu.

Platonov's insinuation of an ontological agenda into his account of utopia-in-the-steppes reveals itself early on in the very motivations supplied for Dvanov's quest for socialism. In the apocalyptic atmosphere of revolution with which *Chevengur* begins, expectations for political and social change translate rapidly into longings for final release from the sorrows of the flesh. Thus Shumilin, the official who sends Dvanov off on his search, worries that his typhus-stricken wife will die unless "socialism is begun as soon as possible." It must already exist somewhere out in the steppes, he reasons, "because people have nowhere to go other than to band together out of fear of misfortune" (70). Dvanov himself has a foreshadowing dream in which a group of people exiled from the "warm places of the earth" build houses in the tundra to secure warmth (70), then another, distinctly Fedorovian one in which his father instructs him to "do something in Chevengur, otherwise why should we lie here dead?" (215). It is, in fact, the imminence with which the concept serves up absolute questions regarding existence that may explain Platonov's persistent attraction to apocalypse and to apocalyptic interpretations of the Russian revolution.

This blending of existential concerns with social engineering is reaffirmed in the sections of the novel dealing specifically with the utopian activities in Chevengur. On arrival there Dvanov and Kopenkin discover a band of apostolic communists in thrall to visions of a radically egalitarian brotherhood in which are to be assembled all the victims of oppression under the old regime. They speak obsessively of "comradeship" (*tovarishchestvo*, a term with distinctly Bogdanovian connotations), resolve to forsake all material belongings (obtaining one another as "possessions" in compensation), and declare even the weeds in the town to be "international property" (174). For all its resemblance to early Soviet dreams of communal life, however, this vision has more to do with longings for redemption from the trials of existence than with any social ethic as such. The very decision to import, as the "proletarian" beneficiaries of this communist utopia, the weak and impoverished *prochie* who serve as the novel's emblem for corporeal suffering suggests that the "regime" under which men presently suffer is as much ontological as political.[43] But the Chevengurians also imagine their utopia as bestowing a list of specific ontological benefits. In their "comradeship" they constantly, even obsessively, embrace one another (a compulsion that lends some credence to Paramonov's claim that the novel is a "gnoseological utopia constructed on the basis of homosexual psychology").[44] Even the bizarre campaigns of voluntary labor, in which the town's residents move its houses and gardens from place to place, are explained by their desire to live in "comradely close quarters" ("*v tovarishcheskoi tesnote*," 182), and the resulting jumble is said to make it look as though "people had pressed close to one another by means of their abodes" (274–75).[45] But as the huddling of the half-naked *prochie* suggests, the principle motivation for all this clinging is the desire for literal, physical refuge from the surrounding world. The characters' especially physical brand of comradeship is but a utopian institutionalization of the assorted acts of huddling, embracing, and sheltering performed along the road to Chevengur.

The rendering of shelter, in fact, becomes perhaps the central utopian activity in Chevengur, and may be viewed as a symbol of how Platonov sees social organization as proceeding *out of* existential conditions. The local soviet vacates the town's only stone building so the "proletariat" will no longer have to sleep in the open, and when Iakov Titych falls ill the remaining Chevengurians set about repairing his leaky roof (through which rain penetrates to fall "on his body," the explicitness of reference underscoring the flesh's involvement in all this). They then initiate a series of altruistic acts that, however ironic and postlapsarian, are aimed at providing shelter and sustenance (they attempt to generate fire, to mill some grain for kasha, and so forth). In an only partly ironic interlude, Iakov Titych himself takes in a cockroach – impressed, in particular, with the insect's apparent stoicism in the face of corporeal hardship. The Chevengurians' ultimate utopian vision is that of a day when even such redemptive sheltering becomes unnecessary. As Chepurnyi watches the *prochie* move the town's houses and gardens closer together he expresses the hope that some day they will *disassemble* the houses "as traces of their oppression" and live completely in the open, "without shelter" (*bez vsiakogo prikrytiia*) warming themselves only with one another's bodies because by then winter will have ceased to exist (267).[46] As with all such sheltering gestures in Platonov, the comradely embraces of Chevengur ultimately derive from desires for the literal preservation of the soul within the body, a point repeatedly underscored by the spatial literalism of the novel's language. (Chepurnyi, for example, is said to live "surrounded by comrades and protected by their sympathy from unavoidable misfortunes," 249; while Prokofii reflects that it is necessary to look after the "life" located "inside" each of the *prochie*, so that it will not "go out of the body and turn into wasted activity," 295.)

For the Chevengurians this dream of utopian, sheltering comradeship expands into the fervent belief that the end of history will usher in a new ontological order in which the world's destructive forces will be suspended and man will enjoy a recovered unity with the natural world. As Gopner puts it to Fufaev, who goes about collecting scrap-metal, the Revolution needs none of the junk belonging to the inhabitants of the old world, because "the new world will be constructed out of an eternal material that will never wear itself out" (155). The Chevengurians abolish labor as a form of suffering necessitated by the struggle against entropy under the old regime (Prokofii declares it to be "a survival of greed and a form of animal-exploitationist passion, because labor gives rise to possessions and possessions to oppression," 190), then they elaborate an edenic vision of reconciliation with the created world. In the fantasy many have read as referring to Campanella they declare that their material needs will henceforth be met spontaneously by the sun, which as the chief "proletarian" of Chevengur is now expected to labor on their behalf.[47] For their own part the steppes surrounding the town will assist the proletariat in acquiring food "without the interference of labor and ex-

ploitation," because nature has now "refused to oppress man
with labor and herself presents the non-possessing eater with
everything nourishing and necessary" (247; a typical example
of the contamination of Marxian terminology with ontological
themes in Platonov's text). This theme of being provided for by
nature is in part a response to Fedorov's lament over the earth's
refusal to serve as a real mother to mankind (cf. the beggar
Firs's vision on approaching Chevengur of how "from the
sunny center of the sky there dripped down nourishment for
men, like blood through the mother's umbilical cord," 178).
However, it also expresses that characteristic Platonovian
hope, apparent in even his earliest writings and a symptom of
his underlying ambivalence toward utopia, of a *passive* victory
over nature demanding the minimum of effort from an
inherently impotent mankind.

The Chevengurians' utopian designs culminate, then, in a
vision of community with every plant, animal, or even thing
(since Platonov expands the category of animacy to include
such extensions of human life as huts and fences) that may be
counted a co-sufferer with man of the vicissitudes of physical
existence. In the novel's persistent ideological pun, existential
afflictions qualify any form of being as a downtrodden member
of the "proletarian class" and therefore as a candidate citizen
of utopia. Chepurnyi, for example, thinks of the weeds growing
in the steppes as "brotherly, longsuffering plants that look like
unhappy people" because they endure, together with the
proletariat, "the heat of life and the death of snows." As a
result it is naturally assumed that they "want communism,"
too – unlike cultivated flowers, which represent something of a
vegetable bourgeoisie and are correspondingly to be banned
from Chevengur. (The town's cattle also "want communism,"
and Chepurnyi at one point refers to the overgrown steppes as
an "International of grasses and flowers".) In a similar mixing
of the biological and political, Dvanov regards some sparrows
he sees in a yard as "a truly proletarian bird, pecking at its
bitter grain," because unlike swallows (which, however
beautiful, fly away in the fall), they remain to "share the cold
and human need... there may perish on the earth from long,

dull hardships all the tender creatures, but such life-bearing
creatures as peasants and sparrows stay behind to wait for a
warmer day" (148).

Even this vision of a reconciliation with nature is underlaid
by Platonov's ontological theme of being's exposure before the
physical world: in the Chevengurians' utopian fantasy the
steppes will not only feed man but shelter him as well. The very
weeds that begin at the outskirts of town ("dusty burdocks ... growing in a brotherly manner among the self-satisfied
grasses") form a sheltering barrier between it and the hostile,
open space of the steppes: "The weeds surrounded Chevengur
with a close defense against the insidious spaces, in which
[Chepurnyi] sensed whole deposits of inhumanity. If it weren't
for the weeds, for the brotherly patient plants that looked like
unhappy people, the steppe would be unbearable" (219).
Among the several monuments to communism produced by the
Chevengurians is one that fittingly depicts a man in *embrace*
with a tree, "under a common sun" (247).

The Chevengurians' hopes for a reconciliation with nature
can be thought of as deriving from that sentimental, vulnerable,
and lyrical side which from the outset had complemented the
more aggressive, world-transforming tendencies of Platonov's
thought. It continues the distinctly pantheistic strain informing
some of the poems in *Golubaia glubina* (the pre-revolutionary
contributions to the volume, which were apparently written
before Platonov came under the influence of Cosmism) and is
represented in later works by the theme of nostalgia for a
childhood period of oneness with the earth. It furthermore
explains the novel's affinities with myths of a "peasant utopia"
(and its difference in this respect from a work like *Kotlovan*, with
its overriding echoes of the production novel and *industrial*
utopias), as well as with that variant of Russian modernist
eschatology that delights in images of a millenarial kingdom
among the beasts (Geller, p. 212). Khlebnikov's apocalyptic
*Ladomir* (1920), for example, envisions horses and cattle
entering into political "freedom" (*Ia vizhu konskie svobody*/*I
ravnopravie korov*), while Zabolotskii treats man's subconscious as
proof of his link with the "awkward beauty" of lower forms of

life.[48] In Platonov these notions have more to do with dreams of surrendering one's defensive posture toward the world and entering into a state of unthreatened community with it, than with any anarchistic flight from order; but the zoological utopias articulated by both Platonov and his modernist peers share common roots in perennial Russian visions of a redeemed material world.

That the Chevengurians' eccentric mix of revolutionary fanaticism with the philosophies of Fedorov and Bogdanov, and their resulting dreams of redemption from the world's hostility, are shown to fail in the novel underscores the pessimism with which Platonov had come to regard the prospects for rescue from man's existential lot. But in fact Chevengur's utopian achievements are never more than incompletely realized and are compromised from the start by the novel's persistent countertendency toward satire. Rather than tragedy, the novel tends toward a kind of despairing farce. The outsiders drawn to Chevengur (Dvanov, Kopenkin, and Serbinov) are never fully convinced that "communism" has been established there, and the utopian institutions they witness are at best ironically diluted versions of their antecedents in Fedorov and Bogdanov. The Chevengurians' relations of "comradeship," for example, may echo Bogdanov's ideal of proletarian communalism, but they equally represent the failure to establish the ontologically more profound relations of "brotherhood" declared by Fedorov to be the prerequisite for resurrection of the dead. Thus the *prochie* remark that they cannot become brothers to one another because they have no fathers, and embrace one another "not out of love, but out of a lack of clothing" (248). The Chevengurians' chastity is a similar instance of mock-realization: they forgo taking the women Prokofii herds in from the surrounding steppes, not in order to put an end to the chain of procreation, but because in their state of chronic orphanhood they need relations of succor and "sheltering" more than conjugal ones. Indeed, the very "shelter" provided in Chevengur's would-be utopia may be seen as a subtle abnegation of the goal of resurrection (that is, the radical remaking of the world) in favor of merely mitigating entropy's effects. The Chevengurians remain a collective of co-sufferers in an immutable world, not of those redeemed from its influence.[49]

It is the episodes of more explicitly ontological disintegration, however, which compose the novel's dénouement and demonstrate Platonov's theme of man's unalleviated subordination to matter. Whereas the Chevengurians believe they have transcended history and entered into an eternal summer whose sun raises up plants for their effortless consumption, the season in fact passes into autumn. In that overabundance of mortality noted so sardonically by Gurvich, Platonov uses this theme to show repeatedly that the natural world is nothing but the domain of "dead" matter. His descriptions of autumn's arrival correspondingly abound in the morbid conceits of decadent prose: pallor, decay, emptiness, fatigue, isolation, loss, silence, and death become the leitmotifs of the novel's second half, and the light of the Chevengurian sun is increasingly replaced by that of the moon:

Overhead, as if in the afterworld, there rose the incorporeal moon, which had already turned toward its setting. Its existence was pointless – no plants grew because of it, and in its light man slept in silence. The light of the sun, which from a distance illuminated the earth's nocturnal sister, contained a certain murky, hot, and living substance; but this light reached the moon already sifted through the dead length of space. Everything murky and living was dissipated out of it along the way, and there remained only a pure dead light. (294)[50]

In what may be a pun on the theme of bolshevik "October," the passing of revolutionary fervor is thus translated into an episode of universal expiration, with overtones of the ephemeral soul's departure from the world of matter (cf. "The Revolution passed like the day... The open spaces of the ravines and the countryside lay in emptiness and silence, having *released the spirit like a mown field*"; emphasis added, 284). Both Geller and Günther speak of utopia's unravelling in the novel as the disintegration of the static "chronotope" of an "eternal" city. An equally important context in which to view the novel's indulgence in lurid decline, however, is that of Morson's observation that, in contrast to utopia's characteristic denial of history, anti-utopia typically asserts historicity and "novel-ness".[51] Platonov's version of that historicity is his reassertion of entropy in the latter half of *Chevengur*.

The events marking utopia's final demise in the novel similarly emphasize the ontological nature of what takes place. The Fedorovian goal of resurrecting the dead (which, if never explicitly espoused, is nonetheless implicit in the Cheven-gurians' utopian program and is alluded to a number of times in the text) is negated when a child belonging to one of the beggar women dies.[52] Chepurnyi desperately tries to revive the boy so he will live "just one more minute" "under com-munism"; but he dies nonetheless and Kopenkin realizes that "there is no communism in Chevengur" (272). Later, when Kopenkin looks out into the steppe to see whether "in the air there might not be some kind of visible empathy for the child," he sees only the changing weather and the wind blowing through the weeds (273).

So, too, does the town's catastrophic rout by a band of marauding cossacks and cadets (or in some readings, the Red Army) contribute to this portrait of a final surrender to matter. For all its complex political overtones (the crushing of spontaneous, anarchic communism by the organizing, burea-cratic center; or the just desserts of infantile leftist extremism) what the episode ultimately depicts is the rupture of that encircling "shelter" which the characters believed had been established, literally and spatially, in Chevengur, and whose implicit model is being's relation to the body and the world. In what for Platonov counts as the extreme of ontological tragedy, the town turns out to be defenseless against an invading external force, and the comparison of that force with a relentless machine suggests it as a metaphor for the forces of matter. Brandishing sabers and rifles, this "machine-like enemy" ("*mashinal'nyi vrag*") moves on the town with the "machine-like force of victory" ("*mashinal'naia sila pobedy*"), crushing what feeble resistance the Chevengurians put up. (Ironically, as it advances the battalion secures for itself precisely the kind of "shelter" the Chevengurians lack: the horsemen are unafraid of bullets because they have "a

commander and order," and even when their commander is
struck by a bullet they fail to break rank – *ne rasstroilis'* – and
remove him into the protective depths of their formation,
360–61.) The coda Platonov supplies for this scene of
Armageddon both reaffirms the return to matter and reiterates
the rejection of utopian-historical solutions in some of the
earlier works. With the corpse of Kopenkin (who had dreamed
of reaching Rosa Luxemburg's grave and resurrecting her)
slung over his saddle, Dvanov abandons the ruined Chevengur
and makes his way back to the site of his father's suicide at Lake
Mutevo. There, in the novel's most explicit negation of
Fedorov, he ends his own life by marching into the waters – to
rejoin, that is, not a resurrected father, but the father's corpse.[53]

### The ideal of "reification" in Chevengur

*Chevengur* thus amounts to a curious combination of utopia and
anti-utopia. The vision of difficult existence that it offers cannot
but be read as a tacit endorsement of its characters' utopian
aims, but in the end the novel narrates the failure of that utopia
to be realized (moreover, in a manner ambivalently poised
between pathetic lament and parodic derision).[54] But beyond
the question of whether Platonov ultimately qualifies as a
utopian, a failed utopian, or some hybrid of the two, his novel's
seminal contribution to the genre lies in the connections it
establishes between its vision of existence and the manner in
which its characters aim to bring utopia about – and both the
vision and the manner are rich in echoes of Platonov's
ideological context.

   It was argued above that one of the central anxieties
informing Platonov's world view has to do with the apprehension that anything belonging to the realm of "spirit"
must be ephemeral or even nonexistent (a view the novel
ultimately confirms in its closing reversion to the dominance of
matter). Even in minor actions the characters display an
obsession with preserving intangible ("spiritual") entities in
material form, as if such an instantiation in matter were a
guarantee against their loss to entropy. Hence, among other
things, their perpetual urge for physical contact and the strange

forms it takes, which so redundantly underscore the novel's theme of physicality. When Sonia serves dinner to Serbinov, for example, he intentionally "touches with his mouth those places where a woman's hands had held the food" (321), and later he steals the sheets on which they have slept together because "in leaving he wanted to preserve an incontrovertible document of her" (326).[55] Such contact plays a particularly important role in the context of death, that ultimate loss to entropy. Despite a certain resemblance to necrophilia, the frequent desire of Platonov's characters to be near, if not in physical contact with, a corpse represents the longing to find, as a kind of ironic surrogate for resurrection, that the person's essence is somehow preserved within his remains. Thus the young Dvanov wants to dig a pit next to his father's grave and lie down in it because even though dead his "father" will be near, "with his shirt soaked in warm sweat and his hands, which once embraced Sasha as they both slept on the shore of the lake" (24). Zakhar Pavlovich similarly wants to exhume his mother's corpse in order to look on her bones and hair, "on all the last, decaying remains of the native realm of his childhood" (37) and plans, when Dvanov appears to be dying of typhus, to dig him up every ten years.[56] In the most literalized version of this theme even the objects with which someone has come into contact become vessels "containing" his otherwise intangible essence. The nomads who immigrate to Chevengur, for example, fondle the objects left behind by the town's former inhabitants as though they were concretizations for the "life" of others: "as though those things were the petrified and sacrificed life of their deceased fathers" (299).

One subtext for this obsession with reification can of course be located in Fedorov's program for collecting the artefacts left by man's ancestors and housing them in a museum. Indeed, the spatial literalism of Fedorov's vision (the ancestral trace preserved within a physical building) closely resembles that in Platonov, including his whole notion of "shelter."[57] The novel's most significant statement about utopia, however, lies in the connection it implies between this preservation urge and the very desire to arrange utopia. The characters' repeated attempts at securing intangibles in physical form turn out to be analogues for their much larger attempt to arrange for the *abstract* ideal of communism the same kind of *instantiation* within the material world.

*Chevengur* is not so much a study in utopian society as it is the portrayal, in Platonov's peculiar way at once sympathetic and derisive, of efforts to bring such a phenomenon about, and it has often been pointed out that the novel's theme is not utopia itself but the *process* of its realization (for example, Geller, p. 216). What distinguishes such efforts in the novel is their "fanaticism," the Chevengurians' belief that they can cause the entity of "communism" to appear immediately and instantaneously in their midst. (This is in fact the feature most often cited in comparisons of Platonov with the medieval chiliasts.) Dvanov's very departure to find "socialism" self-generated in the steppes reiterates, in its impatience with abstractions and eagerness to find them reified within the physical world, his father's march into Lake Mutevo to discover the essence of death. The first word Dvanov hears of Chevengur, moreover, is Chepurnyi's claim that "communism has arrived here" ("*u nas kommunizm*"), and he soon witnesses the precipitous bringing about of that claim as the town's residents move its houses and gardens from place to place and summarily execute its former "bourgeoisie."

The defining feature of this fanaticism, however, is not so much the haste of its desire to have apocalypse now as the *literalism* with which it wants to see its cherished ideal of "communism" arrive within the immediate world. In the characters' minds the ideal from the start acquires overtly spatial characteristics that imply its existence as a finite object, containable within the bounds of the town of Chevengur.[58] When Lui suggests communism be declared "the eternal movement of people into the distance of the earth," for example, Chepurnyi tells him that for the time being it should instead "be *limited to the territory wrested from the bourgeoisie, so we will have something to direct*" (pointing up the availability to manipulation which is an important consequence of reification for Platonov; emphasis added, 193). Later he declares that once "the class of the remaining bastards is exiled beyond the boundaries of the *uezd*, communism will arrive, because nothing else will remain (*bol'she nechemu byt'*, 217)" – as though such things were governed by the laws of physical vacuums.

At its extreme the literalism with which the Chevengurians approach their utopian venture manifests itself in expectations that "communism" will assume some immediately tangible form (cf. the scene in which Dvanov first wonders to himself where socialism can be found, then peers into a room "looking for his *thing*," 90; emphasis added). What these expectations underscore is Platonov's introduction of the ideal into that very world of matter and the body where the drama of man's ontological fate is taking place. On hearing from Kopenkin that communism should be slightly "bitter," Chepurnyi suddenly tastes salt in his mouth (195), and later Kopenkin is said to immerse himself in Chevengur, "feeling its quiet communism as a warm peace in his heart" (266). Indeed, the Chevengurians often speak as though they expect "communism" to manifest itself, literally, within their *bodies*. Telling Chepurnyi to counter the bourgeois instincts of Prokofii and Klavdiia, Kopenkin commands, "lower down some communism for yourself from an idea into your body" ("*Spuskai sebe kommunizm iz idei v telo*"; 189), while Dvanov is attracted to the town's inhabitants because "he imagined their naked pathetic bodies to be the substance of socialism, which he and Kopenkin had sought in the steppe and now had found" (311). People even consume grain in Chevengur "so that communism would become the perpetual flesh of their bodies" (285–86), and Dvanov works to secure food for the *prochie* specifically because "every body in Chevengur should be firmly alive, because only in that body does communism live as a material feeling" (312).

In the context of such literalism the downfall of utopia inevitably defines itself as the failure to bring about "communism's" reification in the extant world, an event reinforced by the motifs of emptiness and wan immateriality abundant in the novel's closing descriptions of autumn and the moon. Kopenkin and Gopner grow disappointed that they cannot "notice" communism ("it hadn't yet become an intermediary substance between the torsos of the proletarians," 306), and when the vagabond woman's child dies Chepurnyi asks, "Then where is [communism] located? Chepurnyi... couldn't clearly feel or catch sight of communism in nighttime Chevengur, although officially communism already existed" (277–78). At this extreme Platonov's theme obviously crosses into the comic, though a better way of putting it would be to say that the novel derives its central satiric device – its means for undermining utopian pretensions – from the very literalism of its characters' expectations, their unrelenting conviction that intangibles must have tangible form.[59] But its parodic apsect notwithstanding, the theme of reification stands at the center of the whole nexus of ontological, ideological, and utopian-social ideas informing *Chevengur*. The prospect of the reified ideal – which one could label Platonov's figure for utopia – promises utopia's presence in its surest form: communicated, as tangible substance, to the body itself (that realm of ultimate authenticity in Platonov's world) and even as an answer to bodily desires. At the same time, as a constituent of the physical world utopia is rendered available by this logic to manipulation by man in a manner reminiscent of Platonov's earlier fantasies about bringing the elements and even the planet itself under man's direct physical control.

*Chevengur* narrates the failure of any such reification to occur. But at the same time in the very (parodic) extremism of its characters' desire to bring reification about it exposes a paradox still closer to the heart of Platonov's utopian thinking. In one sense *Chevengur* shows humanity's profoundest desires to be directed toward something in the realm of spirit (for example, the "ideal" of communism or brotherhood); yet fears about the inevitable ephemerity of spirit dictate that the object of one's desire *must* assume tangible form if it is truly to exist, and this assumption amounts to a tacit concession to the contrary philosophical claim that in the end only matter "matters."

Platonov's theme of failed reification furthermore reveals important, and somewhat unexpected, links between his thought and the utopian genre as a whole. If, as Morson suggests, "all utopias are Platonic" because they deal in the opposition between the real world and the imagined world and for that reason narrate attempts at fusing transcendent with immediate reality (*The Boundaries of Genre*, pp. 86ff), then Platonov (the unintentional pun of whose surname keeps thrusting itself on his commentators) may be seen as addressing in ontologically vivid form the very bases of the genre. The ambivalences of *Chevengur* suspend the didactic element otherwise important to both utopia and anti-utopia, but they also turn it into an "examination, rather than either endorsement or rejection, of the presuppositions of utopian thinking and literature." Platonov's novel thus qualifies as that type of literary work Morson calls "meta-utopia" (p. 146). But Platonov composed his meta-utopia within a very specific ideological context, and the peculiar ontological myth that is its despairing derivative of Fedorovian and *Proletkul't* thought is also shaped in essential ways by his dialogue with Marxism–Leninism. That "official" Soviet world view came with its own program for the utopian reification of communism (in which, indeed, Platonov had taken part through his work as electrician and land reclamation engineer), its own supporting doctrine of the primacy of matter, and, most important, its own forms for self-expression in language. The sense of Marxism–Leninism's uneasy closeness to the premises of his own world view is in the end what produces the partly parodic, partly sympathetic portrayal of utopian events in Platonov's novel. This dialogue was to assume still more explicit form, and to reveal more clearly its implications for Platonov's verbal style, in *Kotlovan* – the major work to follow *Chevengur*, written in the period of high Stalinism when Soviet utopianism itself underwent vigorous revival and Soviet literature emphatically strove to realize "the principle of the identity of the artistic ideal in art and in life."[60]

# CHAPTER 4

# Platonov and the culture of the Five-Year Plan (1929–1931)

The years 1929–1931, which in Platonov's life mark the important interlude between the rejection of *Chevengur* and the vicious attack by Fadeev that made publication of his writing problematic for years to come, coincide almost exactly with the First Five-Year Plan and the associated dominance in literary affairs of the ultraleft Russian Association of Proletarian Writers (RAPP). These events are particularly significant because they denominate the first distinctly Stalinist period in the Soviet Union.[1] In this period Platonov wrote a series of works that tend to be treated as satires but are better thought of as records of his ambivalent relation toward, and complex attempt to assimilate himself to, the culture of the Five-Year Plan.[2]

*Kotlovan* (*The Foundation Pit*; 1930) is of coure the fullest, and most troubled, record of this encounter between Platonov's world view and Stalinism's culture, ideology, and language. But the shorter "satirical" works ("Gosudarstvennyi zhitel'," 1929; "Usomnivshiisia Makar," 1929; "Vprok," 1931) are important for what they reveal of the place that *magnum opus* occupies within the oeuvre as a whole. The ironic and even caricaturizing tendencies of these works set them at odds with the kind of literature advocated by RAPP; but Platonov's attitude toward Soviet power and its claims to be remaking proletarian existence had never been simple, and the satirical elements of these works have more to do with outlining the terms on which he was willing to endorse the Five-Year Plan's renewal of these claims than with any wholesale rejection of its campaign.[3] Indeed, with their tentatively positive portrayal of assorted feats of "socialist construction" these works form a bridge connecting the stories of the mid 1920s, which had valorized smaller deeds of electrification and land reclamation, with the more clearly adaptationalist, "socialist realist" kind of writing Platonov was compelled to produce during the latter portion of his career. What they again demonstrate is that rather than a progression from early, utopian enthusiasm for the Revolution to a bitter disenchantment expressed in satire, what we have is the record of Platonov's repeated, though never fully successful, attempts at reconciling his vision of existence with the Soviet experiment to which he was witness – and which seemed, provisionally, to promise redemption from the trials of physical existence.

The period in which Platonov wrote *Kotlovan* nonetheless stands apart from that of the mid 1920s in that, whereas the *Proletkul't* movement whose ideas so influenced him had occupied something of a utopian fringe in early Soviet culture, and the campaign for electrification had proceeded under the moderate auspices of NEP, the "socialist construction" of Stalin's "second revolution" reincorporated utopian aims and language as a part of "official" Soviet culture. This shift considerably complicated Platonov's response.

The work most positive in its attitude toward the Five-Year Plan, and the first to have been published, is "Gosudarstvennyi zhitel'" ("A Resident of the State").[4] Its hero is an elderly, unemployed member of the Union of Soviet Trade Workers named Petr Veretennikov who "love[s] the transportation system as much as he love[s] cooperatives and the perspective of future construction" (312) and whose detached status enables him to wander around surveying, as an enthusiastic sideline observer, various tableaux of "socialist construction." The terms on which Platonov was willing to accommodate himself to "socialist construction" emerge from Veretennikov's persistent worries on behalf of the state – of which, as the story's assimilationist title proclaims, he is a resident. Veretennikov's primary concern is with what might be called "socialism's progress in the world of things." He thus displays a keen interest in the physical condition of any object belonging to the state (particularly if it is a machine). The story opens with him visiting a train station and observing with delight how an engine moves boxcars "full of social materials" ("*polnye obshchestvennykh veshchestv*"), then crossing to the other side of the platform to watch trains depart for remote areas of the Republic "where people work and await freight" (313). He daily follows the state-sponsored "growth of structures" ("*sledil za rostom sooruzhenii*," 312), is moved at one construction site to see so much "labor and material" in one place, and worries over the fact that the wind is not blowing and the peasants are therefore unable to mill their grain.

Underlying Veretennikov's concerns is the question of how the state is faring in its (for him principal) function as agent in man's struggle against nature. Veretennikov reasons that the state exists to guarantee people their "necessary life," and whenever he encounters material disarray (the vagaries of the elements, birds consuming the kolkhoz's grain, trains coming to a halt) his immediate question is, "Where is the state here?" or "How does the state live in the face of all this?" (313). On the other hand, his enthusiasm for the state takes the form of a literalized vision of it as provider of "shelter" to living beings, a theme clearly reminiscent of the notion of utopia elaborated in *Chevengur*. The motif of a barrier between self and the world appears when he is said to love an old map of Austro-Hungary that he keeps at home because it represents to him a "living state *outlined by borders*, a certain *fenced-off and defended sense of civic life*" (315; emphasis added). His map of the USSR similarly represents to him a "border" made up of "living and faithful troops" behind whose backs "labor peacefully sighs" (315). To this notion is added a curious mix of Fedorovian ideas, Marxist labor theory, and Platonov's own ontological myth which regards the state as a preserver from entropy of reified lives. Veretennikov considers labor to be nothing but the "surrender (*smirenie*) of dissipated life" (that is, the dissipation of life's energies), but believes this "life" is then accumulated in the form of the state, which functions to preserve "the life of living and deceased people." Labor is taken from individuals and transformed into the "common body of the state," but this means that buildings, gardens, and railroads serve as the physical embodiments of the citizens' own transient lives (315–16). (Hence walking through the town Veretennikov touches the bricks of a building and reflects that the people who made them have died, but "from their bodies there remain bricks and boards – objects that make up the sum and matter of the state," 318.)

For all this enthusiasm Platonov's attitude in "Gosudar-stvennyi zhitel'" is precisely accommodationist rather than utopian: Veretennikov has his doubts about the state's occasional lapses in the struggle against nature. What is uncharacteristic about this tale, however, is that Platonov channels these doubts into a moralizing warning to *citizens* who fail to contribute sufficiently to the *state*. As Veretennikov tells a peasant from the famine-stricken village of Kuz'ma, "If we were all real (*strogimi*) citizens, there would be enough for everybody" (318).

As its title already indicates, "Usomnivshiisia Makar" ("Doubting Makar"; 1929)[5] rights the balance of skepticism by intensifying the element of doubt already latent in Veretennikov's tale. Makar Ganushkin, whose very name invokes a gallery of meek dissenters in Russian literature, is a poor peasant and an even more eccentric and peripatetic outsider than Veretennikov.[6] Like Veretennikov, he is a jealous observer of the physical progress of socialism; but he is also, in what suggests itself as an alternative vision of socialism's struggle against nature, an eccentric inventor who tries repeatedly to construct utopian devices in the manner typical of Platonov's post-*Proletkul't* heroes: with empirical ingenuity, out of crude materials found immediately at hand (like Zakhar Pavlovich, who makes a wooden frying pan in *Chevengur*). In his native village he builds a carousel that is supposed to be powered by the wind (but fails to work when none arises),[7] then promises to make, out of metal hoops and rope, a self-propelled vehicle (*samokhod*, which suggests Platonov's perennial fascination with the *perpetuum mobile*) and to that end extracts iron ore from the bottom of a well and melts it down in his wife's stove.

That ambivalence has been intensified in this more schematic and anecdotal tale is signalled by the fact that the picture of socialist construction Makar confronts is at once more utopian and more pessimistic than that encountered by Veretennikov. On the one hand, Makar sets off for Moscow, the "center of the state," hoping to find in it a "city of the wonders of science and technology" (96). Though there are flaws (Makar observes here and there the wasting of precious materials and energy) he nonetheless finds this vision in the process of being fulfilled. In direct anticipation of *Kotlovan* he discovers a state engaged in erecting what a passerby tells him will become "an eternal building of iron, concrete, steel, and bright glass" (98). The workers' dormitory attached to its site already provides a kind of pre-utopian "shelter" in which "the head of the poor class rested on a pillow beneath the ceiling and the iron cover of the roof, and the night wind no longer troubled the hairs on the head of the *bedniak* who once lay right on the surface of the globe" (100).

At the same time that it provides this vignette of utopian activity, however, the tale sounds the ominous warning that utopia is being undermined by bureaucratic intrigue (cf. the identical ambivalence in "Gorod Gradov" and *Chevengur*). Makar meets with bureaucratic opposition every step of the way and encounters his nemesis in the person of Comrade Chumovoi (*chuma* = plague), an official who "thanks to his mind directed the nation's movement forward in a straight line toward the general good" (93). This anti-bureaucratic theme culminates in Makar's famous phantasmagoric dream of the "scientific man" who stands in implacable silence atop a hill, thinking only about the "overall picture" (*o tselostnom masshtabe*) rather than some "private Makar." The statue's face is lit up by the glow of the "distant life of the masses," his eyes made "terrifying and dead" by the remoteness of his gaze. Like the canonic "little man" of Russian literature (Evgenii in Pushkin's "Bronze Horseman"), Makar challenges the idol by asking it, "What am I to do in life in order to be needed by myself and others?" (a phrase that at the same time voices Platonov's general theme of ambivalent desire to be included in the doings of the Five-Year Plan). But when, his curiosity having overcome his fear, Makar touches the idol's "fat, huge body" it collapses "because it was dead" (102–3).[8]

In a manner symptomatic of Platonov's hesitations in this period, however, the tale subsequently retreats from this position of political audacity and shrouds its ending in uncertainty. Makar eventually concedes that the "pen pushers" in the bureaucracy give life a "somewhat retarded but correct movement" (101), while his determination to fight for "the Leninist cause and that of the poor peasant" lands him in an office shared by Chumovoi, where he turns out to be unable to think any better than the ignorant workers and peasants who come to see him. (Chumovoi himself stays on to work for "forty-four years" on a self-defeating "Committee for the Liquidation of the State," eventually dying in bureaucratic oblivion.)

"Vprok (bedniatskaia khronika)" ("For Future Use [a Poor Peasant's Chronicle]"; 1931), the work that provoked Fadeev's vicious condemnation as *kulak* propaganda and purportedly inspired Stalin to write in its margins, "Talented, but a bastard," is a peculiar piece displaying all the ambivalence of Platonov's part hesitating, part entreating efforts to assimilate himself to the culture of the first Five-Year Plan.[9]

The work resulted from a tour Platonov made, at the request of *Krasnaia nov'* (which later apologized in print for its decision) to survey the progress of collectivization in his native Voronezh region.[10] Though in the end highly eclectic and contradictory (or polyphonic, as the case may be), "Vprok" consequently has as its premise the kind of feuilleton Platonov and Pil'niak had earlier co-written in "Che-Che-O," with all its proclivity for satire. Like Veretennikov and Makar, the narrator is "tormented with concern for the whole of reality" (198) and grants that the Revolution has made progress in the struggle against nature. He feels divided, however, over the course of collectivization. That campaign initially threatens to discredit itself in the anecdotal nature of what the narrator's journey reveals, as when he finds the members of one kolkhoz trying to set up an "electric sun" to illuminate their village when "nature's" sun is not out, or when there appears a strange figure dressed up as "God," complete with battery-operated halo, who gathers a considerable peasant following as he marches across the steppe (passages like these particularly irked Fadeev). This satirical vein is extended, and rendered more bitter, in the central theme of class war against the *kulak*, which tends to be treated as a vicious absurdity. In this "Vprok" is obviously a bold response to Stalin's March 1930 article on those "Dizzy with Success."[11] Discriminations between *bedniaki*, *seredniaki*, *kulaki*, and *podkulachniki* quickly become muddled, and the narrator meets a self-defined "fighter against the secondary danger," who cryptically explains that the "secondary danger feeds the primary one" and later exclaims what a delight it is to "knock off both rightists and leftists" (211), while the chairman of one kolkhoz (Kondrov) hits an adversary over the head with a rolled-up copy of the very *Pravda* issue containing Stalin's article! Where this satire merges with allusions to peasant sufferings – as when reference is made to the peasants' flight from collectivization (210) – its travelogue form even suggests analogies with Radishchev's *Journey from St. Petersburg to Moscow* (which, if conscious, are underscored by the ethical–allegorical quality of the names of the kolkhozes, for example "Dobroe nachalo," "Utro chelovechestva").[12]

In contrast to *Chevengur* and *Kotlovan*, however, the episodes of village eccentricity in "Vprok" remain this side of the surreal, and there are indications that the work was genuinely motivated by what Fadeev felt was only its cynically feigned intent: a desire to satirize the particular faults of collectivization while endorsing the enterprise as a whole. At the center of that endorsement stand the largely *unironic* descriptions of a series of collectives that Platonov clearly sees as embodiments of a model approach to the arrangement of rural labor (if not of labor in general).[13] "Samodel'nye khutora" (whose very name has something anarcho-syndicalist about it), for example, consists of four small workshop-huts inhabited by a group of demobilized soldiers who devote themselves to all sorts of minor mechanical repair. The narrator remarks that its leader would make an ideal director of the local Machine-Tractor Station because under him the tractors would never break down (a

Platonovian genius at the mechanics of impoverished resources, he could get them to run on just one cylinder). A similar tone of endorsement attends the account of the kolkhoz "Bez kulaka" and its director Kuchum, who refuses to admit peasants unless they are willing to take on hard work; and of the equally hard-working and productive commune "Nagrazhdennye geroi," the description of whose physical arrangement inside a former estate reads less like a feuilleton or travelogue than the kind of survey of an ideal city or factory common to utopian fiction. (Fadeev, in fact, claims that it is described as an idyllic oasis in the midst of the confusion of collectivization, and accuses Platonov of longing for a Chaianov-like peasant utopia.)[14] Moreover, into his survey of the countryside the narrator of "Vprok" interpolates his own discussions of assorted problems in land reclamation (especially the long disquisition on the drainage problems complicating the raising of sheep in the Ostrogozhsk region and that on the water-supply problems of the village of Ponizovka). Such passages might have come straight out of Platonov's technical reportage of the early 1920s and seem to be "planning" elements in their own right – as though Platonov were proferring these insights as his own contribution to collectivization.

Even more indicative of its uncertainties than these assimilationist appeals for a more "spontaneous" approach to collectivization, however, are the heavy concessions "Vprok" makes to the rhetoric of the class war. Side by side with the discrediting anecdotes so irksome to Fadeev the work also presents satirical attacks on the *enemies* of collectivization, such as the *kulak* Vereshchagin (an inveterate swindler who uses loopholes in the law to cheat the state insurance agency). The lighthearted tone of these episodes seems especially bizarre in contrast to the morbid, anti-collectivist tenor of *Kotlovan*, which Platonov had only recently completed. The narrator furthermore recites, with no apparent irony, the militant class-conscious slogans of the time (for example, "*Kroi bezuprechno i pravykh, i levykh*"; "Curse with impunity both rightists and leftists," 212); claims, at one point, that "not a single *seredniak* has been harmed by dekulakization" (209); and participates in the unmasking of both rightist inertia (Kuchum) and leftist

excess (the very same "Nagrazhdennye geroi" commune),
even dispatching a *donos* of sorts to ensure that they are rooted
out.[15] In the end what emerges from these vacillations between
political satire, carefully negotiated alternative stance, and
outright conformity is simply a record of Platonov's own
anxious attempt to find a place for himself within the culture of
the Five-Year Plan. This dilemma of "inclusion" forms a
recurring theme in his "satires" and stands as something of a
leitmotif for this entire period in his career.[16] Only the most
orthodox Stalinist view, or that western/dissident one convinced that if a writer is good he must at all times have resisted
the regime, would find such uncertainty a psychological and
aesthetic impossibility.

## "KOTLOVAN" AS A PARODY OF THE FIVE-YEAR PLAN NOVEL

While the extent to which it involves itself in Platonov's
ontological concerns and commits itself to his peculiar and
innovative uses of language makes of *Kotlovan* a very different
sort of work from the three just discussed, the tale embodies a
similarly ambiguous response to the culture of the Five-Year
Plan.[17] Its protagonist, Voshchev, is a dolorous outcast who,
like Veretennikov and Makar, finds himself at odds with the
energetic "socialist construction" taking place around him.
His distance from its activity, however, is more ironic and
pathetic than theirs. Where the other heroes are never more
than provisional participants in the events they witness,
Voshchev's journey begins with him being *expelled* (for thinking,
about the "plan of life," in "the middle of production") from
a factory job and thus undergoing the very tragic experience
Platonov was later to describe as *not* befalling the hero of a
classic Stalinist production novel. In Ostrovskii's *How the Steel
Was Tempered*, Platonov remarks, Pavel Korchagin is able to
accomplish his feats of production because he is from the outset
closely surrounded by people of kindred spirit (*rodnoi narod*) and
worker origin; "never will he, to his very death, depart their
ranks, he will never leave the formation of strugglers and
workers" – which is precisely what does happen to Voshchev.[18]

The eccentricity that the other works of this period tend to concentrate in their heroes is here largely externalized as a feature of the episodes of construction and collectivization in which Voshchev takes part, and which supply the premise for Platonov's grotesque inversion of Five-Year Plan intentions and their corresponding representation in Soviet literature. A vacant lot on which Voshchev spends the night turns out to have been chosen as the site for a utopian "Proletarian Home" (*obshcheproletarskii dom*), and Voshchev wins his "inclusion" when he signs on to help dig its foundation. This project, however, turns into an exercise in confusion and absurdity. The Plan undoes itself as ever more utopian conceptions of the proletarian home generate ever larger dimensions for its foundation, until in the end all that is produced is a gaping pit.[19] These events are narrated, moreover, from the perspective of the workers' social "below," where construction means little beyond exhausting labor, rather than from the platonic heights on which, in the standard Soviet production novel, the ideal Plan is administered with foreknowledge of historical destiny.

The latter section of *Kotlovan*, set in a kolkhoz bearing the emblematic name "General Line" and devoted to the theme of collectivization, disintegrates into an even more fantastic and grotesque series of events. In place of the politically straight-forward vision of "class war" contained in more orthodox Soviet works, the incidents in Platonov's tale form little more than random instances of cruelty: kulaks slaughter their livestock to prevent its expropriation, then are themselves terrorized and dispatched down the river on a raft, while the flies that have bred in the livestock carcasses bizarrely mix with falling snow. Into these are interpolated a set of ironically fantastic episodes – as when a group of horses "collectivizes" itself, gathering hay into a communal pile, or when a folkloric blacksmith-bear embarks on a private campaign of dekulakization, sniffing the class enemy out of its huts. The whole is presided over by a nameless "Activist" who is comically terrified by the confusing mandates sent by the Party. At first afraid he will be accused of "lagging behind," he is eventually declared to have overdone it and veered off into the "leftish swamp of right opposition."[20]

That all this is as much a response to something specific and conventionalized – the ideological myths of the Five-Year Plan and their literary embodiments – as it is to the events themselves is evident from the number of constitutive elements *Kotlovan* borrows from the production novel, that most representative genre of Soviet fiction.[21] With the possible exception of the protagonist Voshchev, the gallery of characters that parades across the stage of *Kotlovan* is drawn from the stock of social-political-psychological "types" endemic to Soviet fiction. The engineer Prushevskii, for example, is the "bourgeois specialist" and doubting *intelligent* harnessed to socialist construction, Chiklin is the stalwart and energetic laborer (a kind of proto-Stakhanovite), Safronov the activist and ideologue, Nastia and the assorted other children who appear in the work are the heirs to the socialist future, and so forth. *Kotlovan*'s dominant episodes also conspicuously follow the pattern of what was later to be canonized as socialist realism's "master plot."[22]

If *Kotlovan* may thus be said to define its relation to the Five-Year Plan novel in parodic terms, its parody, like that of *Chevengur*, is of a complex and ambivalent kind. The principles by which it translates the elements of the production novel at first glance appear to be those of grotesque, caricaturing distortion. But the essence of this caricature lies in a kind of hyper-loyalty to the elements' original intent (*after* which they become comic, though even then comedy is tinged with pathos), rather than in its derision. Thus not only is Nastia an oversimplified, slogan-spouting symbol of socialism's future, the village activist given no other name than "Activist," and the group of collectivized peasants consistently denoted, in the singular, by "kolkhoz" (as though the term were a proper name); but Zhachev, whose political role is that of one "disfigured by imperialism" (*urod imperializma*), is *literally* a cripple, and the formerly downtrodden worker who metes out justice to the kulaks is *literally* an "industrious bear." A similar principle governs the production of "comic" episodes in the class-war hi-jinx of the characters' involvement with industrialization and collectivization, whose typical device is to

foreground some ludicrously abrupt application of ideology to
life. The village activist, for example, has peasant women
memorize a newly politicized alphabet, in which the letter "a"
denotes "avant-garde, active member, alleluia-ist, advance,
arch-leftist," and so forth, and which preserves the hard sign
because it "makes for strictness and precision in formulations"
(435). Elsewhere when Pashkin is chided for retrieving a
sandwich that has fallen from the table (since in the coming
year agricultural output will vastly increase) he hides the
morsel in his paper tray, not wanting to look like someone
"living at the pace of NEP" (421). An alternative form
involves some slogan's fantastically "spontaneous" self-reali-
zation, as when the horses collectivize themselves or the bear
takes off on his campaign of dekulakization.

While such caricaturing reduction is the stuff of anecdote,
and places *Kotlovan* manifestly at odds with the epic tenor of
mainline Soviet fiction, it is equally the device of allegory and
as such is allied with Platonov's general inclination toward
philosophical abstraction. Moreover, like the instances of
eccentricity throughout Platonov's works, it is also utopian, in
that the "humor" of its half-witted literalism has consistently
to do with the reception of ideology as though it were
immediate truth, applicable to absolutely every circumstance
of life and containing the secret for life's transformation. As we
have already seen in *Chevengur*, the "logic" this literalism
involves is merely the ironic cousin of longings for a
transformation of the world entertained quite seriously elsewhere in the text.

## PLATONOV'S ONTOLOGICAL MYTH IN "KOTLOVAN"

What distinguishes *Kotlovan* from the other works of its period,
and what qualifies it as perhaps the most important and
representative work of Platonov's oeuvre, is the extent to which
it embeds the mosaic of comic and satirical elements just
discussed in the substratum of Platonov's vision of man's
existence in the physical world (and to which this embedding
additionally focuses the linguistic issues in his relation to Soviet

ideology). As Geller remarks, "Nowhere else was Platonov to manage such a complete fusion of a realistic and concrete social-historical background with an ontological subtext" (p. 254).

As a result of this subtext, the tale's primary tableaux of Five-Year Plan activity turn out to be not just occasions for caricaturing industrialization and collectivization, but the sites of what is perhaps the most visceral physicality of any portrayed in Platonov's works. Indeed, in a certain light *Kotlovan* can appear but a series of episodes of unrelieved brutality, in which even slapstick acquires overtones of morbid corporeality – from the repulsive amputee Zhachev, who has no teeth but has nonetheless managed to acquire a "huge face and fat remainder of his body" and who "moves his hand around in the depths of his pocket" (372) as a group of young girls passes by, to the tale's many killings (all brutal, and often accomplished with bare fist to the sound of cracking bones) and the scenes involving the slaughter of livestock. As if this were not enough, the narrative swarms with Platonov's favored allusions to such "naturalistic" functions of the body as sweating, masturbation, eating, and defecation.[23]

As in Platonov's earlier works, this orgy of physicality ultimately serves to underscore the paradoxical notion that being exists in subordination to a material body from which it is fundamentally estranged (that is, both being's inability to inhabit, and its perennial fears that it will be reduced to, the world of matter). Here again Platonov's narrative manner itself renders the notion of possessing a body problematic by insistently referring to the body as though it were an appendage of, not identical with, the character who resides within (thus, not "Voshchev paled," but "Voshchev's *body* paled from fatigue, he sensed the cold on his eyelids and *with them* closed his warm eyes," 368). Where *Kotlovan* exceeds its predecessors is in carrying the theme of being's dependence on the body to its almost self-parodying extreme (which is also, one should note, the extreme of thematic explicitness). Here as before the energies available to life are severely limited. The workers at the foundation pit, for example, do not even undress at night, saving the energy they might otherwise expend on unbuttoning for the next day's bout of "production" (409). But *Kotlovan* treats this situation as though it were governed by some literal equation, in which the "life" or "mind" of a character represents a part of some finite (and therefore implicitly physical) sum of energy allotted to the body and perforce to be parcelled out among its various activities. Thus, a worker in the foundation pit is said to labor, "releasing the remainder of his warm strength into the stone he was breaking up – the stone warmed up, while Kozlov gradually grew cold" (383), while elsewhere we are told that his mind "increases" after he eats (*"um ego uvelichilsia"*). That such passages are also literalizations of the materialist dictum that "matter determines consciousness," moreover, represents something of an ironic concession to the materialist ideology that at least ostensibly motivated the Five-Year Plan. Indeed, the very heightened self-consciousness with which *Kotlovan* treats these themes may have been triggered by the greater metaphysical explicitness (as well as utopianism) with which the Five-Year Plan advanced its claims.

*Kotlovan* also offers a more uniformly pessimistic vision of existence than its predecessors. From at least the mid 1920s onwards (cf. "Rodina elektrichestva"), Platonov had used the theme of emaciation to depict the world's frictive impact on both the body and the being it contains. But what had earlier tended (whatever its function in revealing the ultimate nature of man's existence) to be the plight of extreme cases who, like the *prochie* in *Chevengur*, wander in from the fringe of events, here afflicts the central participants in socialist construction. When Voshchev arrives at the workers' barracks he finds a group of men sleeping from exhaustion and existing, like the *prochie*, "without any excess of life" (*"kazhdyi sushchestvoval bez vsiakogo izlishka zhizni,"* 375). They are entropy's victims, in whom "being" has been reduced to its ephemeral minimum, but in this they only epitomize the human lot: "as thin as the dead, the close space between the skin and bones of each of them was taken up by veins, and by the thickness of the veins you could tell how much blood they had to pump during the effort of labor"; their hearts "beat close to the surface, in the darkness of each sleeper's vacant body," their "chilled legs helplessly stretched out in old workers' trousers" (375). A similar example of reduction, at the hands of entropy, to a state of emaciation bordering on death occurs when Chiklin takes Prushevskii to see Nastia's mother. Chiklin insists she is the same enticing girl they once saw and have dreamed of kissing ever since, but what they find when they reach her (on the floor of an abandoned, tomb-like factory) is a gaunt woman in the throes of death who is so weak that her daughter has tied a rope around her head to prevent her mouth falling open. In a pleonastic footnote to what is already a scene of pathetic scarcity, Nastia sits rubbing her mother's parched lips with a lemon peel so she will get at least some nourishment from the "lemon remainder" (406; perhaps an allusion to Christ receiving vinegar on the cross).[24]

Closely related to *Kotlovan*'s preoccupation with entropy is its vision of time. Negative, cyclical images of time appear in Platonov's works as early as "Buchilo,"[25] but here the theme is brought into particularly sharp relief through its implicit contrast to the temporal aggressions of the Five-Year Plan, with its "Time, Forward!" mentality and obsession with the precocious overfulfillment of its already overambitious schedules. In *Kotlovan* the "organizers" who administer the Plan are indeed caught up in this desire to mortgage the present for the utopian future (the Activist, for example, "was building a necessary future with the greediness of possession and without regard for domestic happiness, preparing in it an eternity for himself," 423). But for Platonov time is synonymous with entropy and reveals itself in disintegration rather than progress. If in *Chevengur* Chepurnyi is able confidently to announce that they have declared the end to "all of world-wide history," in *Kotlovan* that end perpetually recedes, and all Voshchev can do as he stares up into the "dead mass-like murk of the Milky Way" is to wonder "when there will be passed up there a resolution concerning the end of time's eternity" (422). Whatever the Plan's lust for an instant future, the world in *Kotlovan* is mired in the stasis of an entropic present: "endurance exhaustedly went on in the world, as though everything living were located somewhere in the middle of time and of its own motion: the beginning had been forgotten by everyone and the end was unknown, so there remained only direction" (419). Nor is this temporal theme necessarily as idiosyncratic as it appears. The sense of occupying a limbo between the bourgeois past and the arrival of communism has, in fact, always been endemic to the Soviet experience.

This despairing temporal theme also underlies what in *Kotlovan* represents being's most characteristic response to existence in the world of matter. The word Platonov repeatedly uses for this response is *terpen'e* (as in the above example, "*ustalo dlilos' terpen'e na svete*"), which translates literally as "patience" but in Platonov's usage means something more like "(mere) endurance, survival." *Terpen'e* involves being's longsuffering tolerance of the "resistance" exerted by the world, life's doomed but necessary struggle to postpone the effects of entropy. The tale's episodes of endless digging and of the peasants' strangely indifferent response to their fate under collectivization, which constitute so much of the work's "plot," demonstrate this very theme. As Voshchev discovers while watching a flock of sparrows fly over the foundation pit (who may be a conscious inversion of the biblical "birds of the air" who "neither toil nor reap"), in a scene that replicates Platonov's own impulse to scrutinize the body for evidence of the nature of existence, the struggle is ineluctable, perpetual, and eventually consumes those who undertake it:

они смолкали крыльями от усталости, и под их пухом и перьями был пот нужды – они летали с самой зари, не переставая мучить себя для сытости птенцов и подруг. Вощев поднял однажды мгновенно умершую в воздухе птицу и павшую вниз: она была вся в поту; а когда её Вощев ощипал, чтобы увидеть тело, то в его руках осталось печальное существо, погибшее от утомления своего труда. (383)
[From fatigue they fell silent with the sound of their wings, and under their down and feathers was the sweat of need. They had been flying since dawn, without ceasing to torment themselves for the sake of their offspring and mates. Voshchev once picked up a bird that had died instantly and fallen downward: it was drenched in sweat, and when Voshchev plucked it to see its body he saw in his hands just a sad being that had perished from the exhaustion of its labors.]

*Terpen'e* furthermore represents that languishing in the realm of matter, unvisited by the higher functionings of spirit, to which being is subjected in Platonov's world – that is, the same somnambulant existence into which the *prochie* of *Chevengur*, and later the nomads of "Dzhan," have sunk. In *Kotlovan* Platonov treats this "languishing" as a feature of existence in general, and projects it onto the very landscapes through which the characters pass. When the weary Voshchev lies down in the dusty grass by the side of a road, for example, the surrounding world is said to have given itself up to "mute existence" (*"bezotvetnomu sushchestvovaniiu"*). Surrounded by this "univeral longsuffering existence" (*"okruzhennyi vseobshchim terpelivym sushchestvovaniem"*), Voshchev declares that "everything lives and endures on this earth without being conscious of anything...As if some one person or a few people had drawn our confidence out of us and taken it for themselves" (371). In a later echo of this passage, when he believes that "truth" has perished together with the body of the Activist whom Chiklin has just killed, Voshchev sorrows that he is now abandoned to "unconsciousness in the rushing current of existence and to the submissiveness of the blind element" (that is, of matter; 469).

That this state is one of death-in-life *Kotlovan* underscores in a prolific series of motifs grotesquely mixing life with the grave. The excavation of the pit uncovers a group of coffins that turn out to have been laid away, in expectation of death, by the inhabitants of a nearby village (who when they come to claim them report that the coffins were purchased by "*samooblo-zhenie*," a pun meaning at once "voluntary taxation" and "self-burial"). Nastia – the tale's mascot of the utopian future – even ends up sleeping in one for lack of a bed. Nastia's dying mother also tells her, "I've become like the dead," and when Prushevskii later balks at kissing her corpse, Chiklin retorts that "the dead are people too." A contamination of life with death is, indeed, the ultimate fate of the foundation pit itself, which in the end is turned into Nastia's grave. As the text's descriptive passages repeatedly emphasize, a world given over to matter is essentially *empty*. "The air was empty" (367) is the curiously redundant assertion of one such passage, while elsewhere

Voshchev walks out of the town into "space, where there was...nothing but the horizon and the feeling of the wind on his face" (369). Prushevskii at one point surveys "the empty region of immediately surrounding nature" (400), while later rain begins to fall "apathetically, as if in a void" ("*bezuchastno, kak v pustote*," 425).[26] Indeed, the tale's principal setting is a foundation pit, and it is begun, like so many of the utopian projects in Platonov's works, on a *vacant lot* (*pustyr'*; cf. the empty desert, *pustynia*, which is the setting of "Peschanaia uchitel'nitsa" and later "Dzhan," the empty steppe in which the schemes of "Epifanskie shliuzy" and *Chevengur* unfold). This identification of the apotheosis of matter (that is, the dominance of the merely physical world) with the void appears paradoxical only until one recognizes that the underlying symbol is that of the grave – or rather, to delve yet one level deeper in Platonov's thought, the image, archetypal for his works, of the body bereft of its inner being and hence at once both material and hollow.

## THE UTOPIAN THEME IN "KOTLOVAN"

The focus in Platonov's tale of utopian longings for release from these conditions is Voshchev, a gloomier and philosophically more explicit version of Veretennikov and Makar who embodies Platonov's troubled search for some form of "spirit" to serve as antidote to matter's dominance. Voshchev's repeated lament over his inability to discover anywhere the "sense of life" ("*smysl zhizni*") conveys the double nostalgia for spirit characteristic of Platonov's thought in this period: to find such a "sense" is to affirm the existence of an entity transcending the material order (that is, the spiritual value harbored by life) and at the same time to identify that logical principle behind life whose apperception will rescue the world from the pure, inert "givenness" it threatens to represent.[27] Voshchev wants but is unable to discover an epistemological principle of unity (as he puts it, the "exact arrangement of the world," 370) which might, as in Bogdanov's thought, be used to transform existence itself. But he also reflects typical Platonovian apprehensions

concerning the ephemerity of spirit. His need for truth is
*corporeal* (his body "weakens without the truth," 370) and he
expects, with characteristic literalism, to discover it reified in
the here-and-now, variously wondering if it might not be
harbored in the workers at the foundation pit, buried beneath
the soil they excavate, or locked up within the body of the
village Activist.

Where Voshchev embodies Platonov's general despondency
over the ubiquity and dominance of matter, Prushevskii more
specifically represents a pessimistic reprise of his earlier
idolization of "proletarian consciousness." Prushevskii initially
appears to be Voshchev's opposite, the epitome of a *Proletkul't*-
ish engineer who possesses that very knowledge of the "precise
arrangement of matter" that Voshchev lacks and who knows
that the world "submits to his attentive and inventive mind,"
and that "matter always gives in to precision and endurance"
(379).[28] We are told, however, that from the age of "twenty-
five" (which, if he is an autobiographical character, would be
from 1924 on, that is, the very period in which Platonov began
his own disenchantment with *Proletkul't* ideas), Prushevskii has
felt the "restriction of his consciousness and the end to further
understanding of life, as if a dark wall had risen up before his
sentient mind." (This passage is a clear allusion to the "wall"
confronting reason described by Dostoevsky's Underground
Man.) Prushevskii has reconciled himself to the fact that
knowledge of the "true arrangement of matter" probably lies
on *this* side of the wall, but he now wants to know what lies
beyond it. However, with the metaphysical skepticism characteristic of Platonov in this later period, he surmises that beyond
lies nothing but a "dreary place" ("*skuchnoe mesto*") not worth
striving toward. "Consciousness" can know only matter, and
there is nothing else.

In *Kotlovan*'s episode of "socialist construction" Prushevskii's
despairing intimation that nothing beyond matter exists and
Voshchev's contrapuntal search for some noumenal "sense of
life" confront the ontological claims of the Five-Year Plan.
(With the exception of the self-collectivizing horses, reminiscent
of the peasant-utopian overtones in *Chevengur*, the episode of

collectivization in the tale's second half incorporates few utopian themes.) It is a measure of the complexity of Platonov's response to the period's culture and ideology that, for all the morbidity and irony separating *Kotlovan* from "Gosudarstvennyi zhitel'," "Makar," and even "Vprok," its depiction of "socialist construction" is also far from entirely parodic. Given the Five-Year Plan's "fervid industrial utopianism" and renewed enthusiasm for deploying the machine in the "struggle against nature" – that is, its revitalization, following the gradualism of NEP, of notions that had been central to the *Proletkul't* utopianism of Platonov's youth – it is not surprising that the text includes passages expressing a kind of provisional endorsement of the Plan and its projects.[29] The lure the Plan held for Platonov is reflected in part in the theme, which *Kotlovan* shares with other works of this period, of "whether one will live on into socialism": however much such expectations are tinged with pathos and originate in an outsider's point of view, the characters frequently express the hope that they will live on to inherit the socialist future, or fears that they will not, or they recognize that they will not but children will. The Plan's attraction surfaces still more clearly in the tale's several tableaux of what might be called "utopia-in-progress." Just as Veretennikov and Makar approvingly observe construction and the workings of machines, Prushevskii glimpses from afar a row of recently erected buildings that rise above the "murky oldness of nature" and "the rest of the newly-constructing world" like a utopian island, a "white theme of structures" that "radiates calmly" and looks as though it has been built not only for "use" but for "joy" as well (415).[30] Similarly, on arriving at the barracks Voshchev provisionally decides that the "truth" he seeks is located in the very bodies of the workers, and is relieved to find it so near at hand.

The specific focus for hopes regarding the Five-Year Plan in *Kotlovan*, however, is the edifice of the Proletarian Home itself, the allegorizing connotations of whose label (*obshcheproletarskii dom*) are difficult to convey in English. The most immediate benefit expected from it, the derivative of its role in the Plan's vaunted "struggle against nature," is that it will rescue proletarian man from the elements, that is, provide Platonovian "shelter" from the surrounding world. As Prushevskii remarks, the tragedy of man's present condition lies in the fact that he is forced to live in a world in which "no shelter has yet been arranged" (400). Likewise Pashkin, whose decision it is to expand the foundation pit to accommodate ever larger projections for the Proletarian Home, argues that a less-than-colossal edifice might abandon the descendants of socialism to live "outside, in the midst of unorganized nature" (421). This provision of shelter might seem but a slightly more utopian version of what elsewhere serves as the conventional stuff of the production novel; but Platonov places ontological stakes on the project by implying that what the workers are assaulting as they dig is the very "matter" of the world. "I too now want to work on the matter/stuff of existence" (*"ia teper' tozhe khochu rabotat' nad veshchestvom sushchestvovaniia,"* 376) is Voshchev's remark upon joining the excavation and, as Prushevskii's ruminations in particular make clear, the construction they have undertaken has been conceived in terms central to Platonov's ontological myth. Despite his epistemological doubts, Prushevskii embodies the *Proletkul't* notion of engineering elaborated in Platonov's Voronezh journalism: a manipulator of matter by profession, endowed with knowledge of its "precise arrangement," he regards construction of the Proletarian Home as an assault by sentient being on the recalcitrant "stuff" of the cosmos. That assault proceeds specifically by transforming the "dead body" of the world into habitable structures for man:

Весь мир он представлял *мертвым телом* – он судил его по тем *частям*, какие уже были им *обращены в сооружения*: мир всюду поддавался его внимательному и воображающему уму, ограниченному лишь сознанием косности природы... Но человек был жив и достоин среди *всего унылого вещества*, поэтому инженер улыбался мастеровым. (379; emphasis added)

[He imagined the entire world as a *dead body*, judging by those parts of it that he had already *transformed into structures*. Everywhere the world yielded to his attentive and imagining mind, which was limited only by an awareness of nature's inertia...But man was alive and worthy in the midst of *all this depressing matter*, and for that reason Prushevskii smiled at the craftsmen.]

The notion that the workers are digging up the very "dead matter" of the world is hinted at repeatedly in Platonov's descriptions of the excavation – Chiklin, for example, hammers away at the soil "directing the whole life of his body into blows at the dead places" (379), and later he is said to turn the frozen soil over "in big dead chunks" (472).

This dealing in primary ontological categories, in "matter itself," becomes important in connection with the hopes for ontological redemption tentatively raised in *Kotlovan* by the Five-Year Plan. The utopian solution is prefigured in the characters' attempts to preserve ephemeral essences in physical objects, whose ultimate provenance is again Fedorov's notion of the resurrected body. Like Dvanov in *Chevengur*, Voshchev empathizes with sundry suffering and forgotten "beings" and seeks to avenge their loss to entropy by collecting them. Finding a leaf that, having fallen to the ground, is destined only to rot, he gathers it into a bag in which he stores "all sorts of objects of misfortune and oblivion" ("*vsiakie predmety neschast'ia i bezvestnosti*") and even tells it, "You didn't have the sense of life, and since you are needed by no one and just lie there in the midst of the whole world, I will preserve and remember you" (370–71). His efforts are implicitly identified with the activities of the Five-Year Plan when his gathering of discarded objects in the village is described as a form of "socialist revenge" against entropy:[31]

Он собрал по деревне все нищие, отвергнутые предметы, всю мелочь безвестности и всякое беспамятство – для социалстического отмщения. Эта истершаяся терпеливая ветхость некогда касалась батрацкой, кровной плоти, в этих вещах запечатлена навеки тяжесть согбенной жизни, истраченной без сознательного смысла и погибшей без славы где-нибудь под соломенной рожью земли. Вощев, не полностью соображая, со скупостью скопил в мешок вещественные остатки потерянных людей, живших, подобно ему, без истины и которые скончались ранее победного конца (456).
[He went through the village collecting all the destitute, rejected objects, all the trivia of anonymity and all sorts of oblivion – and he did this for socialist revenge. These worn out, longsuffering, decrepit objects had once touched the flesh of poor hired workers; in them was eternally stamped the weight of a bent-over life that had been wasted

without conscious sense and had perished unknown somewhere beneath the rye of the earth. Without fully comprehending, Voshchev like a miser collected into his bag all these material remains of lost people – who had lived, just like he, without truth and who had died before the victorious end.]

If in *Chevengur* such desires have their utopian redaction in the characters' expectations that "communism" can be realized physically in their midst, in *Kotlovan* they find it in hopes that the Proletarian Home will not just represent a monumental refuge from the surrounding world – a notion utopian in its own right – but will secure the existence of noumenal being in the material world. Indeed, the building is intended to serve as a kind of archetypal utopian *body*, reshaped from the "matter" of the world; its imperviousness to the effects of entropy will provide the "being" within it eternal security. Thus one of Prushevskii's primary concerns is the "arrangement of the soul" (*ustroistvo dushi*) in the building he designs – a phrase implying at once the make-up of the souls of its inhabitants and the provision *for* those souls – and he worries lest his structure be erected in vain, as an "empty building" in which "people live just because of bad weather." Instead he wants it to be filled with people who are themselves in turn "filled with that excess warmth of life, which someone once called the soul" (384; though in characteristic fashion this passage hints at a kind of thermodynamic physicality which subtly implies the soul's reduction to matter). Furthermore in his blueprints he takes specific pains to provide for the building's "indestructibility," since the "solidity of this [building] material, which is destined to preserve men who have hitherto lived on the outside" (390) will be its primary guarantee against the effects of entropy.

The hope held out in *Kotlovan*'s episode of socialist construction, then, is for something that one might call the "perfect instantiation" of being in matter, and the building which is its symbol is both the most explicitly realized version of the theme in Platonov's oeuvre and the idealized embodiment of his (partial) attraction to the ideology of the Five-Year Plan. In a way, given the Plan's metaphoric definition of Soviet industrialization as socialist *construction*, the erection of a building was bound to become the campaign's emblematic act (hence the central role of construction sites, of literal *stroitel'stvo*, in the literature of the time).[32] But the image of the sheltering abode had also long been central to Platonov's ontological myth. It was a *topos* of the Cosmist poetry Platonov imitated in the early twenties (in which it is repeatedly promised that the cosmos will be transformed into a "home" for proletarian man), and it appears in this sense in his journalism when he speaks of erecting a "unified temple of human creation," a "unified residence for man's spirit," the laying of the foundation for which is the task of proletarian art ("O proletarskoi poezii"). Its function in *Kotlovan* as a utopian refuge from the world's frictive influence is also undoubtedly underlaid by Fedorov's idea of the "temple-museum" designed to preserve the artefacts of mankind's perished ancestors. Both that borrowing and the architectural image of the *dom* to which it contributes, however, ultimately derive their significance from Platonov's spatially literalized notion of the soul's residence in its material corpus.[33]

The image of the Proletarian Home in *Kotlovan* further sheds light on the underlying themes in Platonov's dialogue with the ideology of the Five-Year Plan. Platonov's own world view may be thought of as an ambivalent conflation of the otherwise radically opposed tenets of materialist and idealist epistemologies. (The precedents for this conflation, if not the tragic awareness of its contradictions, again lie in Bogdanov and Fedorov.) On the one hand his insistence on matter's tragic dominance over being amounts to the assertion of a fairly primitive form of materialism (cf. its literalizing extreme in the passages showing a character able to think only when he ceases to work). But the key to Platonov's thought lies in the lamentative interpretation he places on this circumstance, an attitude that betrays the deeper adherence to idealism responsible for the unrelieved contradictions in his world view: while the dominance of matter is conceded, spirit is nonetheless valued as living (sentient, suffering) and hence ontologically superior to the "dead matter" in which it is forced to reside. Platonov esentially regards materialism as "correct" – indeed, that its basic assertion is literalized in the novel to the point of near-parody serves as a kind of ultimate, "grudging" assent to

its truth – but what it knows points only to the irremediable
suffering characteristic of being.

What "socialist construction" tentatively offers in *Kotlovan* is
the prospect of an optimistically *materialist* resolution of these
antinomies. Not only does it mount the project for constructing
the Proletarian Home, but it backs up its undertaking with self-
confident proclamations of the primacy of matter.[34] When
Voshchev tells a Party official that the "plan of life" he has
been thinking about might guarantee "happiness," he is
rebuked with the remark that "happiness comes from materialism" ("*schast'e proizoidet ot materializma*," 369), a typically
awkward Platonovian phrase that adds to its ostensible
assertion that "the only way to human happiness is through
adherence to the materialist world view" the implication that
materialism somehow directly *produces* the spiritual experience
Voshchev desires (as if in keeping with its own notions of
"superstructures" arising out of "bases"). Prushevskii voices
the same logic, albeit hesitatingly and ironically, when he
wonders, "Does a superstructure arise out of every base? Does
every production of life material yield as its by-product a soul
in man?" (384; that this thought comes in connection with his
plans for the building further amplifies the building's ontological overtones – the word for "superstructure," *nadstroika*,
hints at construction). In *Kotlovan* even the dream of resurrection is appropriated by Marxism: when Prushevskii tells
Chiklin that the dead cannot be resurrected by "science," the
latter retorts that in fact they can, because "Marxism can
figure everything out" (458). Indeed, the very assumption,
central to the tale's utopian construction project, that one can
arrange the security of being in the world through the empirical
act of putting up a building, that is, through a manipulation of
physical substance, implies a faith in the priority of matter.

*Kotlovan*, however, finally disposes of this materialist optimism in a display of matter's unaltered dominance that is
even more morbid than that in *Chevengur*. The efforts to
organize the collective farm end in an orgy of corporeality, in
which both kulaks and activists meet with brutal deaths and
flies proliferate in the rotting carcasses of slaughtered livestock,[35] while the intention to build the Proletarian Home

produces only greater and greater versions of the void. Just as the end of *Chevengur*'s utopia is signalled by the death of a child, defeat in *Kotlovan* comes with the death of Nastia, whom the tale has made into an explicit emblem of the socialist future. When Nastia dies – from exposure to the cold, that is, from "shelterlessness" – Voshchev wonders like Kopenkin whether communism is possible, now that a child has died under its supposed jurisdiction. The redemptive goals the tale had provisionally attached to the construction of the Proletarian Home are then inverted point-by-point in the closing scene of her burial. Chiklin descends into the now-abandoned foundation pit to dig her grave. That he digs for fifteen hours mocks the towering height that had been planned for the edifice, while the ideal of "perfect instantiation" is parodied in the pains he takes to guarantee the indestructibility and inviolability of Nastia's *coffin*, which he hews from the "eternal stone" of the pit so that "neither worm, nor the roots of plants, nor warmth, nor cold" (474) will penetrate to disturb her ironically lifeless corpse.[36]

*Kotlovan* responds to the temptations of the Five-Year Plan, then, by demonstrating the pathos of Stalinism's naive belief that its plans can succeed – the pathos, that is, of any optimistic interpretation of materialism that holds that successful manipulation of "matter" will automatically yield desired results in the realm of "spirit," together with its utopian corollary that construction of the Proletarian Home will directly, without any intervening order of experience, secure the redemption of "being." The extravagant optimism of these beliefs is exposed by the ultimate recalcitrance of the cosmos, which renders such attempts to overthrow its rule futile and rewards them with further suffering or death. In this sense *Kotlovan* becomes a cautionary tale about the drastic consequences awaiting the utopianism of the Five-Year Plan. Or, to the extent that one assumes an element of self-consciousness in Platonov's efforts to reconcile himself to Five-Year Plan ideology, one might say that *Kotlovan* expresses the pathos of his own tentative faith that the Stalinist brand of materialism might indeed fulfill its promise to complete the "struggle against nature" and secure man's existence in the world. In such a light his position might

be said to be that of an ambivalent idealist, writing in an age
of seductively attractive materialist hegemony.

The unconventionality of Platonov's themes, imagery, and
literary style often make him seem somehow entirely apart from
the mainstream of Soviet literature, but in fact he is one of the
most self-consciously "intertextual" of Soviet writers (a trait
perhaps attributable to the essentially ironic qualities of his
world view).[37] We have seen that many of the episodes and
characters in *Kotlovan* travesty features of the Five-Year Plan
novel; but neither, for all its recondite appearance, is the work's
ontological drama the product of notions entirely idiosyncratic
to Platonov. To understand how at this deeper level *Kotlovan*
also responds to specific elements in the culture of the Five-
Year Plan we must consider the tale's implicit dialogue with
Gladkov's *Tsement* (1925), a work that, in addition to being one
of the primary exemplars of the production novel, was one of
the few that had been written by the time Platonov was
working on *Kotlovan*.

That Platonov had Gladkov in mind when composing his
own parody of the genre is evident from his work's several
patent borrowings from *Tsement*. Nastia, for example, is the
direct descendant of the Chumalovs' daughter Niurka (both
symbolize the socialist future, both die in the end, and both, of
course, hark back to Nellie in Dostoeveskii's *The Insulted and the
Injured*). So too is the grim episode of dekulakization in
Platonov's tale patterned after the expulsion of the bourgeoisie
in *Tsement*: both hapless groups trudge, wailing, through the
streets on their way down to the docks where a ship (*Tsement*)
or raft (*Kotlovan*) awaits them. More important to the dialogue,
however, are those textual elements cohering around Gladkov's
central conceit of the progression from death to resurrection,
and from the factory as idle tomb to the factory as energetic
producer of cement, which in his novel emblemizes the theme
of post-civil-war reconstruction. Thus the many "decadent"
motifs of decay, dust, and rot in Gladkov's novel are echoed in
*Kotlovan*, and both plots get underway at a symbolically marked
site of emptiness (Gleb returns from the civil war to find the
machines of his beloved factory standing idle, its yard a *vacant
lot* overgrown with weeds and overrun by chickens and goats;

Platonov's plot starts at an identical weed-filled *pustyr'*). But where Gladkov deploys his motifs as the prelude to restoration and resurrection, and ends his novel with an orgiastic celebration of abundance and production, the same elements in *Kotlovan* define a condition of lack from which no exit is granted.[38] Indeed, Nastia's burial deep in the rock at the end of *Kotlovan* may be a conscious inversion of Gladkov's description of the crowd in his novel's finale as "a living mountain, stones resurrected as people" ("*zhivaia gora – kamni, voskresshie liudom*," 325).

The ontological drama in *Kotlovan* can thus be viewed as an inversion of the central "myth" of one of the most important Soviet production novels, in which the production of substance, tantamount to the renewal of life, has been translated into a production of absence equated with the perpetuation of death. But the connection between the works is more than thematic and episodic. Early in *Tsement*, Gleb delivers a speech in which he declares, "We are producers of cement. We are cement, comrades, the working class... It's time for us to take up the task at hand: the production of cement for the construction of socialism" (71). Katerina Clark has pointed out that *Tsement* consciously paraphrases economic themes that had been aired in *Pravda* in the period of reconstruction, and that Gleb's speech in all probability derives from remarks made by Zinoviev in a 1919 *Pravda* article entitled "Iustin Zhuk." Praising Zhuk, a worker who, on returning from the war, organized efforts to restore a factory in his native Schlusselburg, Zinoviev invokes "cement" in the same metaphoric sense as Gladkov: "It is through such people that the proletarian state stands. Such people are *the cement of the worker and peasant government*" (emphasis added). Lunacharskii later does the same when, in his review of the novel, he asserts that "On this cement foundation we can build further" (quoted in Clark, p. 74). The "cement" produced in Gladkov's work is thus no ordinary substance, but a realization of the rhetorical figure central to the text's didactic aims (the characters literally produce the "cement" on whose foundation the fledgling Soviet state can reconstruct itself). Both the figure and the manner in which it is used derive from linguistic habits peculiar to Soviet *agitprop* (here represented in the authoritative precedent of a *Pravda* article). That the failure to produce in *Kotlovan* may thus also be seen as a response to a rhetorical device of Gladkov's novel brings us to the subject of language, and of the interconnections between it, Platonov's world view, and the rhetoric and ideology of the Five-Year Plan.[39]

## LANGUAGE IN PLATONOV'S MATURE WORKS

The principal stylistic theme in Platonov's works of this period remains that of the post-revolutionary linguistic confusion arising out of the collision between the colloquial speech instincts of Russia's unlettered masses and the bookish, abstract, figure-laden patterns of the assorted styles of writing and speaking that had early on coalesced into a recognizable "Soviet-speak."[40] In those moments of his texts in which this theme is foregrounded, the conventions of this "Soviet-speak" are violated through a process that first extracts elements from their appropriate context, then subjects them to misinterpretation (usually of the literalizing sort), fragmentation, and grotesque recombination with others like them or with the patterns of colloquial speech.

How the resulting cacophony asks to be interpreted, however, is far from straightforward, and varies from work to work. Contemporary critics often found Platonov's verbal manner unsettling; but in the context of RAPP hegemony, with its debates over the admissibility of Soviet satire, what had been mere incomprehension translated into the politicized charge that Platonov had put on a mask of holy foolishness for the sake of deriding the progress of socialism.[41] Fadeev's devastating review of "Vprok," for example, repeatedly expresses annoyance at what it calls Platonov's "shamming" (*krivlenie*), and accuses Platonov of hiding his true class nature (that is, kulak) behind a stylistic camouflage of "simple-mindedness and holy foolishness" (*prostiachestvo i iurodivost'*).[42] E. Usievich was later to level the same accusations at Zabolotskii, charging that his poetry attempted to cloak its idealist philosophy in a "stylized primitivism, fake naivety and feigned holy foolishness (*iurodstvo*)" that was nothing but a feeble imitation of Khlebnikovian primitivism; and her essay hints ominously at the political stakes involved by mentioning an article in which Stalin had warned that the class enemy would now try to *mask* his activities.[43]

In hindsight such political vilification inevitably appears irrelevant to the artistic merit of the works and even inaccurate, but Fadeev's assumption of a *divorce* between the texts' verbal manner and their authorial point of view is shared by the many later discussions of Platonov's style that interpret its ironies as a wholesale rejection of alien and self-discrediting forms of Soviet speech.[44] In fact an attitude of dismissive verbal irony does figure in some of Platonov's works of the late 1920s and early 1930s and represents a direct extension of the penchant for irony and *skaz* stylization prominent in the early works (from the burlesques of "crude" peasant speech in his village sketches to Pukhov's garbled reception of *agitprop* in "Sokrovennyi chelovek" and Zharenov's rhymed, Smithy-like speech in "Rodina elektrichestva"). Thus the eccentric Chevengurians comically literalize political speech as part of their misguided attempt to apply it directly to mundane events (though as will be seen this attempt has utopian implications), while in *Kotlovan* Safronov's speech consists almost entirely of slogans, Kozlov reads political literature in order to memorize phrases with which to intimidate lesser officials. The hyperactive source of it all is identified in the radio, which "worked all the time, like a blizzard" (409) though the verbiage it spews is described as pure noise. "Vprok" summarizes this line of verbal irony, and distances itself from the garbled forms of speech it portrays, when it explains its awkward locutions as the result of those in power having imposed alien forms of speech on the otherwise sincere feelings of the peasantry:

Но зажиточные, ставшие бюрократическим активом села, так *официально-косноязычно* приучили народ думать и говорить, что иная фраза бедняка, выражающая искреннее чувство, звучала почти иронически. Слушая, можно было подумать, что деревня населена издевающимися подкулачниками, а на самом деле это были бедняки, завтрашние строители новой великой истории, говорящие свои мысли *на чужом двусмысленном, куацко-бюрократическом языке.*" (236–7; emphasis added).

[But the well-off, having become the bureaucratic activists of the village, taught the folk to think and speak in such a *garbled-official* manner that any phrase uttered by a poor peasant that expressed sincere feeling sounded almost ironic. Listening to it made one think that the village was inhabited by mocking *podkulachniki*, but in fact these were poor peasants, tomorrow's builders of a great new history, who were speaking in *an alien, ambiguous, kulak-bureaucratic language*.][45]

Despite the persistence into these works of *skaz*-like verbal irony, however, the verbal manner definitive of Platonov's mature style is one in which, through the process described earlier, verbal oddities are embraced as authorial speech and the distance between textual point of view and that of *kosnoiazychie* is closed.[46] Were one to catalogue by structural type the varieties of semantic and syntactic deformation that Platonov thus absorbs into authorial speech, a preliminary list would include tautology, the contamination of one set expression with another, abrupt truncation of expressions, substitution of "inappropriate" cognates, awkward transposition of elements within an expression, and the imposition of false, "folk" etymologies.[47] More important to the poetic workings of this style, however, is the manner in which, in contrast to dismissive verbal irony, these deformations yield a specific content whose relation to Platonov's vision of existence is felicitous rather than random – or to put it another way, the manner in which the elevation of "deformed" speech to authorial status confers on it its function as an *icon* for textual themes (in the semiotic sense of the term). This iconic function, this simultaneous embrace of post-revolutionary linguistic confusion and reading into (or "out of") its bizarre mosaic the semantics of his own ontology, defines the "unique" achievement of Platonov's prose. The discussion that follows examines the iconic attributes of language in the most representative example of Platonov's mature style, *Kotlovan*.[48]

The *misprision* that is Platonov's overarching linguistic theme generates this kind of poetic content in two recurring contexts of semantic (or referential) ambivalence, which often coincide within particular examples. The first involves ambivalence between the abstract and the concrete, whose effect is to imply a world in which everything is physical and in which, at the same time, everything that takes place is contiguous with the absolute – an apocalyptic world of matter, as it were. When Voshchev walks to the outskirts of town, for example, we are told:

[он] очутился в *пространстве*, где был перед ним лишь горизонт и ощущение ветра в склонившееся лицо" (369).
[he ended up in *open space*, where before him there was only the horizon and the feeling of the wind in his inclined face.]

While the mundane episodic context of Voshchev's walk would lead us to expect some concrete, particular term, such as *pole* or *pustyr'*, the substitution, in a kind of inverse metonymy, of the abstract noun *prostranstvo*, especially in the absence of any particularizing modifiers, produces an odd combination of semantic effects and unsettles our perception of the event. On the one hand, the absolutizing effect of the abstract term makes Voshchev seem to tread an apocalyptic landscape, where, beyond the town, lies not fields but "space" itself. On the other hand, yoked to such a concretizing context, the abstraction itself suffers a kind of demotion to the level of the particular, so that the phenomenon of "space" appears to be a finite area that one can enter on foot.

The second context is that of ambivalence between what might be called "life," "nature" – that realm for Platonov associated with existence as such – and the domain of the political, ideological, and bureaucratic, the confrontation of the two being for him definitive of the Five-Year Plan. If the first type of ambivalence appears the extension of a peasant "crudity" or "abruptness" that insists on viewing the world as consisting of "things," this second type arises out of what might be called the "pathos of bureaucratic existence": the sense (in Platonov, both ironic and utopian) that the whole of one's existence has been subsumed under bureaucracy and is therefore best described using its language. "*Stupai tuda i spi do utra, a utrom ty vyiasnish'sia*" ("Go in there and in the morning you'll be cleared up"; 374), Voshchev is told, in a phrase confusing the clarification of his own intentions with the bureaucratic sorting out of his political identity, while the resurrection of a "dead" metaphor in the descriptive passage, "*Tekushchee vremia tikho shlo v polnochnom mrake kolkhoza*" (424), conflates the bureaucratic cliché "*tekushchee vremia*" ("the present time") with the everyday-existential phrase "*vremia idet*" ("time is running out") – in the process rendering the notion of time strangely concrete.

This persistent tendency of Platonov's prose to engender coincidences of meaning in a context of semantic ambivalence closely resembles the workings of the pun. Like verbal puns in general, semantic ambivalence in *Kotlovan* derives its effects from a perceived coincidence of the "intended" meaning of a word or phrase with an "inadvertent" meaning invoked through some slight caprice of lexical or syntactic context that suggests, if only momentarily or ironically, that both meanings somehow obtain simultaneously and that the realms of experience from which the meanings are drawn are likewise identical. (For example, recall Mitrofanushka's remark in Fonvizin's *Nedorosl'* that "*dver'*" is an adjective [*prilagatel'naia*] because the door to which it refers was put in place by someone [*prilozhena k svoemu mestu*], the humor of which owes much to the apparent premise that grammar and physical actions belong to the same order of things.)

The importance of this kinship with the pun for the iconic functions of Platonov's prose becomes clear when one considers the ways in which, under the auspices of his ironic demonstrations of the "pathos of bureaucratic existence," the semantics of "life" or "being" encounter those of Soviet political phraseology and which, in this tale of the Five-Year Plan, collectively function as a "language of utopia" (encompassing the rhetoric of Marxist–Leninist political dogma, Soviet bureaucratese, the language of political propaganda, and even technical terms drawn from the field of engineering).

Just as *Kotlovan*'s episodes of socialist construction and collectivization incorporate a drama of ontology, Platonov foregrounds the mutual contamination of the semantics of existence with those of utopia. Malapropism in the text of *Kotlovan*, for example, frequently yields the "discovery" of some manifestly political sense within a term drawn from the everyday lexicon of the language. Thus when Chiklin strikes a peasant he has been interrogating about the murders of Kozlov and Safronov, the narrator remarks:

Мужик было упал, но побоялся далеко *уклоняться*, дабы Чиклин не подумал про него ничего зажиточного, и ещё ближе *предстал* перед ним, желая посильнее изувечиться, а затем исходатайствовать себе посредством мученья о жизни бедняка (426–27).
[The peasant was going to fall down, but was afraid of deviating too far, lest Chiklin think something well-off about him; so the peasant stood even closer before him, hoping to get seriously mutilated and then get himself designated a *bedniak* for having suffered.]

That the peasant has in fact been struck by Chiklin urges on the reader the literal (and concrete) sense of *ukloniat'sia*, to avoid, dodge, as *uklonit'sia ot udara* "to dodge a blow," (Ozhegov's dictionary). The use of this verb in the episodic context of the peasant's fears that he will be labelled a "kulak" if he falls, and of his desire to win for himself the status of a "bedniak" by standing up to the blow, however, invokes the expressly political, figurative sense of the word that had gained fateful significance during the Stalinist period: "to deviate," as from the correct Party line.[49] The pun thus ironically asserts the *literal* equivalence of the physical event of falling over ("deviation") to an act of political deviance. Moreover, to the extent that the simultaneity of these two meanings appears apt, it projects the momentary fiction of a world in which concrete events are contiguous with political ones, so that physical gestures reap immediate political effects.

Conversely, in *Kotlovan* the specialized and usually abstract lexicon of Soviet political phraseology can be made to yield up references to some "ontological" aspect of the concrete realm that is the focus of Platonov's vision of existence. For example, in a passage reporting Voshchev's wandering through the collective farm in search of the decrepit objects he wishes to collect as evidence of "being's" tragic struggle against the material universe, we are told of a chart drawn up by the party activist to whom the objects are delivered:

Вместо людей, активист записывал признаки существования: лапоть прошедшего века, оловянную серьгу от пастушьего уха, штанину из рядна и разное другое снаряжение *трудящегося, но неимущего тела* (456–57, emphasis added).
[Instead of people the activist wrote down the symptoms of existence: a shovel dating from the last century, a tin earring from some shepherd's ear, a pair of pants, and all sorts of other outfittings for a laboring but nonpossessing body.]

Here Platonov's pun hinges on a misconstrual of grammatical part of speech. In their conventional, political usage the words *trudiashchiisia* and *neimushchii* function as substantivized adjectives that require no antecedent; they denote, respectively, the socio-political categories of "toiler" and "nonpossessor." Their unexpected conjunction in Platonov's text with the noun *telo*, however, causes them to be read ("inadvertently") in their original etymological state as participals, and in so doing, restores to them the literal meanings of the verbs from which they derive. In its paronomastic conflation the phrase thus contends that Voshchev has retrieved the effects of *bodies* that *toil* but *have nothing* – precisely the interpretation of Marxist–Leninist social morality important to the characters' utopian vision, in which it is believed that a socialist construction project will release them from the trials of corporeal existence. Again, the connotative effect of the pun implies the identity of the political and existential spheres from which the differing denotata are drawn, as though the social oppression of the lower classes were defined fundamentally in terms of their sufferings from the vagaries of corporeal existence.

Similar semantic effects attend Platonov's discovery of "ontological" themes within the technical terminology of construction and engineering, which, as suggested above, forms a natural kinship in the work (and perhaps in Stalinist culture in general)[50] with more expressly political phraseology as a subcomponent of the "language of utopia." As in the preceding example, these paronomasias tend to assert the literal identity of some purely technical notion with a fundamental aspect of "being," often further implying that the business of engineering is by definition to deal in ontological affairs. Thus when

Prushevskii stands looking across the foundation pit toward a distant industrial complex, we are told:

В далеке светилась электрическая постройка завода, но Пруш-евский знал, что там ничего нет, кроме *мертвого строительного материала* и усталых, недумающих людей (384; emphasis added).
[In the distance there shone the electrical structure of the factory; but Prushevskii knew there was nothing there but dead inventory and tired, unthinking people.]

This passage occurs as Prushevskii ruminates on his role as engineer and decides his task is to mount an assault on "matter" itself in order to reshape it into a utopian shelter for the proletariat. Platonov's pun then transfers this theme to the level of style, where it becomes a constitutive feature of the very language of the text: the two notions to which Prushevskii ostensibly refers in his thoughts are *mertvyi material* (literally, "dead material"), which means "material or equipment not being used in production," and *stroitel'nyi material*, or "construction materials," both of which he presumably sees at the factory. However, his "inadvertent" conflation of these compound terms violates their normal syntactic integrity and consequently restores to the epithet *mertvyi* the literal meaning suppressed in the technical lexicon. The coincidence of figurative and literal meanings in the pun consequently reiterates Platonov's view of the utopian project by stating that the factory Prushevskii sees contains "[literally or ontologically] *dead* material *to be used in construction*." "Mortal" puns playing on the latent ontological pretensions of such terminology are, in fact, one of Platonov's favorite ways of underscoring the existential significance he assigns to engineering and construction in the work. This is clear, for example, in the episode in which peasants from a nearby village arrive at the foundation pit to claim the empty coffins the workers have unearthed, arguing that they need them as "*mertvyi inventar'*" (literally, "dead inventory," but in its technical sense, "the means of production"; 62).

Platonov's attraction to paronomastic effects, particularly those brought about through the deformation of some grammatical or stylistic norm, recalls certain exemplars of the *skaz* tradition such as Zoshchenko or Gogol', in whose works a similar, but comically motivated, coincidence of "intended" and "inadvertent" meanings is often used to reveal the misprision of the character who has uttered it. (The rhetoric of the pun, in fact, should be seen as one of the key lessons Platonov derived from his early emulation of *skaz* traditions of the 1920s.) Platonov diverges from the tradition in attenuating the comic emphasis on linguistic ignorance as such, since his work lacks the kind of stylistically orthodox authorial voice – manifest or implied – which ordinarily calls attention to the act of misprision. What Platonov retains from this branch of the *skaz* tradition, however, is the unique ability of comic malapropism to expose linguistic intention – to implicate the erroneous presuppositions regarding meaning and reference from which the flawed utterance arises. In this sense the type of linguistic irony found in *Kotlovan* conforms to Morson's definition of "parody" as an "etiology of utterance," a polemic over linguistic and ideological values in which the parodist aims at revealing the "unstated motives and assumptions" of both the speaker and his world view (p. 113). It testifies, moreover, to the extent to which Platonov had assimilated and moved beyond the mere theme of linguistic confusion that he deploys – in a manner that transcends both a purely satirical, "Zoshchenko-like" debunking of cultural illiteracy and a dismissive satirization of Soviet-speak – what might be called the "rhetoric of linguistic intentions" provided by comic malapropism to reflect the pathos of utopian aspirations in the work.

The immanent "intention" behind the paronomastic style of *Kotlovan* may be perceived in the puns' moment of semantic coherence, when the "intended" and "inadvertent" meanings seem at once felicitously apt, and the figurative and literal senses of an expression appear identical (cf. "Сафронов знал, что социализм – это дело научное, и произносил слова так же логично и научно, *давая им для прочности два смысла – основной и запасной*, как всякому материалу"; "Safronov knew that socialism is a scientific matter and so he also

pronounced words logically and scientifically, buttressing them
with two meanings, a basic one and a spare, as one would any
material," 394).[51] These paronomasias project (or, one might
say, aspire to refer to) a world in which the boundary between
the abstract and the concrete, the particular and the absolute,
has been dissolved, a kind of allegorical universe in which
there exists no division between spirit and matter and hence no
need to draw any parallel distinction in the referential aspect of
language. In particular, as the ubiquitous mutual intersection
of political phraseology and the semantics of "existence"
implies, this is a universe in which ontology and politics belong
to a single plane of experience. The moments of referential
identity on which Platonov's paronomasias turn thus provide a
linguistic analogue to the notion of the reconciliation between
spirit and matter central to the characters' utopian vision. In so
doing they imply a referential domain in which plans for
literally restructuring the cosmos make eminent sense. Hence
the persistent urge in Platonov to regard language as a physical
thing, as in the explanation for why the village women learning
the alphabet continue to use the hard sign:

Потому что из слов обозначаются линии и лозунги и твердый
знак нам полезней мягкого. Это мягкий нужно отменить, а
твердый нам неизбежен: он делает жесткость и четкость
формулировок (435).
[Because out of words are denoted lines and slogans and the hard sign
is more useful to us than the soft sign. It's the soft sign that should be
abolished, while we need the hard sign: it makes for strictness and
precision in formulations.][52]

This image is only a tentative, or ambivalent one, however,
because Platonov's paronomasias never elude the same irony of
semantic disjuncture that in comic malapropism serves as the
grounds for satire – the awakened linguistic prudence of the
reader, which signals that the coincidence of meanings the pun
effects ultimately does not obtain but, like an unstable chemical
compound, breaks down into its separate parts. By reminding
the reader of the ungrammaticality of the utterance, this ironic
disjuncture dissolves the image created in the pun's semantic
conceit and confirms the ultimate impossibility of speaking

about the world in the manner that has been attempted. When all of its features are taken into account, then, the language of *Kotlovan* should be seen as a linguistic icon not of utopian "instantiation" but of the "frustrated instantiation" in which the novel displays utopia's demise. The linguistic irony of the text thus amplifies that of its themes and plot.

Moreover, there emerges from *Kotlovan* the suggestion, never far from any pun encountered in the text, that the urge toward the kind of literalized double entendre discussed above is not just an idiosyncracy of the tale's peculiar narrative consciousness but is endemic to Stalinist utopian thought itself, whose manifest reliance on metaphor testifies to its motivating will toward literalization (and it is perception of these traits in the language of "socialist construction" that explains Platonov's attraction, however ironic, to Stalinism's characteristic forms of expression). In Platonov's texts some of the most common political metaphors from the period of collectivization are made to appear pregnant with their own literalization, afflicted with a seemingly self-generated propensity to overextend themselves to the point of *reductio ad absurdum*. Safronov's use of one of these clichés thus grows into a phantasmagoria of concretizations: "*My uzhe ne chuvstvuem zhara ot kostra klassovoi bor'by, a ogon' dolzhen byt': gde zhe togda gret'sia aktivnomu personalu!*" ("We already feel the heat from the bonfire of class war, but there should be some fire: otherwise how is active personnel to warm itself!"; 420). Elsewhere in the text a party directive warns of "*malozhelatel'nye iavleniia peregibshchiny, zabegovshestva, pereuserdiny i vsiakogo spolzaniia po pravomu i levomu otkosu s ottochennoi ostroty chetkoi linii* ("undesirable manifestations of overdoing it, racing ahead, overexertion, and all sorts of sliding down the left and right slope from the sharp ridge of the precise line"; 464).

It is with regard to this reflection of the culture of the Five-Year Plan, moreover, that it finally becomes appropriate to speak of the literary style of *Kotlovan* as the instrument of a particular kind of parody. In the rhetoric of linguistic intentions provided by the pun, the very existence in the text of the paronomasias we have discussed implies the presence of a "speaker" who utters them in the manner he does because he harbors certain presuppositions about the world to which he uses them to refer. To equate willfully the figurative and the literal, to invoke routinely political phraseology to refer to "existential" phenomena, or to deploy common words as though they literally comport political meanings, implies the assumption of an analogously ordered ontological domain. In the case of *Kotlovan*, the belief that the boundary between matter and spirit has been surmounted and that a socialist construction project can deal directly with the ontological foundation of the cosmos is the very cornerstone of the utopian Five-Year Plan vision provisionally entertained in the tale – and in this sense the paronomasias genuinely constitute a "utopian" mode of speech. But the ironic disjuncture never absent from Platonov's puns then threatens to flaunt not their ungrammaticality alone but also the fallaciousness of the utopian vision from which they derive.

The exposure of referential heresy at this point translates into a larger undermining of world view. In showing the language of the Five-Year Plan to be predicated on a propensity toward this kind of literalization, Platonov suggests that the Stalinist utopian project has been undertaken in the first place because its promoters naively feel the presuppositions on which it rests to cohere in language. Not only do they assume a particular manner of speaking about the world, but on the basis of that (ultimately fallacious) speech they believe their plan for remaking the world to be valid. Nowhere is this logic implied more strongly than when the text foregrounds the "projective" (in the sense of the Russian *proektivnyi*) quality of the Stalinist lexicon, through which Soviet political phraseology appears not only to be capable of referring to the concrete world but also to contain the algorithm for its remaking – as in (yet another) passage describing Voshchev's passion for collecting discarded objects: "*Voshchev...sobiral v vykhodnye dni vsiakuiu meloch' prirody, kak dokumenty besplanovogo sozdaniia mira, kak fakty melankholii liubogo zhivushchego dykhaniia*" ("Voshchev... gathered all sorts of trivia of nature, as a document of the planless structure of the world, as facts of the melancholy of

all that lives and breathes"; 103), where the Soviet politico-
economic neologism *besplanovyi*, ostensibly misapplied to mean
some kind of "cosmic" disorder or chaos, suggests by its very
inclusion that redemption from this chaotic state lies in
implementation of the Stalinist *Plan*.

Here a linguistic practice – the language of Stalinism, with
all its metaphoric conceits – is shown to be the generator of
utopian acts. But it falls victim to the fatal tautology of
believing its epistemological presuppositions (the dominance of
matter over being, which in turn sanctions the Stalinist utopian
scheme) to be ratified in the solecistic linguistic practice (the
naive conflation of figurative and literal at the root of Soviet
political phraseology) to which it has itself given rise (since the
conflation itself is motivated by the presupposition of its
referential aptness). This urge toward ontological and linguistic
fusion, whose motivations Platonov in part shares but whose
tragic disintegration he cannot help but anticipate, is ultimately
revealed as specious by the workings of language itself. The
semantic ironies of *Kotlovan* demonstrate that one cannot speak
in the language of utopia because the world is, finally, not
constituted as that language and the world view from which it
derives would have one believe. "Language" turns out to serve
in the text as primary representative of the recalcitrant stuff of
the cosmos, and it is linguistic parody that ultimately offers the
most incontrovertible, "material" evidence for the fallaciousness of Five-Year Plan utopian schemes.[53] And if puns, in their
semantic multivalence, "illuminate the nature of language in
general," then Platonov's prose sheds light on the complexities
involved in the contrary – utopian – desire imposed on language in the Stalin era to have a world and a manner of
speaking about it free of all antinomies.[54]

In thus turning toward *language* Platonov transposes the
conflict between his own vision of existence and its utopian
materialist competitor (toward which he feels his own brand of
"envy") to the very realm in which Russian culture had from
the symbolists onward sought to resolve the antinomies of spirit
and matter, and in which Soviet culture had most aggressively
and with the greatest *apparent* success asserted the triumph of its

materialist view. Among the traditions of Soviet literature and its response to the language of its epoch, however, his specific brand of verbal parody assigns him a curious place at once central and peripheral.

The self-conscious topicality with which Platonov's major works reflect the language of the Five-Year Plan can be viewed as an extension of tendencies that in the preceding decade or so of Soviet literature had found a variety of representations, from the Futurists' interest in "mass speech" and the language of the street[55] to assorted democratically inspired efforts at last to allow the *narod* its own literary voice. These tendencies were perhaps epitomized in Pil'niak, whose works have been described as having consciously set out to embody the "very distinctive languages of the epoch" and whose principle of "montage" Platonov had himself briefly imitated (and revived from time to time in the wholesale inclusion of "documents," such as the instruction for the electric sun in "Vprok").[56]

The irony with which Platonov tended to reproduce both the language of the Soviet era and its reception by the semi-literate *narod* recurringly invited the labels of satiric *skaz* and disingenuous *iurodstvo*, but his insistence on the grotesque nature of "lower" speech was for him the gateway to things other than purely sociological or political satire (hence his distance from, and apparent aesthetic distaste for, Zoshchenko).[57] Nor, despite many points of resemblance, does his poetic coincide with that of someone like Zabolotskii (in whom a certain intentional childishness of speech is also linked with a posture of empathy for lower forms of being), since Platonov's prose avoids an aestheticizing turn toward "transsense" (*zaum'*) and absurdity by "sincerely" insisting on the existential themes yielded up (as it were, prophetically) by its deformations of the language of Soviet officialdom. What distinguishes Platonov is the extent to which he was capable of rendering explicit the epistemological substratum of language and making it a manifest theme of his works, and it is undoubtedly his view of language as the privileged revealer of linguistic and, behind them, epistemological presuppositions which led him to embrace verbal art as the natural medium in which to conduct

an ideological debate. In thus reading the epistemological face
of language Platonov may have been influenced by Futurism's
cult of the material and insistence on the "thingness" of art,
and the implicit alliance with the "democratic" tendencies of
Soviet literature in which Platonov's poetic places him, his
remoteness from high-brow art of the bourgeois era, was
grounded in a similar sense of language's involvement with the
existential realm. The embrace of lower forms of speech seems
connected in his works with a curiously pathetic rendition of his
sense of proletarian origins, in which awareness of his
emergence from the lower social order(s) is associated, not with
any historical or political sense of self, but with "ontological"
anxieties over having emerged out of the chthonic "filth" of the
earth. As he asserts in an early essay, "I am confident that the
advent of proletarian art will be ugly (*bezobrazen*) ... We grow up
out of the earth, out of all its filth (*iz vsekh ee nechistot*), and
everything that is on the earth is on us as well...But we hate
poverty... We march obstinately out of filth" (Platonova, p.
162).

Platonov's relation to the forms of literature and literary
language that came to be identified with socialist realism was
equally paradoxical. As we have seen, his preoccupation with
the semi-literate folk's reception of post-revolutionary language
and culture somewhat parallels that in Zoshchenko. But, as
Chudakova has argued, where Zoshchenko felt himself to be
suspended between the high culture of the past (whose
expressive possibilities the Revolution had wholly discredited)
and the "low" culture of new, extra-literary forms (whose
expressive potential had yet to be realized), Platonov's works
from the mid twenties on are governed by a distinct, if complex,
sense of "participation" in the language of the present Soviet
era.[58] Indeed, Chudakova's claim is that Platonov was that
very "imaginary but genuine proletarian writer" who Zoshchenko believed had yet to appear (117); and that his writing
was moreover motivated by "the conviction that his word
does nothing more than affix what his milieu has to say about
itself; he attempts to discern its voice" (114).

As *Kotlovan* suggests, Platonov turns out to be uncannily close to some of the latent assumptions of socialist realism. The tale's linguistic ironies subvert an impulse toward metaphoric literalization that, born in the rhetoric of *agitprop*, later surfaced in socialist realism's claims to be translating the "pathos of the Absolute" into "reality itself" (or, in its sentimentalized version, to be "making fairy tale into reality," "*sdelat' skazku byl'iu*").[59] Socialist realism was itself ultimately to realize this goal through quite different and more complexly retrospective, "Red Tolstoyan" means, and Platonov hardly qualifies as a socialist realist author of the Fadeev–Gladkov–Ostrovskii stripe. But his troubled relation to literary officialdom may have had more to do with his uncomfortable exposure of its underlying designs (from the viewpoint of officialdom, his *perverted* manner of "participation" in Soviet language and literature) than from any undivided opposition to it (which he certainly never declared, and accusations of which troubled him). In this sense he deserves to be thought of as socialist realism's incipient metapoet – though it was the resigned attempt more completely to assimilate himself to socialist realism's *actual* forms that was to govern the remainder of his career spent under its auspices.

# CHAPTER 5

# "Socialist Realist" Platonov
## (1934–1951)

My title is not meant to imply the full identity of its terms, but simply to address the theme of the works Platonov produced in the age of socialist realism's hegemony – which for him essentially meant everything written after "Vprok." With some minor exceptions ("Iuvenil'noe more" and "Musornyi veter," and his two plays of the mid 1930s) virtually everything Platonov completed from 1934–1951 was either published in or clearly intended for standard Soviet publication, for which the principles of socialist realism (however malleable from time to time, as Platonov himself shows) were obligatory. We know of no great, unconventional works in the manner of *Chevengur* and *Kotlovan* written for the "drawer" in this period, and the failure of any to surface during his by now virtually complete rehabilitation suggests none indeed exists.[1]

That a discontinuity divides the pre- and post-1934 oeuvre is thus beyond dispute. What we have is two Platonovs, much in the way that one can speak of two (pre- and socialist realist-) Pasternaks or Zabolotskiis, though in Platonov's case there is a distinct irony to the fact that because the later, more "conformist" Platonov most readily lent himself to rehabilitation in the Brezhnev period, many readers came to view him as the representative article. Nor is there any doubt that the changes in Platonov's poetic resulted primarily from external pressure and are attributable to the literary politics of the time. Though Platonov admitted to having committed "crude errors" in the past and publicly claimed to have reformed himself,[2] for example, he consistently avoided the kind of full-blown socialist realism of production plots and the historical struggles of the proletariat, even in his war stories. Instead he sought for himself a place at socialist realism's fringe, and testimony to this idiosyncratic posture can be found in the irate response his works continued to provoke in the orthodox critical establishment to the very end.[3] Still more directly, such items as the note attached to the manuscript of "Dzhan," in which Platonov declares to his editors his willingness to produce a different version of the tale's second half that would portray the *dzhan*'s attainment of "happiness," suggest his assimilation was far from voluntary or organic.[4]

Within this assumption of external pressure on Platonov, however, another view of the discontinuity is possible which may free us from the necessity of choosing one "Platonov" over the other, and which corresponds to what we have come to recognize as the complex workings of socialist realism. From this perspective the essence of Platonov's writing in the thirties and forties lies in an "art of adaptation" to socialist realism, which is neither an inward transcendence of his former artistic self nor alienated capitulation (nor, except in some instances, aesopian camouflaging).[5] Instead the later works are produced out of a process of mediation between, on the one hand, Platonov's world view and the poetics of its earlier expression, and on the other the socialist-realist aesthetic to which he now had to conform. The Platonov of this view determinedly maneuvers to preserve elements of the old (hence the continued uneasiness of his relation to officialdom and its canon) but at the same time works to transform himself into a not-entirely-cynical practitioner of the new. (This experience was, of course, not uncommon among Soviet writers who had survived the purges and strove to assimilate themselves to the realities of the Stalinist era.) In assuming this vantage point I retain the view that it is works like *Chevengur* and *Kotlovan* which establish Platonov's reputation as a major Soviet writer and to that extent culminate his "genuine" evolution. In considering the later works, however, it is important not just to identify the elements surviving from the wreckage of a former poetic, but to assess the meaningful ways in which that poetic itself evolved. It is the subtle infusion into a socialist-realist framework of his abiding themes, and the resulting dialogue with the Stalinist world view, which makes Platonov's post-1934 works such a peculiarly valuable contribution to Soviet culture.

## PLATONOV'S TRANSITION TO SOCIALIST REALISM

Platonov's "adaptation" to socialist realism did not come about at once, however, and in the years 1934–1936 he wrote a series of works whose mixed intentions and lingering penchant for the grotesque link them more closely to *Kotlovan* and "Vprok" than to anything that followed. In them attempts at positive heroes and optimistic plots of socialist construction co-mingle with satiric episodes, farce, and fragments of ontological and utopian themes from the earlier period – the multiplicity of premises reflecting the fitful nature of Platonov's efforts to adjust to the demands of the new era. In a sense these works continue the "dilemma of inclusion" informing their pre-decessors in the period of the first Five-Year Plan. Indeed, they contain a number of passages that fairly transparently agonize over the predicament of the politically dispossessed writer. None of these works was published (or staged) during Platonov's lifetime.[6]

At the center of "Iuvenil'noe more" ("The Sea of Youth"; 1934), for example, stands a conventional socialist-realist plot involving the efforts of an energetic *sovkhoz* worker named Nadezhda Bostoloeva to overcome bureaucratic inertia, supply shortages, and the obligatory practical difficulties on the farm, to ensure that her collective overfulfills its quota for meat production.[7] To this scheme Platonov adds glimpses of utopian technology, as though still negotiating his accommodation to socialist realism on the terms of his works of the 1920s: Vermo erects a windmill whose energy will be used to heat barns in the winter, while the aquifers of the title's "sea of youth" are tapped for irrigation by a device that uses electromagnetical rays to "vaporize" the layers of rock in which the water is "entombed." Underlying this semi-utopian vision, however, is a series of characteristically grotesque existential themes. Thus the emptiness of the steppe landscape in which the isolated *sovkhoz* is located is emphasized (it is a *pustynia*) and the terrain is said to be suffused with *ennui* (*skuka*). The tale also displays the familiar preoccupation with the more repulsive aspects of corporeality, as when rats run over Bostoloeva's body at night, or when one of the characters produces a sausage made from the penis of a bull killed by the local kulaks.[8] Still more subversive of the Bostoloeva plot are the tale's several hints at an underlying attitude of historical pessimism. Vermo "participates in the proletarian animation of life" and works toward the "joy that stands at the heights of our history," but he experiences persistent doubts and struggles with "his despair that life is dreary and people cannot conquer their pitiful madness in order to create the future time" (his name encapsulates this ambivalence – "*vera*" + "*der'mo*," that is, "faith" + "crap").[9] Umrishchev likewise believes that calamities arise from people behaving like adolescents and "interfering" in history, and makes his motto the phrase "*ne suisia*" – "don't get involved" (cf. the forest watchman in *Chevengur*).

The most complex of these transitional works is the play "Sharmanka" ("The Barrel Organ"; 1934), whose thematic center is correspondingly difficult to locate.[10] On the surface it is a double satire on the themes of capitalist envy of socialism and the bureaucratic tendencies of the Soviet state. A Danish food specialist named Stervetsen (*sterva* means "carrion" and is used as a term of vulgar abuse) and his daughter Serena visit the Soviet Union looking to "buy" the country's soul and take it back to a spiritually bankrupt Europe. They end up in a remote region at a supply cooperative headed by a typical "organizer-bureaucrat" named Shchoev, who issues commands to his subordinates through a megaphone and whose organization turns out to have long ago been liquidated to make way for natural gas exploration. Though they are ultimately ambiguous characters, the cultural workers Alesha and "Miud" (an acronym for "International Youth Day") who arrive from the capital to help further progress toward socialism figure as the *raisonneurs* situated between these two satiric fields.

What thematic center the play possesses would seem to lie in the theme of Stervetsen's desire to procure a "soul" for Europe,

which appends to the cliché about capitalist envy an element of
Platonov's earlier ontological mythology. Europe, says Stervetsen, is undergoing a crisis because its soul has exhausted itself,
while that of Soviet Russia is vibrant and somehow oddly
guaranteed by its Marxism (it is the "superstructure" of Soviet
society and is produced "like industry"; 42). In this the play
might appear to reconcile the ontological yearnings of the
earlier works with the claims of Stalinist culture. However, the
lines of meaning in the play are far from clear and the episodes
repeatedly engage in reversals of expected meaning and veer off
into the grotesque and the absurd (much of it difficult to stage:
one scene calls for a thousand birds to descend on the metal roof
of Shchoev's office, another for a robot who has hitherto been
walking around to be dismembered). Thus Stervetsen is a
decadent capitalist, but it is he who searches for soul amidst
episodes of grotesque physicality; the Soviet Union possesses
"soul," but that entity turns out to be nothing more than an
object that they "manufacture" like an industrial good. The
scene that epitomizes this ambivalence, in which the Soviet
system appears to satisfy existential needs but in fact does not,
is the "evening of the testing of new forms of food" organized
by the bureaucrat Shchoev. On the one hand, his project is a
utopian one that creates food out of meager resources at hand
(they have managed to make flour out of fish, soup out of
bones, kvas out of wild honey, acid from ants, pancakes from
weeds – all of the dishes served to the guests from a conveyer
belt used as a table). But the eating of such artificial food is
tantamount to ingesting the "base matter" of the world
("We'll put the whole of nature into food," Shchoev vows,
"we'll feed everyone with cheap eternal matter," 29), and
during the dance that follows the dinner all the guests vomit.

Ultimately what center this somewhat confused satire has
may lie in a self-reflective theme of authorial doubt, or more
specifically, of Platonov's anxieties over having produced works
denounced as kulak propaganda. This theme is embodied in
the figure of Alesha and his robot Kuz'ma, the "iron man"
whom he and Miud have brought with them for agitational
purposes. When he first appears, Kuz'ma spouts the "correct"
political slogans of the class war, and the fact that he is a

"mechanical man" may allude to Platonov's own ultra-loyal *Proletkul't* phase. Mid-way through the play, however, Kuz'ma breaks down and begins to utter only counter-revolutionary remarks or gutteral terms of abuse ("*khkhady*," "creeps"). Alesha's response is to regret that he has created an "opportunist," and, in a scene that in its writerly-suicidal overtones deserves to be placed alongside Maiakovskii's remark about "stepping on the throat" of his own song, he *disassembles* the robot and considers writing a document of self-criticism. When his companion Miud, the only upright character left at the end, leaves, she dismisses Alesha as a "foul capitulator" ("*gad-prismirenets*," 56). This moment of self-castigation is ambivalent, however, since it is not clear whether Platonov means his own capitulation to *kulak* ideology or to the Stalinist regime.

"Musornyi veter" ("Garbage Wind"; 1934)[11] marks the morbid extreme, in manner and theme if not chronologically, in this series of works written during Platonov's transition to a more "socialist realist" self (it has the distinction of having annoyed Gor'kii with the "irreality of its contents" which "border on gloomy madness"; *Gor'kii i sovetskie pisateli*, p. 315). In the story Al'bert Likhtenberg, an emotionally dispossessed citizen of Nazi Germany, is imprisoned for assaulting a monument to Hitler and is taken to be executed; he escapes miraculously, only to commit suicide by cutting the flesh off his own legs in order to feed a starving woman. Platonov dedicates this tale to a German worker imprisoned in one of Hitler's concentration camps, but myriad hints prompt a reading of the work as a denunciation of Stalinist Russia instead. In this light it constitutes both an early exemplar of Soviet aesopian writing and the darkest expression we have of Platonov's relation to his own society.[12]

Whether "Musornyi veter" intends to denounce fascism or Stalinism, its most important feature is its anticipation of the punishment awaiting anyone who raises his hand against absolute power – a lurid reworking of both "Usomnivshiisia Makar" and its Pushkinian subtext in which one readily discerns an autobiographical theme. Likhtenberg is a typically exhausted Platonovian hero who avoids involvement in corporeality (in particular by hoping to escape sex with his wife; in this he prefigures Nikita in "Reka Potudan'"). The totalitarian world he inhabits, however, is ruled by a repulsive, self-satisfied physicality, epitomized in its nauseating "garbage wind."[13] The face of the leader depicted on the monument has "greedy lips that love food and kisses" and "cheeks fattened by world-wide glory," while its inhabitants have been subjected to a perversion of Makar's cheery, quasi-materialist vision of labor "preserved" in the property of the state: at one point Likhtenberg stares into the idling motor of a truck and sees "thousands of people transformed into metal, heavily breath-[ing] in the motor and no longer demand[ing] socialism or truth, feeding on cheap gases alone" (116). The price for Likhtenberg's failed rebellion against *both* these orders – the ontological regime and the political one that mirrors and intensifies it – is, like that of Perri in "Epifanskie shliuzy," a brutal immersion in the "filth" of matter. Likhtenberg receives a savage beating in which his ears are cut off and his penis crushed, then is flung onto a garbage heap. There he literally ingests filth by eating the bits of discarded food that come his way (later in prison he catches a rat gnawing at his leg, and consumes it whole). When Likhtenberg's corpse is discovered at the end of the tale, he looks so horrendous that those who find him decide that they have found not a man but the corpse of a monkey someone dressed in human clothes.

The immediate suggestion is that Likhtenberg's bizarre torture is a display of Freudian castration anxiety, but other readings may be more plausible. Freudianism's assertion of the priority of the somatic in human life is in fact superseded in Platonov by a much broader sense of the corporeal, within which sex serves as but one, albeit vivid, metonymic point of reference among many. For him it is a sign of the abhorrent physicality of existence, whose prominence has as much to do with Fedorov as with Freud. Moreover, Likhtenberg is in the event quite complacent about his castration (he calls the penis a "monotonous, docile reactionary," 120), which anyway frees him from the fleshly activities forced on him nightly by his wife. Indeed, "Musornyi veter" seems to indulge a masochistic delight at the prospect of destroying the corporeal self (Likhtenberg's offer of his own flesh to the starving woman is important here as well). The tale's traumatic quality, however, may ultimately have more to do with Platonov's fears over the silencing of his literary voice. Once castrated, Likhtenberg wonders why his torturers did not tear out his *tongue* instead, since as the agent of thought it is the real "prostitute" among the human faculties (120).[14]

Platonov's turn toward a more conformist literary manner, together with his tentative "rehabilitation" in the eyes of the literary establishment, began with a series of works written in 1933–1934 and devoted to Central Asian themes.[15] Since up to this point his most aggressive opponents had belonged to RAPP, some form of leniency was to be expected following the April 1932 Central Committee decree which disbanded that organization and declared the formation of the Union of Soviet Writers (to which Platonov was admitted as a member; Geller, pp. 321–22). The real opportunity for "inclusion" in the new literary order, however, came in the form of an invitation to travel with a writer's "brigade" to Turkmenia in late 1933 and early 1934 to prepare a volume celebrating the tenth anniversary of the formation of Soviet Turkmenistan. The most eagerly "participatory" work to result from these travels was the sketch "Goriachaia arktika," which in the vein of Stalinist heroism asserts the similarities between the transformation of the desert and the conquering of Arctic wastes, then elaborates a series of projects for reclaiming the desert for cultivation. As Geller notes, the sketch is full of sovietisms of a kind Platonov had parodied only recently in *Kotlovan*, but it was, curiously, rejected for publication (pp. 323–24, though he does not say by whom the sketch was rejected, or for what reason).

Of the two works that were published, "Dzhan" (1933–1935) makes concessions to the socialist-realist aesthetic but manages within that framework to provide a culminating version of Platonov's earlier ontological myth.[16] The tale has as its premise a conventional Stalin-era rescue expedition, in which the hero Nazar Chagataev is dispatched from Moscow to find his native people, return them to their homeland, and in so doing bring them forth into Soviet society.[17] Its true focus, however, is the state of dream-like oblivion in which the *dzhan* languish, which is in essence a reprise, in self-consciously mythic guise, of the themes associated with the wandering vagabonds of *Chevengur*.

Like the *prochie*, the *dzhan* are a nation (or rather anti-nation) composed of orphans, fugitives, and other assorted dregs of humanity who have been displaced from settled existence into a futile, ceaseless wandering. The desert through which they roam turns out to be an ideal symbol for "the world" as it appears in Platonov's earlier works:[18] it is emptiness incarnate (*pustynia*) and the very "hell" of the world (29), and hence is variously depicted as a pit and a tomb (it is the place where the desert "drops its land down into a deep depression, as if preparing itself a grave," 14). Devoid of water – the symbol of life and of the organic throughout Platonov's works, and often the object of utopian desires, as in "Epifanskie shliuzy," "Iuvenil'noe more" – the desert further epitomizes the inorganic matter of which the world consists (and which it forces its inhabitants to ingest; several times the *dzhan* and Chagataev must eat sand in an attempt to quench their thirst). As a realm defined by scarcity, the desert also allows Platonov to show the *dzhan* subsisting on an excruciatingly meager diet (often nothing but dry desert grasses), which reduces them to the familiar condition of emaciated, "worn-down" victims of the world's opposition.

Under these conditions, which here assume a more absolute and allegorical form than in the earlier works, the *dzhan* succumb to that extreme of existential tragedy in Platonov's vision: an existence pushed so close to the brink of nonexistence that there remains no strength for any higher faculty (such as "consciousness") that might exert itself against the world.[19] The designation of this hapless tribe as the "*dzhan*," a term Platonov translates in a footnote as a Turkmen word for "a soul in search of happiness," is thus an ironic one, since in their case "soul" comes to mean something like "naked existence, without the mitigating presence of bodily reserves."

(Consider the comment that their "soul" is nothing but the "ability to feel and experience torment," 112; or the description of the desert as "wide-open and dreary, like a mournful, alien soul," 20.)

What distinctly marks this as a late text, however, is its attempt to fuse Fedorovian and Stalinist views. The *dzhan* exemplify Fedorov's *bespamiatstvo* by languishing in a double oblivion: they are a tribe forgotten by the rest of the world, and they have "forgotten" themselves in a state of somnambulance (in contrast to their rescuer Chagataev, who at the beginning of the story is said to have "awakened" – "*opomnilsia ot minuvshego dolgogo vremeni*," 7). In combination with Platonov's spatially literal vision of being's residence in the body, this theme then gives rise to a symbolic opposition between "dispersion" and "collection" or "preservation". As elsewhere in Platonov, deep anxieties are generated by the prospect of the self undergoing the traumatic dissolution of its defences against the outer world (under the onslaught of, for example, entropy or the elements), and the tragedies of oblivion and death are correspondingly attended in "Dzhan" by motifs of scattering. Chagataev first finds his people living among some reeds whence they had come ten years earlier and "scattered themselves" ("*narod ... rasseialsia*"), and his initial attempt to return them to staid existence ends with them wandering off in separate directions toward the horizon. With more distinctly ontological overtones, the ribs of a Red Army soldier Chagataev discovers among the ruins of a fort similarly "had spread out in different directions (*razoshlis' v raznye storony*), as if for breathing after death" (46). Conversely, life begins with (one could say for Platonov is defined by) an act of collecting or gathering. Like many other characters in Platonov's works, Chagataev periodically checks to see whether his body is "whole" (*tsel*, 14) and at one point feels sorry for his bones, which his mother "once gathered (*sobrala*) for him out of the poverty of her own flesh" (77).

In this context Chagataev's Party-sponsored rescue expedition becomes a redemptive gathering that in itself will retrieve the *dzhan* from death, a reprise on a higher ideological plane of the collecting of discarded and forgotten objects by Dvanov and Voshchev. Here it is explicitly "Soviet power" that "collects (*sobiraet*) all the outcasts and forgotten" (15), as Chagataev at one point reflects, and one of the first "civilizing" acts performed by his companion Aidym when the *dzhan* have been gathered in their ancestral homeland is to *sew together* for them clothing out of whatever scraps of cloth she can gather. As typical as this event is for Platonov, the influence of Stalinist culture on its representation here is undeniable. Platonov may well have been inspired by the fact that the Turkmen nation whose ten years of official existence he had been dispatched to help celebrate had been similarly formed out of fragments by the Soviet state. Platonov's spatialized sense of being's relation to the world thus merges in this tale with a characteristic Stalinist obsession with unity and the inviolability of borders (cf. the Soviet anthem, "*Soiuz nerushimyi*," "Inviolable union").[20]

"Dzhan" thus negotiates its accommodation to the demands of socialist realism in a hybrid of Stalinist heroism with Platonovian rescue from dispersion in the material world. It nonetheless dilutes any suggestions of Stalinist "progress" by suspending its plot in a series of mythic allusions that assert the trans-historical, essentially timeless and allegorical, nature of its events.[21] Nor, in the famous double version of the tale's ending, is the outcome of Chagataev's mission entirely clear. The truncated *Prostor* version is not necessarily the more optimistic (as Geller and others suggest), since its assertion that the *dzhan* will find "happiness" individually and "beyond the horizon" hardly signals the success of Chagataev's expedition. But the longer version retains some ambivalence, or at least open-endedness, as well: in it Chagataev succeeds in collecting the *dzhan* once again, but he quickly departs for Moscow with Aidym, leaving the question of their ultimate fate unsettled.

### PLATONOV'S "ADAPTATION" TO SOCIALIST REALISM

The important works of Platonov's "second" career adapt themselves to the socialist-realist aesthetic by exchanging the more *outré* components of the earlier works (their grotesquery, satire, and utopian plots) for a more conventional narrative manner based on psychologism, domesticity, and at times even a distinct sentimentality. The psychologism is primarily that of family or romantic relationships (less frequently, that of laborers in their work, for example, "V prekrasnom i iarostnom mire") and it is most important for the turn inward it signals, away from the world-historical stage of attempts to found communist utopias or fulfill the Five-Year Plan (though that domain persists at the edges of, and in a certain competition with, these works' narrative vision). In keeping with this inward turn Platonov's later stories also shift their events to a domestic milieu. The action now takes place in some apartment or home (only rarely, as in "Bessmertie," in an office), rather than on the site of a utopian project. The result of these changes in narrative manner is a certain "domestication," even diminuzation, of the Soviet world. In contrast to the earlier works, where Soviet institutions, officialdom, ideology, and so forth appear as the objects of satire, the same elements appear in the later works as "givens," as if they were a part of the "natural" landscape. This domestication is of a subtly ambivalent kind, however, since once the socialist milieu has been "naturalized" in this manner it becomes the setting for the characters' typically melancholy thoughts and humble (versus energetic, Stakhanovite) lives.

The concessions Platonov makes to the socialist-realist aesthetic do not, of course, represent a complete break with the concerns of the past and still less the inauguration of an entirely different poetic. They signal, rather, the transformation of those concerns into new forms, which merit attention, not only as the "post—" history of Platonov's evolution into the author of *Chevengur* and *Kotlovan*, but also as the embodiments of his response to the Stalinist world view.

The psychologism these later works elaborate seems on the surface to derive wholly from the conventions of Soviet fiction, with its ritual confrontations between individual desires and the priorities of socialist construction, collective labor, the Soviet *narod*, and so forth. But even at their most quotidian and conformist Platonov's later psychological themes are informed by a lingering, "eccentric" philosophism which has the characters seeking to define their existential position in the world (never a given in Platonov's works). In fact their assorted psychological dilemmas continue in conventional guise a tension that had defined many of the earlier works: that between the subjective experience of being (in which is grounded Platonov's ontological vision, and which for him represents the domain of "ultimate reality") and the prospect of world-historical solutions to its dilemmas (which in the end typically fail or are called into doubt).

To put it in terms more appropriate to the stories in question, Platonov may be said to "adapt" to the demands of socialist realism by undertaking, in the realm of his characters' psychology, a series of mediations between two competing sets of values.[22] The first may roughly be labelled "the distant" (or still better in the noun form permitted by Russian, *dal'*) and is associated with such phenomena as socialist construction (especially in far-off regions), the future, technology, the abstract organization of human life, and so on – that is, everything that had hitherto been associated in Platonov's works with utopian aspirations and that here is subsumed within the utopianism of the Stalinist state. The second value may correspondingly be labelled "the near" (Russian *bliz'*). It primarily involves intimate relations with individuals (rather than mankind as a whole), particularly as these entail or promise physical contact (be it filial or romantic/sexual embrace). The "near" offers the succor of shelter, warmth, and that immediacy of physical possession that in Platonov's earlier works serves as antidote to the ephemerity of spirit (and here to absence, loss, the abstractness of the remote). Because of its link to explicitly socialist values, however, the "distant" in these works is not available for ironization or discrediting, and Platonov repeatedly tries his hand at reconciling it with its (for him, at this stage) far more attractive antithesis. At its most successful this kind of mediation manages to fuse the priorities of the intimate with those of the utopian far-away in some "idyllic" rather than ironic manner – quite similar to the exuberant moments of "contact" with the socialist "far-away" in the later Pasternak, which have been described as an adaptation in a "semi-official" key to the post-symbolism of

the Soviet thirties (Zholkovskii, "Fro: Piat' prochtenii," p. 42).
Even at such moments, however, ambivalence remains more
characteristic of Platonov's works than tranquil reconciliation.

"Bessmertie" ("Immortality"; 1936)[23] is the most out-
wardly accommodationist of these later works, and for that
reason has been dismissed by many as a regrettable attempt to
contribute to the literary iconology of the "new Soviet man."
Even here, however, Platonov's hesitations show through, and
contemporary apologists for the work found it necessary to
explain its peculiarities in terms of the "complex" nature of
that Soviet man's development.[24]

In this story Platonov establishes the socialist-realist cre-
dentials of his hero, Emmanuil Levin, by patterning him after
the conventional Soviet notion of the "model administrator/
Party worker, selflessly devoted to the tasks of socialist
construction." The official in charge of a small railway station,
Levin involves himself personally in even the slightest details of
its workings and so absorbs himself in service to the
transportation system that he sleeps only briefly, and in his
clothes, lest something require his attention. This conventional
attribute is further underscored by allusion to the even loftier
model of Kaganovich, whose phonecall to Levin reveals him
also to be working late into the night, "not sparing himself."

More particularly, and already somewhat at variance with
the standard models for the positive Soviet hero, Levin
embodies an ideology of self-denying love for "others" who are
far away. At least on its surface this love represents a categorical
endorsement of the values Platonov associates with "distance."[25] Platonov attributes Levin's self-sacrifice to his ability
to "turn away from himself the hands of his wife or friends"
(123–24) in order to visit the station at night, and to feel more
for the goods loaded on the trains (and destined for those "far
off") than for the "loyalty of friends or love for a woman." For
Levin humanity takes priority over people because the
"pleasure of a single beloved" means nothing if it does not
"serve the cause of feeling and understanding those many
beings hidden behind that one person" (124). The central
symbol for this quality is Levin's knapsack (*kotomka*): the
emblem of an itinerant existence (that is, one devoted to

"distance"; cf. the vagabonds who wander off in search of utopia in Platonov's earlist poems and stories), it was sewn out of rags and so emblemizes the voluntary poverty of self-denial. Though it itself always remains empty, "it seemed that out of this sack, and out of the hands of the man who carried it, there always came good(s)" ("*vykhodilo dobro*," 117). Levin's efforts to wean his subordinates from their selfish concerns introduces them to the same principle of self-denial, which is further mirrored in the cook, Galina, who finds living "for herself" boring and now lives for others by looking after Levin and sharing his concern for the transportation system – though even this is not enough, because Levin tells her it is a waste to serve just one man.

This essay by Platonov into what might be called a "Soviet caritative ideal," however, is underlaid by hints that such an existence poses a threat to the intimacy, warmth, and physical contact – the values of the "near" – that for Platonov redeem man from his isolation in the world. Levin's self-sacrifice, for example, is attended by masochistic and even suicidal overtones (his gloominess was one of the favorite complaints of orthodox critics).[26] Thus his labors on behalf of a remote mankind turn out for him to be a means of "exhausting himself in labor and cares," and he turns out to undertake them so willingly because he considers himself a "temporary, transient being." Platonov's socialist hero moreover hungers for the kind of immediate, intimate contacts that cannot be provided in his lonely martyrdom to socialist society. His service condemns him to separation from his wife and daughter in Moscow, and thus to caressing *himself* in bed ("*Levin sam pogladil i polaskal rukami svoe telo*," 124). The sight of a female passenger, who steps down off the train as a concrete embodiment of the humanity Levin serves, similarly leads him to recall a former lover who "disappeared somewhere without fame, without a name" and who has never thought of him again because she "probably doesn't know how to feel that which is far away" (120).

The way Platonov attempts to mediate between Levin's opposing impulses is to suggest that an intimate warmth can somehow be infused into the apparatus of Stalinist institutions.

"Any system of work is just the play of an isolated mind if it is not warmed with the energy of the hearts of all the workers," Levin reflects, sitting in his office (118); and later, in thinking of how to handle his subordinates, he decides it is "necessary to warm the other man with one's breath, *hold him near* so he does not grow numb (*"chtoby...ne mertvel"*), so he feels that he is needed" (118; emphasis added). But this very formula hints at the lingering priorities of the "near," and the story in the end provides no antidote to Levin's somber isolation. Indeed, one of his main hopes regarding the far-off socialist future for which he sacrifices intimate contacts is that in it station-masters will be able to sleep nights, take vacations, and "live in a family with their wives and among their own children (*sredi rodnykh detei*, 120)."

"Fro" (1936) much more forcefully asserts the values of the "near" (which is to say that it more openly questions the values of Stalinist utopianism) than does its mirror image "Bessmertie," with which it appeared side by side in the same issue of *Literaturnyi kritik*. When Fro's husband Fedor leaves at the very beginning of the story "for far away and for a long time, almost irretrievably" to work on a construction project in Siberia (that is, he leaves for the "socialist far-off") Fro is plunged into intense longings for his return and becomes an avenger of intimate relations and all they connote in Platonov's world. As her name elliptically denotes, she is Aphrodite, a goddess of love so absorbed in the desire for her partner's return that she neglects the father with whom she lives and even herself, and dreams only of being loved in return.[27] "Fro" thus makes particularly clear the connection between the psychologism of the later stories and Platonov's earlier ontological themes. In an echo of the utopian works' many efforts to reify the non-material and so counter its ephemerity, Fro aggressively preserves every surrogate form of physical contact with Fedor that she can find. Immediately after his departure, for example, she touches the iron of a mailbox with her finger to reassure herself that it is solid and that "no one's soul *contained in a letter* will be lost from here" (emphasis added; cf. the similar scene in "Sokrovennyi chelovek").[28] Later she jealously scrutinizes

an express train she sees that, because it would have passed
Fedor's train on its way west, was "next to her husband after
she was" (much as Kopenkin in *Chevengur* envies the clouds he
sees passing overhead, which are on their way to Germany and
so to "contact" with Rosa Luxemburg). Alone in their bed
she seizes on a hair of Fedor's she discovers between the pillows,
then greedily smells the pillowcase "which had not been
washed since the last time her husband's head had raised itself
from it" (141; Serbinov similarly steals Sonia's sheets in
*Chevengur*). Where Levin had been forced to caress himself at
night, Fro sighs, "Ah, Fro, Fro, if only someone would embrace
you" (141).

The set of values opposed to Fro's thirst for intimacy is
represented in this study by Fedor, who departs at the opening
to help build socialism in Siberia and dreams of ranging even
farther afield, "maybe even to China," in pursuit of that aim.
Where Fro responds instinctively to nature (to which she
appeals for Fedor's return, and whose sun penetrates her
apartment to light her body), Fedor's more utopian domain is
that of technology and machines. He has the ability "to sense
the voltage of an electrical current as if it were some personal
passion" (138), is constantly coming up with inventions, and
mentally resides not on earth or in nature, like Fro, but "a
hundred kilometers up in the stratosphere" where there are
atmospheric conditions "capable of guaranteeing man eternal
life" (146). Fro temporarily accommodates herself to this
opposing ideal when, at Fedor's urging, she begins to take
technical courses. She attends the lectures, however, not out of
any devotion to socialist society and its future, but because she
lives by imitating her husband in all things. She stops attending
once Fedor is gone, and even while there "her" semantics
ironically keep intruding upon the text: the courses are on
"*sviazi* i signalizatsiia" ("communications," or more literally
"*ties* and signalization"), and in them she learns about such
things as "uitstonovskie *mostiki*" ("wheatstone *bridges*") and
"zheleznye *serdechniki*" ("*iron cable cores*," literally "(*little*)
*hearts*") (138–39).

Rather than a conversion tale, then, Fro's story is one of

failed attempts to reassert the priority of the "near" over the "far." When the subterfuge of a telegram falsely reporting her to be near death succeeds in luring Fedor back, Fro seems to have secured the immediate "possession" her ardent soul desires. Shutting themselves off from the world, the couple embrace because, in explicit competition with utopian values, "they wanted to be happy immediately, right now, before their future diligent labor had yielded its results for personal and universal happiness" (146; essentially an ironic reprise of the reification theme in *Chevengur*). But in this world of Platonov's later works, Fro's desires cannot be reconciled with, and in the end must cede priority to, those of Fedor. Fro promises to work hard so that everyone in the country will someday live better; but she repeatedly procrastinates getting out of their bed and taking up her new life, until Fedor one day leaves ("for China, to make communism or something," as her father reports to her, 148).

Fro thus becomes a double figure of loss, at once, as her name metathetically suggests, an Orpheus whose efforts to retrieve a lost loved one are undone by the intemperance of her own desires, and a Euridice abandoned to the pit and to a life among the shades (at the station Fro works in a pit shovelling slag, and the claim of her telegram is that she is near death).[29] Nor is she alone in this experience: she herself neglects her father, one of her friends has lost a husband to prison, the little boy whose harmonica playing soothes her is "orphaned" while his parents work – the whole of it adding up, as Zholkovskii puts it, to an atmosphere of "estrangement, emptiness, gaps, the absence of a single center in which might come together [these heroes] oriented toward their separate 'far-offs'" ("Fro: Piat' prochtenii," p. 26). Though the ending of the story ostensibly shows Fro overcoming her narrowly egoistic desires, and so appears to elevate the value of the "distant" over that of the "near," it sustains an emphasis on intimate contact that renders the accommodation highly ambivalent. (Hence the story's dual readings as either the reform of an individualist or the critical review of utopia from an individual's point of view.)[30] In Fedor's absence Fro has been comforted from time to time by the sound of a boy from the apartment upstairs playing the harmonica. When Fedor leaves the second time she calls the boy in to her because, we are told, she has decided that this "person" (*chelovek*) is that very "humanity (*chelovechestvo*) about which Fedor spoke tender words to her" (148). Fro thus appears to shed her preoccupations with a romantic object in favor of maternal relations with a child, whom she embraces instead of the absent Fedor and as a surrogate for the whole of mankind. But surrogate relationships have been portrayed in a largely negative light throughout this story – Fro rejects the erotic advances of a dispatcher she dances with at the workers' club "because she loved someone far-off" (136), while her father is emphatically named "Nefed" (that is, "Ne-Fedor") – and anyway her embrace of the child covertly perpetuates her desire for Fedor. It has erotic overtones, since the boy assumes Fedor's place and Fro is in her nightgown, and the very gesture appearing to signal Fro's transcendence of her narrow desire is subtly prompted by the fact that the "humanity" she embraces in the child is that "about which Fedor spoke tender words to her." The rewards of the "near" are to be relinquished, in other words, only if the "distant" promises to return them in some other form.

"Reka Potudan'" ("The Potudan' River"; 1937)[31] engages in mediation of a different sort from that in "Fro." In it an identification of the "near" with the physical act of sex (rather than with shelter or warmth) occasions a revived awareness on Platonov's part of the attractions of a life devoted to ascetic, utopian "distance," and thus reveals some of the complexities of Platonov's thought even in this most conformist period. (Hence, perhaps, the retrospective cast of the story, which is set in the early 1920s and resembles some passages of *Chevengur*.) The story's central theme might be stated as "the difficult overcoming of alienation from one's own physical existence."[32] Nikita Firsov is a demobilized soldier who returns from the Civil War to his native town, where he begins to court a young medical student named Liuba (that is, "love"). He at first must temper his desires and worries that Liuba will not have him, a poor demobilized soldier. Having nonetheless decided to marry in the spring, they walk the frozen river Potudan' whose waters beneath the ice mirror their own postponed marital bliss. When the moment comes, however, Nikita proves unable to consummate the marriage. Liuba is tolerant, but Nikita, a kind of prodigal spouse, flees to a self-imposed exile in a different town, where he subsists by clearing garbage from the local marketplace. He is retrieved by his father, who informs him that in her grief Liuba had attempted to drown herself in the Potudan'. Nikita returns and, more hesitantly than triumphantly, at last consummates the marriage.

Contained within this tale of the psychology of love (or rather impotence) is the conflict between two principles closely linked to Platonov's ontological vision. The first is the imperative, dictated by a utopian reaction against the nature of present existence, that one reject corporeal life (the "givenness" of the world, in Paramonov's phrase). The ethical corollary of this imperative, and an important motivation for Nikita, is that one must not inflict an involvement in corporeality on others. The second principle, more typical of the mediating quality of Platonov's later works and only tentatively (or reluctantly) introduced into the text, states that one cannot flee one's own corporeality and that it is necessary in the end to reconcile oneself to such things as desire and physical love – in short, to a place in an unreconstructed world.[33] "Reka Potudan'" thus takes its place in Platonov's oeuvre as a revision of the schematic opposition of sex and procreation to utopian "consciousness" that had been typical of his earlier works; and to that extent the story represents a weakening of his otherwise antagonistic posture toward existence.[34]

The argument against involvement in the corporeal runs throughout "Reka Potudan'." As often in Platonov, there is little food (the characters inhabit a time when "hunger and need had excessively tormented the human heart"), Nikita contracts typhus, Liuba's family has died during the war and her friend Zhenia dies of typhus shortly after Nikita's return. The story's entire opening section, in fact, ambivalently mixes its ostensible theme of "new post-revolutionary beginnings" with motifs of alienation and despair. The returning soldiers

have felt within themselves the "great world-wide hope" of the
Revolution, and make their way home as if to live for the first
time." But they return in *late* summer (Nikita at one point lies
down in "September grass" that has "already grown tired of
growing here since spring"), and are said to "barely remember
themselves" ("*smutno pomnia sebia*," 178; cf. the theme of
"forgetting oneself" in "Dzhan"), while Nikita looks on his
native region "as though he were from some other place." The
story's somewhat anachronistic turn toward the theme of post-
civil-war ruin – quite out of step with the enthusiasm of the
Stalinist 1930s – would in fact seem to be motivated by the
renewed sense that theme facilitates of the material world's
hostility toward man.

Nikita initially manifests the traits of a "utopian" psychology
that refuses to partake in such a world. Timid and passive, the
antithesis of a lustful male, his premarital relations with Liuba
are those of an asexual "caring" in which he visits her daily to
"help her live," displaying concern for her physical welfare and
stoking the stove so she has light (not heat!) by which to
study.[35] Nikita's relationship with Liuba, however, must
compete with that with his father, which represents the
Fedorovian valuation of ties with "fathers" over those with
wives. Nikita's father, who in his own day failed to marry
Liuba's mother, is "orphaned" by his son's absence and when
Nikita returns he weeps on his chest "as though he had come
to his rest." When Nikita obtains some rolls he does not give
them to his father but saves them for Liuba, and when the
father visits the ailing Nikita he brings presents only for him.

Nikita's crisis of impotence is precipitated by this very
rejection of the corporeal "given" of his existence. The sexual
act expected of him has been foreshadowed in a surreal dream
of corporeal excess he has on the road home, in which a "small
fat animal" suffocates him with its "hot fur," trying to claw
with its "clutching paws" into the very center of his soul (cf.
the description of Likhtenberg's wife in "Musornyi veter" as
"furry" and animal-like).[36] In the event itself he undresses, as
if ashamed of his body, behind the wardrobe, while Liuba
unabashedly disrobes in the center of the room.[37] Platonov

presents Nikita's inability to perform the act, however, less as an erotic failure, the absence of desire, than as the assertion of an ethical principle demanding the rejection of corporeality. Nikita "timidly" embraces Liuba, "afraid of harming something in her special body" (194); he is "unable to torment Liuba for the sake of his own happiness" (195), and so fails to perform the act. Liuba's tolerant response further underscores the nature of Nikita's failure: she thinks he is unable to have sex with her because he loves her too much, and decides that if he were to love her less then "he could be strong." As Krasnoshchekova points out, it is "weakness" which in Platonov's physiologico-ethical world figures as the higher value, a sign of spiritual wealth, whereas "strength" arises out of the ascendancy of reason over feelings and signals the impoverishment of the characters' emotional world – though it is "strength" that renders them capable of mundane survival, and "weakness" can lead to their ruin.[38]

The exile Nikita imposes on himself by fleeing to the Kantemirovka bazaar on the one hand continues his flight from involvement in the corporeal. He goes there to "forget himself" and takes up an existence essentially the same as that of the *prochie* or the *dzhan*, allowing the bustle of the market to "distract him from memory of himself and from his own interests." By fall he only seems to "live" on earth, while in reality he merely "exists in oblivion (*bespamiatstve*), in poverty of mind, in lack of feeling" (202). Nikita's apparent muteness is particularly interesting in this regard, since it implicitly links the loss of one's voice with castration and thus recalls the anxieties over the writer's fate evident in works of the early 1930s (especially "Musornyi veter," where the connection is made explicit). But Nikita's flight is also, paradoxically, a rite of passage and expiation that leads to reconciliation with his own existence and the physical demands of his marriage[39] (hence, perhaps, the importance as a prelude to his return to corporeal life of his immersion in the "filth of the world" at the bazaar, where he subsists by removing garbage and cleaning latrines). The opposing tendencies of "Reka Potudan'" are reconciled in the final scene, which like that of "Fro" sustains a measure of ambivalence. Upon his return, Nikita finally relinquishes his posture of detachment from the world by attempting to embrace Liuba. But he feels "shame" and asks her whether "it hurts," and only when she reassures him that she "feels nothing" does he manage to perform his conjugal duties. He does so, however, only because he discovers in himself the "cruel, pitiful strength" necessary for the act, and he feels nothing exceptional beyond the fact that his heart now "shares its blood with [his] poor, but necessary pleasure" (204). Moreover, the story's post-nuptial coda points not to any new-found delight in physicality, but to the persistence of the material world's hostility toward man: Liuba asks Nikita to stoke the stove because she feels cold, her "thin body" having "been chilled in the cool twilight of the/a late time" (204). In this late, accommodationist text, then, Platonov concedes the necessity of corporeal involvement and relinquishes the principle of a life founded on its rejection; but he refuses to endorse such involvement as a moral good. And though it would be stretching things to read "Reka Potudan'" as a transparent political allegory, the parallelism between the ontological and the political regimes established throughout the earlier works suggests that Nikita's reluctant acceptance of existence-as-is reflects Platonov's own struggle to find a place for himself in a Stalinist world.[40]

# Conclusion

If domesticated plots, psychologism, and the suspension of irony toward the Soviet world are the means by which Platonov acquiesces to the demands of socialist realism, what becomes in these works of 1934–1951 of his literary style, in which, I have argued, is invested so much of his identity as a writer?[1] The short answer to this question is that verbal effects produced through the deformation of Soviet ideological clichés are the most evident sacrifice of Platonov's later period. From the mid 1930s on, Soviet rhetoric is no longer subjected in his works to the kind of awkward literalizations typical of *Chevengur* and *Kotlovan*. Indeed, as a distinct genre of speech "Soviet-speak" virtually disappears from the texts altogether, which is to say that the later texts no longer orient themselves overtly toward a language of "utopia."[2] Phrases whose awkwardness would earlier have signalled some important underlying theme thus appear embedded in the later texts in a normalizing context of psychological or other "realist" motivation.[3]

Yet semantically productive violations of standard literary Russian persist into Platonov's later prose, where they support a familiar orientation toward existential themes. The later texts preserve the atmosphere, if not of egregious deformation, then at least of unlettered, "primitive" speech, often through a kind of empathetic infection with the speech habits of the characters themselves.[4] An example of how this more subdued style manages to introduce the kind of "philosophical" orientation that had figured so importantly in the earlier works can be found in "Liubov' k dal'nemu," whose decidedly awkward opening phrase casts the entire tale in a quasi-allegorical mode:

"*V Moskve, na sed'mom etazhe, zhil tridtsatiletnii chelovek Viktor Vasil'evich Bozhko*" ("In Moscow on the seventh floor there lived a thirty-year-old human being named Viktor Vasil'evich Bozhko"). In this locution, whose semantic effects precipitate out of an "illiterate" failure to mention the building in which the hero lives, it is as though Moscow were conceived of as a single building (an echo, perhaps, of the Proletarian Home in *Kotlovan*), and the hero were not an individual Bozhko but "humankind" itself ("*chelovek*").

This creation of unexpected meanings through subtle manipulations of syntax rather than through egregious deformation is in fact typical of the later works. It attains its perfection in passages that restore to the simplest existential Russian verbs (*byt'* and its contextual cognates) their full, active meanings.[5] In the opening passage of "Glinianyi dom v uezdnom sadu" ("Clay House in a Provincial Yard"), for example, a sequence of ostensible copulars is transformed through a series of barely discernible syntactic misplacements into a drama of being:

В уездном саду *была* деревянная кузница. Вокруг нее *росли* лопухи и крапива, далее *стояли* яблоневые и вишневые деревья, а между ними *произрастали* кусты крыжовника и черной смородины, и выше всех *был* клен, большое и грустное дерево, давно *живущее* над местным бурьяном и всеми растениями окрестных дворов и садов. (116; emphasis added)
[In a provincial yard there was a wooden smithy. Around it were growing burdocks and nettles, farther on were standing apple and cherry trees, and between them were growing up bushes of gooseberry and blackberry. Taller than the rest was a maple, a large and somber tree that had been living for a long time above the local weeds and all the plants of the surrounding yards and gardens.]

Ordinarily the verbs *byla*, *rosla*, *stoiala* would have the semantically "empty" function of asserting, "there is/was." But like so many of the earlier works, this text refuses to take the notion of existence for granted. Instead of simply noting the presence of the various plants it draws attention to their existence as an active process and even a struggle. Thus the first sentence asserts "*byla ... kuznitsa*" in place of the expected, semantically empty "*stoiala*," and the result is something roughly equivalent to the English "In the yard a smithy *was*" as opposed to "In the yard there was a smithy." The chain of predicates *byla – rosli – proizrastali – vysshe vsekh byl* ("there was" – "there were growing" – "there were growing up" – "higher than all there stood" then projects an active process of emergence and ascent.[6] A "primitive" manner of speech revealing within itself the semantics of existence: this preserves the essence of Platonov's earlier style, minus only its potential for ideological parody. In this regard if the style of Platonov's later works resembles anything, it is not the modernist grotesque of his masterpieces of the late 1920s to 1930s but the post-modernist manner of the paintings of Komar and Melamid or Dmitrii Prigov's verse, in which irony similarly protrudes from beneath a posture of feigned naivety and an ostensibly accepting, domesticated depiction of the Soviet world.

That an ambivalence of this sort should survive into Platonov's later prose, however, is characteristic of the place he occupies within Soviet culture in general. In a curious and perhaps unique way Platonov was all along both insider and outsider to the Soviet world, and he was himself aware of this duality from an early stage. He was an insider not only because of his working class origins and early support for the Bolshevik cause, but also because he shared with the state its ultimate desire for a total remaking of human existence. In intellectual terms Platonov belongs to the extraordinarily fertile pro-liferation of utopian philosophies in Russian culture of the early twentieth century, and his writings respond to that movement at a level of specificity unexpected in someone raised at such a remove from the centers of Russian culture.[7] Platonov moreover belonged to a generation that had seen the politics, social organization, economy, and cultural forms of an old world destroyed, and the creation of a new world attempted, in a very short period of time. The expectations raised by these drastic changes were large: to someone like Platonov, with one foot in the village, even the introduction of electrical lighting into impoverished huts could appear a utopian event. Platonov's involvement in these revolutionary transformations was direct. Among writers he was one of the very few who actively participated, however briefly, in the reshaping of Russian physical reality; and it was this poverty-born hope for an utter transformation of existence, together with his tolerance of the notion that the Soviet state might somehow, someday, achieve such ends, which caused him to *hesitate* between utopia and anti-utopia even in his period of dissatisfaction.

If the hopes raised by events of the revolutionary period were large, for someone like Platonov who sincerely believed in them their subsequent deflation was correspondingly great. Platonov found intolerable the bureaucratism and coercion that attended Stalinist efforts to "construct socialism," and suffered considerably as a writer and a citizen in those darkest years of Soviet history. But the root cause of his disaffection resides on a deeper and more important level that makes itself felt even in his most enthusiastic, early phase. Platonov's relation to "official" Soviet culture was so troubled precisely because he shared some of the fundamental tenets of its materialist world view. For Platonov, however, this assent derived from an extremely pessimistic sense of man's place in the world (and the expression of this existential despair occupied him in text after text). It was for this reason that he found himself unable to endorse the blithe optimism associated with Stalinist utopianism and in the end failed to discern any possibility for altering existence – while seeing every reason to do so. The logic behind this contradiction has to do, not just with some lingering general notion of man's spiritual nature, but more specifically with a quintessentially Russian desire to see spirit at last find a home in some redeemed form of matter. In this broadest sense the vision of existence elaborated in *Chevengur* and *Kotlovan* might be thought of as an attempt to work out the contradictions between traditional Russian religious sensibilities and the Marxian materialism of the post-revolutionary age.

The same combination of exclusion and belonging also characterizes the stunning achievement of Platonov's literary style. Because his works put "Soviet-speak" on display in a manner so evidently intended to subject its underlying intentions to irony, their exclusion from the conformist culture of the 1930s was a foregone conclusion. Yet so many "Soviet" things come together in Platonov's prose – the speech of workers and peasants, the language of engineering and science, the Russian utopian philosophical tradition and its characteristic expressions, the phraseology of Marxist–Leninist theory, *agitprop* slogans – that one would be justified in calling it the most quintessentially Soviet prose of the century. In this regard it is virtually unprecedented; even the canonical works of socialist realism adopt a manner more traditional, less preoccupied with reflecting the speech situation of their day, than that found in Platonov.

Perhaps Platonov's greatest achievement, however, is that in formulating his peculiar linguistic parody he revealed how much of the Soviet mindset was itself predicated on linguistic phenomena, and indeed belonged to a broader effort in Russian culture to resolve epistemological dualism in the domain of language. The intersection of so many concerns in Platonov's writings – ideology, philosophy, social commentary, Soviet rhetoric, socialist construction, the historical experience of Russia's unlettered *narod* – is sure to guarantee a plurality of critical approaches to him for some time to come, especially as the Soviets continue to reassess their cultural past. But the analysis of verbal style is likely to remain central to Platonov studies. Indeed, as I have attempted to show, it is in his attitude toward, and his uses of, language that the multifarious issues in Platonov's thought come together. At the same time this study has managed to suggest only some of the ways in which language is important to his works. Brodsky may be correct in stating that on the heights of Modernism "there is no hierarchy," but down below in the world of scholarship one anticipates the day when, along with a more richly informed biography, full archival access, and a complete collected works, the study of Platonov's prose will attain the kind of prolificacy characterizing that of Joyce, Musil, or Kafka.

# Notes

## INTRODUCTION THE PROBLEM OF READING PLATONOV

1 V. V. Gol'tsev, in "'... Ia derzhalsia i rabotal'. Stranitsa biografii Andreia Platonova," *Pamir* 6 (1989): 105.

2 M. O. Chudakova, *Poetika Mikhaila Zoshchenko* (M: Nauka, 1979), p. 117.

3 Anthony Olcott, "Andrej Platonov. The Citizen-Artist," (Diss., Stanford University, 1976), p. 27. Platonov appears to have changed his name from Klimentov sometime in the early twenties, for reasons that remain unclear but probably had to do with the fact that his father's first name was Platon (he may have been inspired by Fedorov's notion of the importance of the "fathers" of the human race; in the thirties he also used the pseudonym "Firsov," derived from his father's patronymic, Firsovich). For a discussion of Platonov's name change, see Joe Willwerth Shepard, "The Origin of a Master: the Early prose of Andrej Platonov," (Diss., Indiana University, 1973), p. 74n; for a list of the various pseudonyms Platonov used in the course of his career, see Olcott, p. 355. Curiously, though Platonov was technically of working-class origin, in a questionnaire he filled out in 1924 he lists himself as a "*meshchanin*"; see E. Inozemtseva, "Platonov v Voronezhe," *Pod"em* 2 (1971): 98.

4 Andrei Platonov, *Golubaia glubina. Kniga stikhov* (Krasnodar: Burevestnik, 1922), pp. v–vi.

5 G. Antiukhin, "Put' v literaturu," in his *Filologicheskie ocherki* (V, 1966), p. 17; cited in Thomas Langerak, "Andrei Platonov v Voronezhe," *Russian Literature* 23–4 (1988): 440. Mention of Platonov's invention is made in M. Iu., Preface to *Golubaia glubina*, p. ix.

6 Platonov's relations with the Bolshevik Party remain one of the unsolved riddles of his early biography. In a letter to Voronskii he claims to have been a member of the Party from 1920–1921 ("until

the end of that year, after the purge had already taken place," he remarks), but left "on my own for a juvenile and unforgiveable reason" ("*po mal'chishestvu i neprostitel'noi prichine*"), and was readmitted as a candidate member only in the spring of 1924; Inozemtseva, "Platonov v Voronezhe," p. 100. Shepard suggests Platonov may have left out of solidarity with Smithy members such as Kirillov and Gerasimov, who were angered by what they felt to be NEP's corruption of communist ideals; Joe Willwerth Shepard, "The Origin of a Master: The Early Prose of Andrej Platonov," (Diss., Indiana University, 1973), p. 59. A more intriguing reason is reported, however, by the Polish scholars Wiktoria and René Śliwowscy (who claim to have their information from Platonov's brother): Platonov was incensed that during obligatory *subbotniki* he was forced to clean up other people's garbage. Wiktoria and René Śliwowscy, *Andrzej Płatonow* (Warszawa: Czytelnik, 1983), pp. 29–30. See also Oleg Lasunskii, "'V drugikh partiiakh ne sostoial.' Novoe ob Andree Platonove," *Literaturnaia gazeta* No. 23 (6 June 1990): 6.

7  See the 1942 autobiographical sketch in N. Kornienko and E. Shubina, eds., "O zhivykh i mertvykh," *Literaturnoe obozrenie* 9 (1989): 34. See also the questionnaire Platonov filled out in 1923 (Inozemtseva, 97) and his 1946 autobiographical sketch (in F. Levin, "Andrei Platonov," preface to A. Platonov, *Izbrannye rasskazy* [M: Sovetskii pisatel', 1958], p. 6).

8  V. A. Chalmaev, *Andrei Platonov. Ocherki zhizni i tvorchestva.* (V: Tsentral'no-Chernozemnoe knizhnoe izd., 1984), p. 32.

9  In an employment questionnaire he filled out in 1924, he claimed to have been a land reclamation engineer (*meliorator*) since 1921 and an electrical technician since 1917; Inozemtseva, 98.

10 Platonov served first as chairman of the region's hydrophication committee, then director of its land reclamation bureau, head of the section concerned specifically with agricultural land reclamation, head of the efforts to electrify local agriculture, and, in 1923, chair of a committee assigned the task of building a hydroelectric station on the Don river; Inozemtseva, 100. Shklovskii gives the following account of his meeting with Platonov in the field: "Comrade Platonov is a land reclamation engineer. He's a worker, about twenty-six years old... Platonov is very busy... The desert is encroaching. Water seeps away to beneath the earth and there flows in huge subterranean rivers... Platonov spoke also of literature, of Rozanov, and about the fact that it's impossible to describe sunsets and that one ought not to write stories (*nel'zia pisat' rasskazov*)." Viktor Shklovskii, *Tret'ia fabrika* (M: Artel' pisatelei "Krug," 1926), pp. 126, 129.

11 M. Platonova, "'…Zhivia glavnoi zhizn'iu' (A. Platonov v pis'makh k zhene, dokumentakh i ocherkakh)," *Volga* 9 (1975): 163; reprinted in Andrei Platonov, *Gosudarstvennyi zhitel'* (M: Sovetskii pisatel', 1988), pp. 551–58.

12 The best source on this period in Platonov's career is Thomas Langerak, "Andrei Platonov vo vtoroi polovine dvadtsatykh godov (opyt tvorcheskoi biografii). Chast' pervaia," *Russian Literature* 21 (1987): 157–82.

13 Langerak points out that at the 15–22 February 1926 Moscow meeting of the First All-Russian Meeting on Land Reclamation (*Pervoe Vserossiiskoe Meliorativnoe soveshchanie*) Platonov was elected to the *Vserabotzemles* organization. On 15 May he was relieved of his post in Voronezh to take up this new position, probably starting work in Moscow in early June, only to leave it shortly thereafter. By autumn of that year, however, he was working for Narkomzem. Langerak dismisses the opinion of Platonov's widow (Platonova, 176) that agents of the "Industrial Party" (*Prompartiia*) had maneuvered to remove Platonov and thus sabotage land reclamation work in the Voronezh region, citing the fact that Platonov left his Voronezh position voluntarily; "Andrei Platonov vo vtoroi polovine," 160–1.

14 See V. Verin's comments in "Videt' zvuki, slyshat' zvezdy," *Tekhnika – molodezhi* 5 (1987): 52.

15 Platonov himself remarked that during 1926–1927 his "faith was shaken" ("*ia zakolebalsia*"); see "'…Ia derzhalsia i rabotal'," *Pamir* 6 (1989): 105. L. Shubin comments that during the revolutionary period Platonov was in the grip of utopian fantasies concerning the immediate transformation of the world by means of "consciousness" which did not match up to the complex nature of reality, and that reality later "contributed its own correction" of those ideas; "Andrei Platonov," *Voprosy literatury*, 6 (1967): 44. See also Elena Tolstaia-Segal, "Naturfilosofskie temy v tvorchestve Andreia Platonova 20-x–30-x gg.," *Slavica Hierosolymitana* 4 (1979): 223; Mikhail Geller, *Andrei Platonov v poiskakh schast'ia* (Paris: YMCA Press, 1982), ch. 2, "Somnenie," pp. 63–172; Vladimir Vasil'ev, *Andrei Platonov. Ocherk zhizni i tvorchestva* (M; Sovremennik, 1982), "Platonov protiv Platonova," pp. 45–71.

16 These four months are one of the few periods in Platonov's life for which there exists (or has been published) documentary material providing insight into his personal experiences and attitudes. See the letters written to his wife in Moscow; Platonova, 164–7.

17 From *Iz istorii sovetskoi literatury 1920–1930-kh godov. Literaturnoe nasledstvo*, t.93 (M, 1983), pp. 609–10; quoted in Langerak,

"Andrei Platonov vo vtoroi polovine," pp. 160–61. At one point Platonov's Tambov correspondence suggests that writing had become something of a surrogate for the wife he sorely missed. "So long as I have in me a heart, brain, and this dark will to create, my 'muse' will not betray me. She and I are truly one. *She is the sex in my soul (Ona – eto moi pol v dushe)*" (Platonova, 165; emphasis added).

18 See Langerak's publication of "Antiseksus" in *Russian Literature* 9 (1981): 281–96.

19 Chief among these was Georgii Litvin-Molotov, who in 1925 had joined the executive committee of Gosizdat, and in 1927 was made director of *Molodaia gvardiia* publishers, which that year issued Platonov's first collection of stories, *Epifanskie shliuzy*, and the following year brought out *Sokrovennyi chelovek* (containing the eponymous story and "Iamskaia sloboda"). Litvin-Molotov had sponsored Platonov's early career as a journalist, and as the head of the *Burevestnik* publishing house in Zadonsk in 1921 had issued Platonov's collection of verse, *Golubaia glubina*. Andrei Novikov, M. Trishin, and V. I. Narbut are the other Voronezh connections who helped Platonov; Langerak, "Andrei Platonov vo vtoroi polovine," pp. 167–70.

20 See, for example, *Gor'kii i sovetskie pisateli. Neizdannaia perepiska. Literaturnoe nasledstvo*, t.70 (M: Izd. Akademii Nauk SSSR, 1963), p. 103; see also Langerak, "Andrei Platonov vo vtoroi polovine," p. 177, n. 34. Pil'niak also speaks positively of Platonov as a Soviet writer who, together with Olesha and P. Pavlenko, does not belong to any literary "system"; "O teorii sotsial'nogo zakaza," *Pechat' i revoliutsiia* 1 (1929): 71.

21 Gor'kii's remark is quoted in L. Anninskii, "Otkrovenie i sokrovenie," *Literaturnoe obozrenie* 9 (1989): 8. On their mutual influence see especially Elena Tolstaia-Segal, "'Stikhiinye sily': Platonov i Pil'niak (1928–1929)," *Slavica Hierosolymitana* 3 (1978): 89–109. Tolstaia-Segal points out the similarities between Pil'niak's *Krasnoe derevo* (1929; reworked as *Volga vpadaet v Kaspiiskoe more*, 1930) and the co-authored "Che-Che-O." She also suggests that the whole of *Krasnoe derevo* may be about Platonov, and in her reading *Kotlovan* then becomes Platonov's response to *Volga vpadaet*.

22 *Novyi mir* 12, 1928: 249–58.

23 Though see the synopsis published in the journal *Rabis* 46 (31 Nov. 1928): 7 (reproduced in Langerak, "Andrei Platonov vo vtoroi polovine," p. 170), which suggests the work's similarities to both *Chevengur* and *Kotlovan*.

24 Langerak points out that overtly negative responses to Platonov

appear only after the publication of "Che-Che-O," and that these were almost certainly tied to the recent hegemony of RAPP and its attacks on Pil'niak; "Andrei Platonov vo vtoroi polovine," pp. 169–72; also Tolstaia-Segal, "'Stikhiinye sily'," p. 96.

25 On "Vprok" see A. Fadeev, "Ob odnoi kulatskoi khronike," *Krasnaia nov'* 5–6 (1931): 206–9; on "Makar" see L. Averbakh, "O tselostnykh masshtabakh i chastnykh Makarakh," *Na literaturnom postu* 21–22 (1929): 10–17 and A. Selivanovskii, "V chem 'somnevaetsia' Andrei Platonov," *Literaturnaia gazeta* 10 June 1931. On Stalin, see commentary to Andrei Platonov, "Tekhnicheskii roman," *Ogonek* No. 19 (3277) (May 1990): 19.

26 E. Mindlin, *Neobyknovennye sobesedniki* (M: Sovetskii pisatel', 1968), p. 420.

27 See commentary to Platonov, "Tekhnicheskii roman," 19–20.

28 Anninskii, "Otkrovenie i sokrovenie," pp. 10–14. See also the stenogram of the "literary evening" in the Writers' Union devoted to Platonov; reproduced in "'Ia derzhalsia i rabotal'..."

29 See commentary to Platonov, "Tekhnicheskii roman," 19.

30 See Śliwowscy, p. 167. It has been suggested that Platonov escaped arrest because (following "Vprok"?) Stalin knew of him and his arrest would thus have required the General Secretary's personal order; see Geller, 367.

31 Joseph Brodsky, "Catastrophes in the Air," in his *Less Than One. Selected Essays* (New York: Farrar Straus Giroux, 1986), p. 281.

32 L. Shubin, "Andrei Platonov," *Voprosy literatury* 6 (1967): 28.

33 Sergei Zalygin, "Skazki realista: realizm skazochnika," *Voprosy literatury* 7 (1971): 126 and 128.

34 Edward J. Brown, *Russian Literature Since the Revolution*, Revised and Enlarged Edition (Cambridge: Harvard University press, 1982), p. 234.

35 See, in particular, her "Naturfilosofskie temy v tvorchestve Platonova 20-kh-30-kh gg," *Slavica Hierosolymitana*, 4 (1979): 223–54; and "Ideologicheskie konteksty Platonova," *Russian Literature*, 9 (1981), 231–80. N. G. Poltavtseva, *Filosofskaia proza Andreia Platonova* (Rostov-na-Donu: Izd. Rostovskogo un-ta, 1981) also claims Platonov as a writer of "philosophical prose," while his "aesthetic philosophy," is taken up in N. M. Malygina, *Estetika Andreia Platonova* (Irkutsk: Izd. Irkutskogo un-ta, 1985). See also Boris Paramonov, "Chevengur i okrestnosti," *Kontinent* 54 (1987): 333–72.

36 See, for example, Tolstaia-Segal, "'Stikhiinye sily'," and "K voprosu o literaturnoi alliuzii v proze Andreia Platonova: Predvaritel'nye nabliudeniia," *Slavica Hierosolymitana*, 5–6 (1981): 355–69; A. Zholkovskii, "Fro: Piat' prochtenii," *Voprosy literatury*

12 (1989): 23–49; Hans Günther, "Andrej Platonov und das sozialistisch-realistische Normensystem der 30er Jahre," *Wiener Slawistischer Almanach*, Bd. 9 (1982): 165–86.

37  S. I. Piskunova comments on Platonov's relation to primitivism in her "Mudrost' zabroshennykh knig," *Voprosy filosofii* 3 (1989): 32–34.

38  Geoffrey H. Hartman, *The Unmediated Vision* (New York: Harcourt, Brace, and World, 1966), pp. 78–79.

39  In this section I have drawn on the condensed version of Fedorov's (enormous and repetitive) *Filosofiia obshchego dela*, in N. F. Fedorov, *Sochineniia*, Filosofskoe nasledie, t.85 (M: Mysl', 1985), and on the commentary in S. G. Semenova, "N. F. Fedorov i ego filosofskoe nasledie," introduction to Fedorov, *Sochineniia*, pp. 5–50; Mikhail Geller, *Andrei Platonov v poiskakh schast'ia* (Paris: YMCA Press, 1982), pp. 7–54; Ayleen Teskey, *Platonov and Fyodorov. The Influence of Christian Philosophy on a Soviet Writer* (Amersham, UK: Avebury, 1982); Shepard, pp. 43–53; and Stephen Lukashevicz, *N. F. Fedorov (1828–1903). A Study in Russian Eupsychian and Utopian Thought* (New York: Associated University Presses, 1977).

40  Quoted in Semenova, "N. F. Fedorov i ego filosofskoe nasledie," p. 5.

41  In my account of Bogdanov I have drawn on his *Filosofiia zhivogo opyta* (M: Gosudarstvennoe izd., 1920), and on discussions of his thought in: K. M. Jensen, *Beyond Marx and Mach. Aleksandr Bogdanov's 'Philosophy of Living Experience'*, Sovietica Vol. 41 (Dordrecht, Holland: D. Reidel, 1978); James C. McClelland, "Utopianism versus Revolutionary Heroism in Bolshevik Policy: The Proletarian Culture Debate," *Slavic Review* 39 (3) (Sept. 1980), 403–25; and S. V. Utechin, "Philosophy and Society: Alexander Bogdanov," in Leopold Labedz, ed., *Revisionism: Essays on the History of Marxist Ideas* (New York: Praeger, 1962), pp. 117–25.

42  V. I. Lenin, *Materializm i empiriokrititsizm* (M: Izd. politicheskoi literatury, 1984), p. 226.

43  In addition to establishing a truly collective form of social existence, the proletariat would, in Bogdanov's account, create its own, utopian form of culture which would concern itself with synthesizing all existing forms of knowledge, from the purely practical and technical to scientific theory, the speculative claims of philosophy, and even religion. Its goal would be to unite the insights each discipline affords into the nature and processes of "organization" as such, in *both* the logical and the physical realms, in order to establish a grand meta-science of organization,

which Bogdanov christened "techtology" (*tektologiia*), or the "general organizational science" (*vseobshchaia organizatsionnaia nauka*, whose anticipation of cybernetics has often been noted). See his *Tektologiia. Vseobshchaia organizatsionnaia nauka* (its three volumes were first published in 1913, 1917, and 1922, and subsequently reissued in a number of editions).

44 My summaries of Grot and Kavelin are taken from Andrzej Walicki, *A History of Russian Thought from the Enlightenment to Marxism* (Stanford: Stanford Univ., 1979), pp. 358 and 362.

45 See the discussion in Katerina Clark and Michael Holquist, *Mikhail Bakhtin* (Cambridge: Harvard Univ., 1984), Ch. 2, "Nevel and Vitebsk, 1918–1924," pp. 35–62.

46 J. D. Elsworth, *Andrey Bely: A Critical Study of the Novels* (Cambridge: Cambridge Univ., 1983), p. 134.

47 The first quotation is from Isaiah Berlin, "The Energy of Pasternak," in Victor Erlich, ed., *Pasternak. A Collection of Critical Essays* (Englewood Cliffs, NJ: Prentice-Hall, 1978), p. 40; the second is from Yury Lotman, "Language and Reality in the early Pasternak," p. 29 in the same collection.

48 Peter Alberg Jensen, "The Thing As Such: Boris Pil'njak's 'Ornamentalism'," *Russian Literature* 16 (1984): 81–100.

## 1 CONSCIOUSNESS AND MATTER: PLATONOV IN VORONEZH AND TAMBOV (1917–1926)

1 Principally Platonov published in the organs of the Voronezh provincial committee of the Bolshevik Party, *Voronezhskaia kommuna* and *Krasnaia derevnia*, but the list includes *Krasnoe znamia*, *Krasnyi voin*, *Ogni*, *Izvestiia soveta oborony Voronezhskogo ukreplennogo raiona*, *Krasnyi luch*, and others, and eventually extends beyond Voronezh to the Moscow journals *Kuznitsa*, *Krasnaia niva*, *Oktiabr' mysli*, and *Plamia*; see Vasil'ev, p. 24. In 1919 Platonov contributed some sixteen items, most of them poems he had written before the Revolution, but in 1920 the tally rises to 112, with a predominance of articles and essays. See the bibliography of Platonov's works for these years published by V. Maramzin *et al.*, in *Ekho* 4 (1979): 189–90, and 1 (1980): 149–58.

2 For brevity's sake, I treat the Voronezh journalism more or less as a single text. The Soviet scholar V. Eidinova adopts the same approach to this body of material; "K tvorcheskoi biografii A. Platonova," *Voprosy literatury* 3 (1978): 213–28. For a careful study of how Platonov's ideas developed from year to year, see Langerak, "Andrei Platonov v Voronezhe."

3 See, for example, "K nachinaiushchim proletarskim poetam i pisateliam," *Zheleznyi put'* No. 19 (April 1919): 25–26; "O kul'ture zapriazhennogo sveta i poznannogo elektrichestva," *Iskusstvo i teatr* 2 (22 August 1922): 2–3; reprinted in A. Platonov, *Sobranie sochinenii v trekh tomakh* (M: Sovetskaia Rossiia, 1985), t.3, pp. 521–22. Bogdanov, as Langerak points out, did not believe proletarian culture would follow immediately from the events of October 1917, and Platonov was closer on this score to such proletkul'tists as Gastev; "Andrei Platonov v Voronezhe," p. 454.

4 "Proletarskaia poeziia," *Kuznitsa* No. 9 (1922); reprinted in Andrei Platonov, *Sobranie sochinenii v trekh tomakh*, t.3, pp. 523–28. See also "U nachala tsarstva soznaniia," *Voronezhskaia kommuna* No. 12 (1921).

5 In her insightful discussion of the Voronezh journalism, Eidinova ("K tvorcheskoi biografii A. Platonova," pp. 220–22) notes Platonov's eagerness to perceive the world as embodying the "polar opposition of life's bases," the chief among these being the dichotomies between the spiritual and the material, intellectual and emotional motivations, and the domain of nature versus that of machines.

6 *Voronezhskaia kommuna* No. 293 (26 December 1920).

7 See "O liubvi," TsGALI f.2124, op.1, ed. khr. 32, ll.5–8; and my publication in *Russian Literature* 23–24 (1988): 390–95. "O nauke," *Krasnaia derevnia* No. 89 (25 June 1920): 2.

8 *Krasnaia derevnia* No. 99 (7 July 1920): 2.

9 "Bor'ba mozgov," *Krasnaia derevnia*, No. 171 (3 October 1920): 2.

10 *Iskusstvo i teatr* 2 (22 August 1922): 2–3.

11 "Da sviatitsia imia tvoe," *Krasnaia derevnia* No. 99 (7 July 1920): 2. On the epithet "dead," see Tolstaia-Segal, "Naturfilosofskie temy," p. 225.

12 *Krasnaia derevnia* (22 August 1920). Quoted from copy in TsGALI, f.2124, op.1, ed. khr. 109 (1), l.60.

13 "Vospitanie kommunistov," *Krasnaia derevnia* No. 119 (30 July 1920): 2.

14 *Ogni* No. 2 [19] (11 July 1921): 1.

15 Quoted from the manuscript in TsGALI, f.2124, op.1, ed. khr. 32; see my publication of the essay in *Russian Literature* 23–24 (1988): 387–89.

16 TsGALI, f.2124, op.1, ed. khr. 34, ll. 1–2.

17 *Voronezhskaia kommuna* No. 284 [936] (15 December 1922); quoted from copy in TsGALI, f.2124, op.1, ed. khr. 109 (1).

18 *Voronezhskaia kommuna* No. 43 (1583) (no date): 3; quoted from copy in TsGALI, f.2124, op.1, ed. khr. 109 (1).

19 *Krasnaia derevnia* No. 175 (9 July 1920): 2.

20 *Voronezhskaia kommuna* No. 189 (25 August 1921): 2.

21 *Nasha gazeta* (13 November 1921); quoted from copy in TsGALI f.2124, op.1, ed. khr. 109 (1).

22 *Krasnaia derevnia*, No. 89 (25 June 1920): 2.

23 Similarly in "O liubvi" Platonov remarks that man adapts himself to the world "and so *partially* (*otchasti*) triumphs over it."

24 V. Akimov, "Rabochii klass – eto moia rodina," Afterword to Andrei Platonov, *V prekrasnom i iarostnom mire* (L: Lenizdat, 1979), p. 414.

25 *Kommunisticheskii voskresnik detiam* (6 December 1920): 3.

26 *Krasnaia derevnia* No. 174 (8 October 1920): 2–3. Reprinted in Fol'ker Levin, ed., "Andrei Platonov," *Starik i starucha*. Arbeiten und Texte zur Slavistik b.33. (München: Verlag Otto Sagner in Kommission, 1984), pp. 21–24; my quotations are from this text. Another early story containing a protagonist and themes similar to "Stranniki" and "Volchek" is "Serega i ia," *Krasnyi luch* (Zadonsk) No. 1 (July, 1921): 2–3; reprinted by G. Antiukhin in *Pod"em* 6 (1966): 91–93.

27 *Krasnaia derevnia* No. 206 (16 November 1920): 3. This story reappeared as one of seven under the heading "Zapiski potomka" in Platonov's first collection of prose, *Epifanskie shliuzy* (M: Molodaia gvardiia, 1927), pp. 217–20. Reprinted in *Starik i starucha*, pp. 113–15; quotations from this text.

28 *Repeinik* No. 10 (29 April 1923): 3; in *Epifanskie shliuzy* as one of four tales under the heading "Iz general'nogo sochineniia," pp. 275–78. Reprinted in *Starik i starucha*, pp. 149–51.

29 *Voronezhskaia kommuna* No. 243 (29 October 1920): 3. Reprinted in *Starik i starucha*, pp. 25–27.

30 *Voronezhskaia kommuna* No. 176 (6 August 1922); in *Epifanskie shliuzy* under the title "Pamiat'" as part of the section "Zapiski potomka," pp. 207–11. Reprinted in *Starik i starucha*, pp. 105–8.

31 *Krasnaia gazeta* No. 128 (10 August 1920): 2; in *Epifanskie shliuzy* under the section "Zapiski potomka," pp. 214–16. Reprinted in *Starik i starucha*, pp. 111–12. For a list of the minor stylistic differences between the newspaper and book versions of the text, see *Starik i starucha*, pp. 209–10.

32 *Krasnaia derevnia* No. 14 (21 January 1921); also under the title "Ivan Mitrych" in *Epifanskie shliuzy*, pp. 212–13. Reprinted in *Starik i starucha*, pp. 109–10.

33 *Krasnaia derevnia* No. 21 (30 January 1921): 2–3. Reprinted in *Kontinent* 10 (1976): 339–42, and in *Starik i starucha*, pp. 28–29; quotations from the latter text.

34 Mark Rose, *Alien Encounters* (Cambridge: Harvard University Press, 1981), p. 44.

35 *Voronezhskaia kommuna* No. 252 (7 November 1922): 2. Reprinted in *Russian Literature* No. 9 (1981): 297–301, and in *Starik i starucha*, pp. 37–42; quotations from the latter. I have in mind the original story of that title, not "Satana mysli," *Put' kommunizma* (Krasnodar) 2 (March–April 1922): 32–37, and elsewhere, which Platonov later issued under the same name.

36 *Kuznitsa* 7 (December 1920–March 1921): 18–22; quotations from Andrei Platonov, *Sobranie sochinenii v trekh tomakh*, t.1 (M: Sovetskaia Rossiia, 1984), pp. 25–31.

37 "Ocherednoi," *Zheleznyi put'* No. 2 (5 October 1918): 16–17. One might note a number of descriptive motifs common to these two episodes, as well as to that portrayed in "Satana mysli": the cycling, spiralling, or circularity of the given device, its destruction through an explosion, and the penetration at the moment of that explosion of some encircling shell. These spatial motifs later lend themselves to symbolization of the soul within the body, a notion already anticipated in the reference to the beam's "releasing its [inner] might."

38 *Put' kommunizma* (Krasnodar) 2 (March–April 1922): 32–37. Quotations from *Sobranie sochinenii v trekh tomakh*, t.1, pp. 32–40. The story sometimes appears under the title "Potomki solntsa."

39 For example, in "Proletarskaia poeziia," *Kuznitsa* 9 (1922); reprinted in Platonov, *Sobranie sochinenii v trekh tomakh*, t.3, p. 523.

## 2 LEARNING THE LANGUAGE OF BEING
### (1926–1927)

1 Andrei Platonov, *Sobranie sochinenii v trekh tomakh*, t.1 (M: Sovetskaia Rossiia, 1984), p. 56. Unless otherwise indicated, all other references in this chapter are to this volume of this edition.

2 Tsiolkovskii is merely the best-known example, and Platonov could have borrowed the notion from a variety of sources. Fedorov had written that man must learn to steer the earth like a cosmic ship, and that man would eventually colonize the planets. In Bogdanov one finds such statements as "Mankind must conquer the universe and settle the far-off reaches of space, having conquered the solar system. Human beings will be immortal"; quoted in Tolstaia-Segal, "Ideologicheskie konteksty Platonova," *Russian Literature* 9 (1981): 242.

3 The tale was composed in the same year as "Lunnaia bomba" but first published only in 1968, in the collection *Fantastika 1967*.

*Vypusk 1-yi* (M: Molodaia gvardiia, 1968). The notes to the 1984 three-volume Soviet edition of Platonov's works (t. I, p. 455) indicate "7.XI/1926–27" as the authorial dating of the work.

4 The title of the work in which Popov's mentor Professor Shtufer (i.e., German *Stoff*, "matter") sets forth his views, *Mendeleev's System as the Biological Categories of Alpha-Beings*, clearly alludes to V. I. Vernadskii's *Biosfera* (1926). Vernadskii (1863–1945) speaks of the aggregate of living organisms in the biosphere as "living matter" which, as it transforms the rays of the sun into tissue, continually draws inorganic, "dead" matter into an unbroken cycle of life processes. Vernadskii also argued that under the influence of scientific achievement and human labor the biosphere gradually enters a new state, that of the "noosphere," or sphere of reason. His ideas were particularly influential in the second half of the 1920s when "Efirnyi trakt" was written. Vernadskii's role in organizing a commission to study the Siberian permafrost seems also to have inspired the subplot of the lost civilization of the *aiunity* in Platonov's tale. See *Bol'shaia sovetskaia entsiklopediia*, 3rd edition, ed. M. A. Prokhorov (M: Sovetskaia entsiklopedia, 1971), vol. 4, pp. 1595–97. Tolstaia-Segal argues that Bogdanov's theory of "techtology," in its efforts to identify the principles underlying all forms of both matter and being, had acquainted Russian readers with both the term "*biosfera*" and the notion of "*zhizneraznost'*" before the 1926 publication of Vernadskii's book ("Ideologicheskie konteksty Platonova," 241). Platonov was certainly steeped in Bogdanovism, though the coincidence of the publication date of Vernadskii's work with the writing of "Efirnyi trakt" suggests he was at least prompted to reconsider these themes by the appearance of *Biosfera* itself. The popularity of the notion of an essential link between matter and being among the utopian metaphysicians who attracted Platonov is further attested by Tsiolkovskii's claim in *Nauchnaia etika* (1930) that "everything is living, and only from time to time finds itself in nonbeing, in the form of dead, unorganized matter"; (quoted in connection with the purported "buddhism" of Platonov's later works in Tolstaia-Segal, "Ideologicheskie konteksty," 244).

5 It is in reference to "Efirnyi trakt" that Platonov writes Mariia Aleksandrovna from Tambov that he has been "forcing" (*nasiloval*) his muse over 150 pages of a work; Platonova, 165.

6 In English the titles are, respectively, "Electricity's Native Land"; "How Il'ich's Lamp Was Lit"/"About Il'ich's Extinguished Lamp"; "Teacher of the Sands"; "Masters of the Meadow."

7 Quoted from Andrei Platonov, *V prekrasnom i iarostnom mire* (Leningrad: Lenizdat, 1979), p. 233.

8 Katerina Clark's description of Lenin's view of electrification in her *The Soviet Novel. History as Ritual* (Chicago: Univ. of Chicago, 1981), p. 96.

9 Gladkov's *Tsement* abounds in this pathos of decay, and even Lenin himself sounded such themes, for example, when he warned that unless the entire economy were electrified, the Soviet state was threatened with remaining a backward realm of "small peasant holdings"; quoted in Clark, *The Soviet Novel*, p. 93. Cf. also the depiction in "Rodina elektrichestva" of electrical wiring strung above wattle fences and the title of M. Isakovskii's nearly contemporary collection of poems, *Provoda v solome*, 1927.

10 This is particularly true of the two less anecdotal stories, "Peschanaia uchitel'nitsa" and "Rodina elektrichestva"; the exception is "Lugovye mastera," which was published separately for the series *Dlia molodoi derevni*, its differences reflecting the series' agitational purpose. See Langerak, "Kommentarii k sborniku A. P. Platonova, 'Epifanskie shliuzy'," in André van Holk, ed., *Dutch Contributions to the Tenth International Congress of Slavists. Sofia, September 14–22, 1988. Literature* (Amsterdam: Rodopi, 1988), p. 167.

11 This description of the icon is clearly patterned after Babel's "Pan Apolek."

12 First published in the collection *Epifanskie shliuzy* (M: Molodaia gvardiia, 1927), pp. 3–61.

13 Tolstaia-Segal says "Epifanskie shliuzy" reflects Platonov's new-found skepticism toward the potency of "idea" vis-à-vis the world as well as toward the imperative for "action" (*delanie*); "'Stikhiinye sily'," p. 95.

14 Platonov's symbols perhaps also beg a psychoanalytic interpretation; but even their most explicitly sexual connotations ultimately lead back, through man's experience of the somatic, to the more general corporeality Platonov regarded as the primary form of existence; see Chapter Five.

15 Tolstaia-Segal also notes that it is in "Epifanskie shliuzy" that the theme of statehood (*gosudarstvennost'*) begins to figure prominently; "'Stikhiinye sily'," p. 95. The science fiction works have their governments that sponsor (failed) utopian projects and their societies (or sometimes mankind as a whole) that are to benefit from them, but their presence is largely reduced to the function of explaining the vast resources at the scientist-hero's disposal and of aggrandizing the stakes of taking on nature (as in "Satana mysli"

and "Lunnaia bomba," where mass industrial accidents accompany the projects' construction). The tales of reclamation at times anticipate the concerns of "Epifanskie shliuzy," as when the jealous kulaks of "O potukhshei lampe Il'icha" burn down the electrical generator built by the hero, but the significance of Soviet state sponsorship of their various efforts to irrigate and electrify the countryside remains unaddressed in these works.

16 On the popularity in the later twenties of the theme of the "muzhik" see E. A. Krasnoshchekova, "A. Platonov i Vs. Ivanov (vtoraia polovina 20-kh godov)," in V. P. Skobelev, ed., *Tvorchestvo A. Platonova* (V: Izd. voronezhskogo un-ta, 1970), pp. 147–56; reprint Ardis, 1986.

17 On Platonov's use of historical sources see: Vasil'ev, pp. 79ff; Langerak, "Kommentarii k sborniku A. P. Platonova 'Epifanskie shliuzy'," pp. 145–49; T. A. Nikonova, "Kommentarii k povesti A. Platonova 'Epifanskie shliuzy'," in Skobelev, ed., *Tvorchestvo A. Platonova*, pp. 204–20.

18 On Eurasianism in Platonov and Pil'niak see Tolstaia-Segal, "'Stikhiinye sily'," pp. 92–94.

19 In a 1922 article for *Voronezhskaia kommuna* Platonov had himself reported on the local Gubispolkom's order that an electric power station be built on the site of the locks (near the settlement of Chizhevka, adjacent to Platonov's own Iamskaia sloboda). "The station will be fitted out in the structure left by Peter the Great, whose remains still stand," Platonov states, then predicts the three dams to be constructed will mark a new era for the Voronezh region. See "Voronezhskaia gidro-elektricheskaia stantsiia," *Voronezhskaia kommuna* 284 [936] (15 December 1922): 2.

20 V. Strel'nikova, "'Razoblachiteli' sotsializma," *Vecherniaia Moskva* 28 September 1929. On connections in Soviet literature between Peter and Stalin see Clark, *The Soviet Novel*, pp. 133–34.

21 The first appeared in the *Epifanskie shliuzy* collection, the second in *Krasnaia panorama* (L), September (9), pp. 3–20, and October (12), pp. 3–10 (later also in the 1929 collection *Proiskhozhdenie mastera*). Langerak claims Platonov's redaction was extensive enough that one should speak of two distinct variants of the work, though the ambivalence already inhabits the original version published in *Epifanskie shliuzy*. See Langerak, "Kommentarii k sborniku A. P. Platonova 'Epifanskie shliuzy'," p. 156.

22 One Soviet scholar speaks of Platonov and Zabolotskii as representatives of a line in Soviet prose of the 1920s concerned with translating everything into the "natural-philosophical" terms of life-nature-death and hence with examining social

themes in the light of a philosophical effort to scrutinize the "flesh of the world." She also mentions Filat in "Iamskaia sloboda" as representing a "condition on the threshold of emergence from natural-elemental ties with the world." See Natal'ia Vasil'evna Kornienko, Abstract of "Filosofskie iskaniia i osobennosti khudozhestvennogo metoda Andreia Platonova," Cand. Diss., Gos. Pedagogicheskii Inst. im. Gertsena (L), p. 17.

23 The importance of this adaptation of economic themes to his notion of ontology may be judged from the fact that Platonov had devoted to it two of the sketches in the *Epifanskie shliuzy* collection. "Mavra Kuzminishna" describes an old woman whose miserly habits enable her to live fourteen years without spending a kopek of her meager savings (she raises vegetables in her house, uses dishes discarded by others, and so on). "Ekonomik Magov" likewise recounts the painstaking care that has allowed the hero to wear a single pair of boots for twelve years and own the same pencil since childhood. Even such anecdotal treatments link the characters' miserly calculations to the physical economy of the body's efforts to sustain itself in a world begrudging subsistence: "Mavra Kuzminishna fed herself, chewing the food thoroughly and for a long time, tormenting her stomach and salivating profusely, by means of which she gained a high output of usefulness from her food...in the summer she would sit in the warmth and sunshine, multiplying the caloric reserves of her body" (*Epifanskie shliuzy*, p. 222). Indeed, the same "economic" theme is sounded in the description, in "Rodina elektrichestva," of the old woman's "stingily accumulated mind."

24 At least one Soviet text, *Istoriia russkoi sovetskoi literatury* (M: Vysshaia shkola, 1986), includes its synopsis of Platonov's works of the twenties in the context of a discussion of "the problem of the spiritual content of the self in the new Soviet society"; pp. 128ff.

25 Voronskii is quoted in Platonov, *Sobranie sochinenii v trekh tomakh*, t.1, p. 458. As the genre of ironic confrontation between the autonomy of the protagonist and the social hierarchy through which he travels, the picaresque is in fact eminently suited to Platonov's theme, and in the late 1920s he appears to have turned to it whenever the impulse toward satire and irony predominated over that toward tragedy (for example, in parts of *Chevengur*, "Usomnivshiisia Makar," "Gosudarstvennyi zhitel'").

26 See V. A. Pronin and L. N. Taganov, "A. Platonov – poet (sbornik *Golubaia glubina*)," in *Tvorchestvo A. Platonova*, pp. 130–39. See also Briusov's remarks in his review of *Golubaia glubina*, which in a manner characteristic of many early responses to Platonov (cf.

Gor'kii's comments on *Chevengur*) notes both the technical awkwardness and the (apparently indefinable) "uniqueness" of the poems; "Sredi stikhov," *Pechat' i revoliutsiia*, 6 (1923): 69–70.

27 Respectively:

"Ехидный мужичок похлюпывал носом и не шевелился. И нельзя было понять, спит он или сейчас хитрит…С обрыва сигнул другой такой же мужичок, будто брат его, но только еще жиже и тоще, а на вид душевней. -Хтой-та-эт? Што за епишка? Откель бы…И пахуч же враг!" Andrei Platonov, *Starik i starucha. Poterjannaja proza*, ed. Volker Levin. Arbeiten und Texte zur Slavistik, 33 (München: Otto Sagner, 1984) p. 111.

Жил некоим образом человек – Евдок, Евдоким; фамилию имел Абабуренко, а по-уличному Баклажанов. Учил его в училище поп креститься: на лоб, на грудь, на правое плечо, на левое – не выучил. Евдок тянул по-своему: а лоб, а печенки…" Levin, p. 93.

28 For example, "Был двор на краю города…Тут я жил. Ходил домой я через забор. Ворота и калитка всегда были на запоре, и я к нему привык"; "Даже когда лезешь через забор, посидишь на нем секунду-две, оттуда видней видно поле, дорогу и еще что-то далекое темное, как тихий низкий туман"; "А узнавать есть чего, хоть бы то, отчего мы хотим знать все, если узнавать нечего, все живет само собой в черноте и пустоте" ("Volchek," 1920).

29 For example, "Он был когда-то нежным, печальным ребенком, любящим мать, и родные плетни, и поле, и небо над всеми ими. По вечерам в слободе звонили колокола родными жалостными голосами, и ревел гудок, и приходил отец с работы, брал его на руки и целовал в большие синие глаза."

*versus*: "Он вырос в великую эпоху электричества и перестройки земного шара. Гром труда сотрясал землю, и давно никто уже не смотрел на небо – все взгляды опустились в землю, все руки были заняты. Электромагнитные волны радио шептали в атмосфере и межзвездном эфире грозные слова рабочего человека."

30 "И иногда, редко, тайно от самих себя, при безумных взрывах энергии в машинах и в Массе, мы смутно ощущали эту податливую, слишком покорную мягкость материи…Мы тогда напряглись, регуляторы ставили на полную скорость, мы размахивались и ударили в пустоту и сами падали…"

31 "*Ia napisal "Epifanskie shliuzy" v neobychnom stile, otchasti slavianskoi*

*viaz'iu--tiaguchim slogom"*; Platonova, 165. The reference to the tale's "unusual" style reflects the consciousness with which Platonov was beginning to cultivate his unorthodox verbal manner; in a later letter he asks that not a word of the text be changed by the collection's editors (insisting on "the necessity of preserving my style exactly," 165).

32 Tolstaia-Segal claims this for the poems in *Golubaia glubina*; "'Stikhiinye sily'," p. 106 and n. 54. See also Krasnoshchekova on the opposition between "extreme rationalism" and "intuitivism" in the early Platonov; "Andrei Platonov i Vsevolod Ivanov," pp. 56–74.

33 One might note here the general similarity between Platonov's stylistic evolution and that of his ultimate progenitor, Gogol. Like that of Gogol, Platonov's emerging style often provoked accusations of mere ineptitude and ungrammaticality, while the antipodal position occupied in Gogol's conception of literary language by Derzhavin's odes might be roughly compared with the role played in Platonov's works first by declamatory Smithy phrases, later by utopian *agitprop* rhetoric. See the remarks in Abram Terts [Andrei Siniavskii], *V teni Gogolia* (Paris: Syntaxis, 1981), pp. 337–42.

34 Geller, p. 91, identifies the quasi-Petrine style of "Epifanskie shliuzy" as the first instance of this utopian discourse (specifically, he calls it *"iazyk 'prozhekta'"*).

35 This is particularly true of the works he contributed to the "peasant" newspaper, *Krasnaia derevnia*: for example, "Chul'dik i Epishka," "Pop," "Erik."

36 The relation between the *mature* Platonov and Zoshchenko (which will be commented on in the next chapter) is somewhat more complex. See also Chudakova, *Poetika Mikhaila Zoshchenko*, p. 118, on Platonov's dislike of Zoshchenko.

37 Features which were, as Selishchev points out, the inevitable result of translating what had been the parlance of a highly educated, conspiratorial coterie into propaganda for the masses; *Iazyk revoliutsionnoi epokhi* (M: Rabotnik prosveshcheniia, 1928), especially Chapter Two; reprint Zentralantiquariat der Deutschen Demokratischen Republik (Leipzig, 1974), p. 133. See also A. P. Tsvetkov, "Iazyk A. P. Platonova," Dissertation, University of Michigan, 1983, Chapter Three, "Revoliutsiia i iazyk." Even here, though, Platonov's relation to post-revolutionary babel is ambivalent. If the satirical orientation of his stories of the mid twenties may be seen as coinciding with the Party's efforts to shore up the linguistic orthodoxy of "Soviet" Russian speech

(through such efforts as the campaign against illiteracy, with its 1923 All-Union Society *Doloi negramotnost'*, or the converse but related debate over the proliferation of empty rhetorical clichés in the Soviet press, as in Lenin's 1924 "Ob ochistke russkogo iazyka") Platonov nonetheless remains the chronicler of post-revolutionary linguistic confusion. His ambivalence toward orthodoxy is reflected even at an early stage in the fact that several of his purely journalistic pieces might have prompted Kalinin's complaint about the "vulgarizing" tendencies resulting from attempts to write even news items in a special "language for peasants" (Kalinin expressed his dissatisfaction at a 1924 conference of peasant correspondents for the newspaper *Bednota*; see *Ocherk istorii russkoi sovetskoi literatury* [M: AN SSSR, 1954], p. 94).

38 On the unconventionality of the example from "Peschanaia uchitel'nitsa" see the interesting remarks in Elisabeth Markstein, "Der Stil des 'Unstils': Andrej Platonov," *Wiener Slawistischer Almanach* Bd. 2 (1978): 115–19. Tolstaia-Segal has in a somewhat different context spoken of this process as the means by which Platonov sought to overcome the heterogeneity of Pil'niakian stylistic montage; "'Stikhiinye sily'," p. 106.

39 The question of Platonov's relation to any specific modernist aesthetic is an intriguing one for which there exists no easily documented answer. Against such a connection argue his provincialism and his failure, uncharacteristic for the avant-garde, to associate himself with any of the movements devoted to the destruction of conventional literary language (with the exception of this fairly brief bout of *podpil'niakovshchina*). In its favor argue, in addition to the strong evidence of the works themselves, his enthusiasm for some of the aesthetic theories of LEF and a number of suggestive passages in his early works. For example, the avant-garde aesthetic seems whimsically invoked in the scene in "Rodina elektrichestva" in which the narrator discovers a painting by Picasso and a "women's bidet" (an allusion to Duchamp?) stashed away in a barn – the setting itself functioning as a kind of absurdist montage of aesthetic object, everyday artifact, and village primitivism.

40 *Novyi mir* 3 (1928): 270. S. G. Bocharov's definition also implies the presence in Platonov's prose of certain Modernist tendencies derived from *skaz*: "*Difficult expression* is the very inner quality of Platonov's language…"; "'Veshchestvo sushchestvovaniia'. Vyrazhenie v proze," in *Problemy khudozhestvennoi formy sotsiali-sticheskogo realizma*, t.2 (M: Nauka, 1971), p. 311.

41  See Tsvetkov, "Iazyk A. P. Platonova," p. 31; on the parallels between Platonov and eighteenth-century Russian see Markstein, "Der Stil des 'Unstils'," pp. 129–43.

42  That is, Platonov's works readily fit the conventional definition of the avant-garde as "[deriving] from the dichotomy between conventional, clichéd language and experimental linguistic forms that dislodge those clichés." Jochen Schulte-Sasse, "Foreword: Theory of Modernism versus Theory of the Avant-garde," in Peter Bürger, *Theory of the Avant-Garde*, Vol. 4 in Theory and History of Literature (Minneapolis: Univ. of Minnesota, 1984), pp. vii–viii.

43  From Khlebnikov's "Ka" quoted in Patricia Carden, "Ornamentalism and Modernism," in George Gibian and H. W. Tjalsma, eds., *Russian Modernism. Culture and the Avant-Garde, 1900–1920* (Ithaca: Cornell Univ. Press, 1976), pp. 49–64. Carden cogently argues that "ornamentalism is simply the name attached to the appearance of Modernism in Russian prose"; for her perceptive remarks on the modernist tendencies of Remizov's archaicism, see p. 58.

44  Gumilev's "Vosmistishie": "*I simvol gornego velich'ia,/ Kak nekii blagostnyi zavet,/ Vysokoe kosnoiazychie,/ Tebe daruetsia, poet*". Quoted in Nancy Pollack, "Mandel'shtam's *Mandelshtein* (Initial Observance on the Cracking of a Slit-Eyed Nut OR a Couple of Chinks in the Shchell)," *Slavic Review* Vol. 46 No. 3/4 (Fall/Winter 1987): 466. She in turn cites O. Ronen, *An Approach to Mandelshtam* (Jerusalem: Magnes, 1983), p. 168.

45  See N. A. Kozhevnikova, "Iz nabliudenii nad neklassicheskoi ('ornamental'noi') prozoi," *Izvestiia AN SSSR. Seriia literatury i iazyka*, t.35 No. 1 (1976): 55.

46  For example, in works by Neverov, Leonov, Vs. Ivanov. See N. V. Dragomiretskaia, "Stilevye iskaniia v rannei sovetskoi proze," in G. L. Abramovich *et al.*, ed., *Teoriia literatury* (M: Nauka, 1965), vol. 3, pp. 139–43. See also Bocharov's remarks on the general theme of "trudnoe vyrazhenie" in Soviet prose, especially in the works of Vsevolod Ivanov, pp. 327ff.

47  On concretizations see also Markstein, "Der Stil des 'Unstils'."

48  Langerak, "Andrei Platonov v Voronezhe," pp. 437–68, especially pp. 454–58; also Tolstaia-Segal, "Ideologicheskie konteksty Platonova," pp. 247–50.

49  Platonov's paraphrase in this essay of Potebnia's theory of the word – he defines it as a "three-faceted symbol of reality" comprising idea, image, and sound – works toward a similar mooring of language in matter. On Platonov's use of Potebnia see

also remarks in N. M. Malygina, *Estetika Andreia Platonova* (Irkutsk, 1985), pp. 98–99.

50  Borovoi notes the importance for Platonov's style of conjunctions of intent, such as *chtoby*, which often link description of the character's mundane situation to some universal goal; "'Radi radosti'. Andrei Platonov," in L. Borovoi, *Iazyk pisatelia* (M: Sovetskii pisatel', 1966), pp. 179–218.

51  For seminal discussions of the role played by notions of "matter," "the abstract," and "the concrete" in Platonov's prose, see Bocharov, and V. A. Svitel'skii, "Konkretnoe i otvlechennoe v myshlenii A. Platonova-khudozhnika," in *Tvorchestvo A. Platonova*, pp. 7–26. For a different definition of the central Platonovian trope see Tsvetkov, *Iazyk A. P. Platonova*, chapter six, "Podstanovka v svete leksicheskoi semantiki," pp. 159–88.

52  Kozhevnikova, 60. Realized through a variety of devices derived from verse (such as metonymic transfers of attributes from abstract whole to concrete part, or vice versa; metaphors based on visual similarities; the recovery of latent, usually literalized, etymological meanings) this ornamentalist penchant for materialization engendered situations of referential ambivalence often strikingly similar to those in Platonov's prose (cf., for example, the simultaneity of literal and figurative meanings of the adjective *ostryi* imposed in the phrase from Vsevolod Ivanov's *Tsvetnye vetra* – "*oster, kak osoka, neulovim vzgliad*," 63; or her discussion of a series of examples in which the abstract nouns *tishina* and *molchanie* are "materialized" through their conjunction with various verbs denoting concrete actions; "*tishinu mozhno polomat' (slomat', vzlomat'), razorvat' (vzorvat'), raskolot', rasporot', vskryt', kromsat', kroshit' i t.d.,*" 66).

53  J. D. Elsworth, *Andrey Bely: A Critical Study of the Novels* (Cambridge: Cambridge University Press, 1983), p. 134; see also his discussion of the ego's encasement within the body, p. 124.

54  On metonymy, see Roman Jakobson's seminal "Randbemerkungen zur Prosa des Dichters Pasternak," in his *Selected Writings*, Vol. V, ed. Stephen Rudy and Martha Taylor (The Hague: Mouton, 1979), pp. 416–32. The quotation is from A. K. Zholkovsky, "The Window in the Poetic World of Boris Pasternak," *New Literary History* Vol. 9 (Winter 1978), No. 2: 286. For convergent locutions see A. Zholkovskii, "Tekhnologiia chuda i ee razoblachenie," *Russkaia mysl'*, No. 3600 (20 December 1985): 9.

55  As part of a rejection of history, "because reality is experienced as the domain of phenomena guided by other principles than those

of human reason or cause and effect"; Peter Alberg Jensen, "The Thing as Such: Boris Pil'njak's 'Ornamentalism'," *Russian Literature* 16 (1984): 90.

56 That rhetoric consists primarily of *agitprop*, the language of Soviet political posters (*plakatnyi iazyk*), the phraseology peculiar to Marxism–Leninism, and the neo-bureaucratisms of the Soviet state.

57 Platonova, 161. See also the train episode early in *Chevengur* in which the slogan "*Sovetskii transport – eto put' dlia parovoza istorii*" (1989 Sovetskii pisatel' edition, p. 90), as well as the discussion of the Revolution as a "locomotive" in "Che-Che-O," *Novyi mir* 12 (1928): 258.

58 See, for example, the "positive" literalizations of Smithy clichés attempted in "V zvezdnoi pustyne," *Ogni* (V), No. 1 (4 July 1921): 2–3; reprinted in Levin, ed., *Starik i starucha*, pp. 30–36. See also my discussion of this in "On the Genesis of Platonov's Literary Style in the Voronezh period," *Russian Literature* 23–24 (1988): 374–8.

## 3 *CHEVENGUR* AND THE UTOPIAN GENRE

1 Langerak cites the Litvin–Molotov letter from a private archive; "Andrei Platonov vo vtoroi polovine 20-kh godov (opyt tvor-cheskoi biografii)," p. 162. In her notes to the published letters Platonov's widow asserts that he never wrote the "fantastic story"; Platonova, "Zhivia glavnoi zhizn'iu," p. 166.

2 See "Puteshestvie s otkrytym serdtsem," *Literaturnaia gazeta* No. 41 (6 Oct. 1971): 7; also Langerak, "Andrei Platonov vo vtoroi polovine," pp. 172 and 178, n. 43.

3 Proofs apparently exist and are housed in TsGALI, fond 2124, op. 1, ed. khr. 80; see D. Ia. Taran, "Rannia proza Andriia Platonova," *Radian'ske literaturoznavstvo* 9 (1969): 49; cited in Langerak, "Andrei Platonov vo vtoroi polovine," p. 172.

4 Still later Gor'kii offered a guarded but favorable reading of Platonov's play "Vysokoe napriazhenie" ("High Tension"), then a shocked reaction to "Musornyi veter." For the cor-respondence regarding *Chevengur*, see *Gor'kii i sovetskie pisateli*, pp. 313–14; and L. Anninskii, "Otkrovenie i sokrovenie," *Literaturnoe obozrenie* 9 (1989): 3–21.

5 Parts of the novel were published separately as stories, for example, "Proiskhozhdenie mastera," "Potomok rybaka," "Prik-liuchenie" (1928); later "Smert' Kopenkina" (1971). For years the "novel" existed as the story "Proiskhozhdenie mastera" plus

the Paris YMCA edition, *Chevengur*; but the Paris edition contained errors and omitted a "missing link" between the published story and its text – see Langerak, "Nedostaiushchee zveno 'Chevengura'. Tekstologicheskie zametki," *Russian Literature* 22 (1987): 477–90. Even the first Soviet publication (*Druzhba narodov* 3 (1988): 96–156; and 4 (1988): 43–156) lacked the opening section (i.e., "Proiskhozhdenie mastera"), though it restored the missing link and corrected the egregious errors of the Paris edition. The 1988 printing by Khudozhestvennaia literatura thus represents the first complete, corrected edition of the novel (so far as one can tell without access to the archives).

6  Many have commented on this aspect of the novel's structure. Hans Günther, for example, labels its structure "episodenhaft"; "Andrej Platonov: Unterwegs nach Tschevengur," in *Literarische Utopien von Morus bis zur Gegenwart* (Königsten/Ts.: Athenäum, 1983), p. 200. See also the discussion of paratactic plots in my dissertation, "Linguistic Devices in the Prose of Andrej Platonov" (Cornell, 1984), especially pp. 152ff.

7  Tolstaiai-Segal suggests Platonov should be regarded as an "ideological" writer, in several senses of the term: namely, that he authored manifestly political works, such as "Makar;" but also that his works are the embodiment of a consistent and complete philosophical system, and that he is a writer primarily concerned with "ideas," in the Dostoevskian tradition; "Ideologicheskie konteksty Platonova," p. 232.

8  Cf. Platonov's remark in a letter to Gor'kii about his "honest attempt to portray the founding of a communist society"; *Gor'kii i sovetskie pisateli*, pp. 313–14n.

9  As Geller notes (*Andrei Platonov*, p. 186), NEP was announced at the Tenth Party Congress, which ran simultaneously with the suppression of the Kronstadt uprising – another tragic outburst of revolutionary "spontaneity."

10  See Geller, *Andrei Platonov*, p. 235; also Vladimir Verin, "'Ia zhe rabotal sovsem s drugimi chuvstvami'," *Literaturnaia gazeta* No. 17 (5187) (27 April 1988): 4.

11  Günther suggests he represents the emerging Stalinist-bureaucratic tendencies of Soviet communism. "Andrej Platonov: Unterwegs Nach Tschevengur," p. 195.

12  Cf. also the satire on "socialism in one *uezd*" in "Che-Che-O"; see Geller, *Andrei Platonov*, p. 211.

13  Platonov's Polish biographers cite multiple instances of dualism or doubling in the novel: for example, the ambivalence implied in the name "Dvanov" (perhaps realized in a doubling of the

heroes, Sasha-Prokofii); the description of the "little observer" within Dvanov; Platonov's dream of himself at the writing table, reported in a letter to his wife; Śliwowscy, *Andrzej Płatonow*, p. 74.

14 Note that a similar ambivalence inhabits "Gorod Gradov": the provincial location and pretensions of the Gradovians would seem to discredit their various schemes, which are identified with petty bureaucratism; at the same time, those schemes contain a vision of the kind of utopian transformation of the countryside for which Platonov had himself at one time agitated.

15 See the prefatory remarks to the novel's publication in *Druzhba narodov* 3 (1988): 96:

> ...Platonov's manner of depicting reality calls to mind the art of caricature. But in fact the way in which Platonov weaves his artistic fabric is more reminiscent of the philosophical and esthetic principles of painters of so-called "naive" art: everything is real, but at the same time deformed; people, animals, buildings, plants all appear as concentrations of metaphoric meanings, as large-scale metaphors which lay bare the primordial, essential, and archetypal bases of human existence.

16 "...*roman ros, kak derevo--sloiami*"; "Andrei Platonov," *Voprosy literatury* 6 (1967): 307.

17 "Da die Figuren des Romans, ihre Handlungen und Dialoge, die gegenständliche Welt und die raumzeitlichen Strukturen des Romans ein engmaschiges netz von übertragene Bedeutungen, eine zweite Bedeautungsebene von philosophischen Dimensionen bilden, scheint es angemessen, *Tschevengur* als allegorischen Text zu betrachten"; "Andrej Platonov: Unterwegs nach Tschevengur," p. 196. See Tolstaia-Segal's insightful comments on the uniformity of "forces" at work within the linguistic fabrics of Platonov's texts and the ideological bases of his poetics (in its very "texture," she says, a text from Platonov's mature period is the "portrait" of an idea); "Ideologicheskie konteksty," p. 233. For similar assumptions regarding the thematic priority of ontology in Platonov, see Boris Paramonov, "Chevengur i okrestnosti," *Kontinent* 54 (1987): 333–72.

18 In general *Chevengur* is rich in Fedorovian allusions. See Ayleen Teskey, *Platonov and Fedorov. The Influence of Christian Philosophy on a Soviet Writer* (Amersham, UK: Avebury, 1982); though Teskey's study falls foul of the risk facing "influence" studies by tending to present Platonov as a mere exponent of Fedorovian ideas.

19 A prototype for these episodes in which the connection between procreation and the sorrows of existence is still more explicitly drawn can be found in "Semën" – a work published in 1936 but

apparently written around 1926, which Platonov calls autobiographical (see Platonova, "Zhivia glavnoi zhizn'iu," pp. 166
and 177, n. 20). The story interestingly describes birth as flight
from a still more tormenting form of (non)existence. Seven-year-
old Semën, the son of another family overburdened with children,
spends his days looking after younger siblings and helping them
scavenge for food. When his mother is about to give birth yet
again, Semën asks his father whether before they are born babies
are "dead." The father says they are, but adds that since they
obviously struggle to enter this world they must be even worse off
there (in death). The story's ending provides further evidence for
Platonov's familiarity with Rozanov: after the mother dies in
childbirth, Semën puts on her dress and takes charge of the
household, a bizarre episode which may have its precursor in
Rozanov's discussion in *Liudi lunnogo sveta* of ancient sects of
eunuchs whose members put on women's clothing to symbolize
their renunciation of sexual desire. See Tolstaia-Segal, "Ideologicheskie konteksty," pp. 249ff.

20 Andrei Platonov, *Chevengur* (M: Sovetskii pisatel', 1989), p. 306.
Subsequent quotations are from this edition.

21 Miroslav Drozda, "Khudozhestvennoe prostranstvo prozy A.
Platonova," *Umjetnost Riječi* 2–4 (1975): 99.

22 A. Gurvich, *V poiskakh geroia* (M-L: Iskusstvo, 1938), p. 65.

23 For a somewhat different treatment of the theme, see Jurij
Striedter, "Journeys Through Utopia. Introductory Remarks to
the Post-revolutionary Russian Utopian Novel," *Poetics Today*,
Vol. 3:1 (1982): 33–60. Drozda, "Khudozhestvennoe prostranstvo prozy A. Platonova," p. 91, comments on "open spaces"
in Platonov: "Platonov's texts are those of *wide, unlimited spaces.*
The desert, the steppe, the vacant outskirts of town, the naked
foundation pit excavated for some future tower of Babel, a
landscape with a train passing in the remote distance – this is an
environment in which man finds himself bereft of shelter ... and in
which nature provides no surrogate for an intimate abode.
Platonov's heroes are *cast into nature as into infinite matter, into the
cosmos*" (italics in original). Geller, *Andrei Platonov*, p. 182,
describes Dvanov's expulsion as his transition from the "static"
chronotope of "Proiskhozhdenie mastera" to the "dynamic" one
of his quest for socialism. See also Gurvich's remark, *V poikakh
geroia*, p. 68, about how Platonov's heroes love open spaces as a
form of "sweet poison" (*sladkaia otrava*), as well as Mikhail
Epshtein's discussion on the Russian love of open space in
"Teoreticheskie fantazii," *Iskusstvo kino* 7 (1988): 69–81.

24 See Tolstaia-Segal, "Naturfilosofskie temy," p. 254; and in general her essay's discussion of the interrelation of matter and spirit in Platonov.

25 The YMCA Press (Paris, 1972) edition of *Chevengur* has the adjective "*pobochnyi produkt*" ("by-product") here (p. 326), which in context sounds more like Platonov than the Sovetskii pisatel' edition's "*porochnyi produkt*" ("flawed product").

26 Tolstaia-Segal notes a certain coincidence of Platonov's interest in death and the transformation of matter with the mysticism of Fedor Sologub; "Naturfilosofskie temy," p. 239n.

27 Cf. the death of the machinist from a wound to the head, the contrast of whose red blood to his aged exterior surprises Dvanov, 46–47; and Dvanov's wounding by the anarchists, when his "strength and consciousness" are said to flow out through the wound, 95.

28 The episode almost certainly alludes to Garshin's "Chetyre dnia," which describes a similar encounter with a soldier's corpse.

29 See Tolstaia-Segal, "Naturfilosofskie temy," p. 223.

30 Since the *prochie* are nomads, they may represent Platonov's response to the Eurasianist notion of Russia's "Turanian" origins; see Tolstaia-Segal, "'Stikhiinye sily'," pp. 91ff.

31 Even abstract afflictions can assume the form of an eroding physical force. Dvanov's meek and empathetic stepfather Prokhor Abramovich, for example, is compared with the grasses living at the bottom of a hollow: "from above there pour on them waters from melting snow, in the summer downpours and, in the wind, sand and dust; in the winter they are buried under heavy and stifling snows. Always and at every moment they live under blows and the heaping on of burdens, and for that reason the grass in hollows grows bent over, ready to bow down and let flow over them misfortune" (26).

32 Tolstaia-Segal suggests that the condition of "memorylessness" (*bespamiatstvo*) may be linked for Platonov with an ideal of anti-egoism that is opposed to the rapaciousness of such "smart" characters as Prokofii and that might provide the basis for a society organized as an anti-individualistic Fedorovian "supra-organism"; see "Ideologicheskie konteksty," p. 250. The novel certainly portrays episodes of anti-egoism – the young Dvanov, for example, empathizes with all the creatures and things around him which suffer from the world's hostility, and moreover is said to have "no sense of himself as a solid object" (45). But Platonov's attraction to this condition may ultimately have as much to do with quasi-suicidal desires to surrender to the world (specifically,

by dissolving oneself in it). See also Gurvich's remark about the typical Platonovian hero being "incapable of attention to his own self," *V poiskakh geroia*, p. 98.

33  Tolstaia-Segal suggests Platonov may have been influenced by the theosophical writings of Gurdzhiev, in particular his doctrine of the "recovery of memory of oneself" as the winning of superiority over all the levels of consciousness; "Naturfilosofskie temy," p. 227.

34  See also the attraction of Dvanov's father to fish as creatures existing *halfway* between life and death, and the Chinese riding on the train who claim that "we love death." Tolstaia-Segal comments on Platonov's general interest in the living/nonliving boundary and its frequent expression in the transformation of one essence into the other (as in the soldier's death); "Naturfilosofskie temy," pp. 224–25. Drozda, "Khudozhestvennoe prostranstvo prozy," p. 95, also notes Platonov's characteristic attraction to people existing on the boundary with death.

35  Though perhaps not; one could plausibly read Fedorov's call to restore ancestral links through the resurrection of the "fathers" as a response to deeper, ontological yearnings surpassing the desire even for resurrection itself (a similar rupture is posited when he speaks of the "non-nativeness" of the present cosmos, whose relation to man is that of a "wet-nurse" rather than a true mother).

36  Geller, *Andrei Platonov*, p. 197 and Tolstaia-Segal, "Ideologicheskie konteksty," p. 259, for example; the connection is tenuous, since we have no way of knowing whether Platonov read Freud, and in any event it is the *loss* of the father, not his repressive presence, which forms the tragedy for Platonov. Freud was not the only one to write on the topic of fathers – Fedorov is the more plausible source. A Freudian reading of the novel is another matter, one with which this study is not immediately concerned.

37  The brief and anecdotal "Erik," for example, already contains a grotesque version of the creation myth, "Rodonachal'niki natsii" portrays a flood that destroys an old world and efforts to build a new one, while "Ivan Zhokh" devotes itself to the theme of peasant utopias. On Platonov's utopian themes see especially Geller, *Andrei Platonov*, Ch. 3 ("Soblazn utopii"), pp. 173–252; J. Striedter, "Journeys Through Utopia," and David M. Bethea, *The Shape of Apocalypse in Modern Russian Fiction* (Princeton: Princeton University Press, 1989), Ch. 3, "*Chevengur*: On the Road with the Bolshevik Utopia," pp. 145–85. Bethea notes that during this progress toward utopia in the steppe Dvanov's mode

of transportation changes from the locomotive, that symbol of modernity and history, to horseback and for a time even to travel by foot (pp. 167, 175). He also suggests that through its steppe setting *Chevengur* enters into dialogue with the Russian literary tradition headed by the famous troika ride in Gogol's *Dead Souls*, questioning "the possibility of effecting *any* change over the expanse known as the steppe" (175); see also his comments on the spatial qualities of the novel's steppe location, p. 180.

38 Though Tolstaia-Segal suggests this ideal comes out of Bogdanov's later notion of *tovarishchestvo*; "Ideologicheskie konteksty," p. 240.

39 They prefer instead a "class caress" (*klassovaia laska*), which is defined as "close infatuation with a similar proletarian person" (233–34). On the "ignorance" of isolated rural masses as the appropriate site on which to erect utopia consider Dvanov's love of "ignorance" over "culture": the former is a "clean field," the latter already crowded with plants. He is glad the Revolution has cleared the fields of Russia, and is "in no hurry to sow anything – good soil will produce on its own something unprecedented and valuable, so long as the winds of war don't bring in the seeds of capitalist weeds" (122). Prokofii declares "mind" to be "as much a form of property as is a house, from which it follows that it will oppress the unlearned and the weak" – to which Kopenkin's response is that one should then "arm all the fools" (190). Pashintsev, too, loves "stupid muzhiks" over "educated bourgeoises" (132). On the anti-sexual theme see Paramonov's polemical, though somewhat narrow, account.

40 See Geller, *Andrei Platonov*, p. 213; Bethea, *The Shape of Apocalypse*, p. 158; and Langerak, "Kommentarii k sborniku A. P. Platonova *Epifanskie shliuzy*," pp. 150–56. The important source on folk utopian legends is K. V. Chistov, *Russkie narodnye sotsial'no-utopicheskie legendy XVI–XIX vv* (M, 1967).

41 Tolstaia-Segal, "Ideologicheskie konteksty," p. 254. On millenarial strains in Bolshevism, see S. Bulgakov, "Dusha sotsializma," *Novyi grad* 1 (1931): 49–58.

42 On chiliasm and Campanella in the novel, see V. Varshavskii, "'Chevengur' i 'Novyi grad'," *Novyi zhurnal* 122 (1976): 193–213; Geller, *Andrei Platonov*, pp. 218ff; Günther, "Andrej Platonov: Unterwegs nach Tschevengur," p. 193. Tolstaia-Segal rather unconvincingly suggests that the author "N. Arsakov" is Nikolai Aksakov, "like Rozanov, a member of Strakhov's circle"; "Ideologicheskie konteksty," pp. 261–62.

43 The eccentricity and half-wittedness of the Chevengurians represents a similar candidacy for ontological redemption – even

as it supplies the comic motivation for their peculiar form of radicalism – through its allusion to the manifest sympathy for the "unlearned" in Fedorov's account of society's tragic division into the "learned" and the "unlearned."

44 Paramonov, "Chevengur i okrestnosti," p. 334. Cf. also the latent homosexual connotations in the "secret relations between comrades" (286).

45 Tolstaia-Segal says that the Fedorovist strain in Platonov causes him to value settledness – the prerequisite for gathering the remains of ancestors – over itinerance; "Naturfilosofskie temy," pp. 248–49. The novel seems more ambivalent than she suggests, however; see its contrary ideal of "wandering": the *prochie* eventually refuse to take up permanent residence in any of the town's abandoned houses and one of the vagabonds named Lui insists that communism is "eternal motion" and repeatedly urges Chepurnyi to issue a declaration to that effect. The existential rationale for such perpetual "wandering" is outlined when Shumilin recalls having read in a "scientific book" that "the force of gravity, the weight of a body and life decreases from speed, which must be why people living in misfortune [always] try to move. Russian wanderers and pilgrims continually wandered for the very reason that on the move they dissipated the weight of the nation's grieving soul" (71).

46 Tolstaia-Segal, apparently referring to the ideal of collectivism held by the Chevengurians, speaks of their "dream of destroying the physical enclosedness of the individual" as the most striking utopian notion in *Chevengur* ("Ideologicheskie konteksty," p. 241); but this seems to skew Platonov's emphases, which instead fall on preserving "containment," as when the *prochie* embrace one another not out of brotherhood but to remain warm.

47 As Prokofii puts it, in typically confused terms, this "solar system will give the strength of life to communism on its own, just so there's not capitalism around; every kind of work and effort is the invention of the exploiters, so they could receive an abnormal surplus over and above the solar products" (251).

48 Geller, *Andrei Platonov*, p. 217, points out the Khlebnikov parallel. On Zabolotskii, see A. Makedonov, *Nikolai Zabolotskii. Zhizn', tvorchestvo, metamorfozy* (L: Sovetskii pisatel', 1968), p. 152; quoted in Tolstaia-Segal, "Ideologicheskie konteksty," p. 105. Platonov here may also be responding to the idea of *vseponimanie* ("universal understanding") set forth in Bogdanov's later writings as the "law of the new conscience" of proletarian man leading to the "true understanding of the inner life of every living thing," and

as such providing the means to "complete mastery of the secrets of life's organization"; Tolstaia-Segal, "Ideologicheskie konteksty," pp. 240, 250.

49 Cf. also Chepurnyi's disappointment on seeing the motley band rounded up to serve as the "proletariat" of Chevengur: he had been expecting the "united heroes of the future" but instead in front of him he sees "people without any class appearance or revolutionary sense of honor... some sort of nameless others living without any meaning whatsoever, without pride, and apart from the approaching worldwide triumph" (251). Even the altruistic labors the Chevengurians perform for one another are overshadowed as "first acts" by their implicit allusion to the first labors performed by man after the Fall (especially since labor was to have been abolished in Chevengur).

50 Tolstaia-Segal sees in the theme of moonlight an allusion to Rozanov's *Liudi lunnogo sveta*, with its discussion of the "sexless" nature of Christian sectarianism (especially in association with the *prochie*, who appear "as though their whole lives they had warmed themselves and been illuminated, not by the sun, but by the moon," 255); "Ideologicheskie konteksty," pp. 265ff.

51 Geller, *Andrei Platonov*, p. 189; Günther, "Andrej Platonov: Unterwegs nach Tschevengur," p. 199; Gary Saul Morson, *The Boundaries of Genre. Dostoevsky's 'Diary of a Writer' and the Traditions of Literary Utopia* (Austin: University of Texas Press, 1981), p. 118.

52 Kopenkin, for example, dreams of resurrecting Rosa Luxemburg and grows disenchanted with Chevengur precisely because he decides that in it she could never be resurrected nor could a "new" Rosa Luxemburg be born. During his journey Dvanov passes a village cemetery whose weatherbeaten crosses "reminded the living who wandered past them that the dead lived their lives in vain and want to be resurrected" (95), and later has a dream in which his father appears and charges him to "do something" in Chevengur, otherwise "why should we lie here dead?" (215).

53 The name of the lake may itself emblemize the novel's rejection of utopia, "Mutevo" (from *mut'*, "murk") inverting the name of Lake "Svetloiar" (from *svet*, "light") on whose shores stands the utopian Kitezh-grad of peasant legend.

54 See Bethea's similar remark, *The Shape of Apocalypse*, p. 158, that Platonov's position is "neither fully utopian nor fully anti-utopian."

55 In general the novel interprets the sexual act as the leaving of a physical trace of oneself (that is, a kind of preservation) within another person: as Serbinov dies, he comforts himself with the

thought that at least Sonia will go on living and "preserve in herself a trace of his body," (363).

56 Kopenkin similarly longs to travel to Germany to be near the grave of Rosa Luxemburg, even to the point of envying the clouds overhead that will soon pass over (that is, be in immediate contact with) her native Germany.

57 For a concise summary of Fedorov's notion of the museum, see S. G. Semenova, preface to N. F. Fedorov, *Sochineniia*, pp. 37–38; see also Tolstaia-Segal, "Naturfilosofskie temy," p. 234.

58 Perhaps it is this quality in particular that suggests the importance of Bakhtin's notion of "chronotope" for this novel; see Geller, *Andrei Platonov*, pp. 181ff; Günther, "Andrei Platonov: Unterwegs nach Tschevengur," p. 199.

59 Consider such "eccentric" behavior as the weekly transportation of houses and gardens from place to place, Kopenkin's attempt to slash radio signals in the air with his saber, the Chevengurians' awe before the "element of higher mind" issuing from a Party circular, the mock allegories of Kopenkin as Don Quixote and Pashintsev as a "knight of revolution" really dressed in armor.

60 Igor Golomstock, *Totalitarian Art* (New York: Harper Collins, 1990), p. 185.


4 PLATONOV AND THE CULTURE OF THE FIVE-YEAR PLAN (1929–1931)

1 The Plan ostensibly covered the years 1928–1933, but was first voted on by the Sixteenth Party Conference only in April 1929 and declared complete by the end of 1932; see Adam B. Ulam, *Stalin. The Man and His Era* (New York: Viking, 1973), p. 322. RAPP's hegemony similarly lasted from 1929 to the 1932 creation of the Union of Soviet Writers. In 1929 Platonov worked as an employee of Rosmetroves, where a friend had found him a job; he and his family first lived in a decrepit hotel near the Sukharev market, then found a small room in the Zariad'e district. From 1931 to the end of his life Platonov lived in a two-room apartment at Tverskoi Boulevard No. 25. See Chalmaev, *Andrei Platonov* (Voronezh, 1984), p. 115.

2 This ambivalence – which is not the same as opposition – is one of the defining features of Platonov as a Soviet writer. A recently published fragment of an essay Platonov wrote in 1930–1931 (apparently in response to the questionnaire "Kakoi nam nuzhen pisatel'?" sent out by the journal *Na literaturnom postu*) contains an eccentric bid for inclusion in the process of the Five-Year Plan, in

which Platonov essentially tries to out-RAPP RAPP by asserting the need for writers' *direct* (that is, technical, extra-literary) involvement in socialist construction. See "Velikaia Glukhaia" in Andrei Platonov, *Vozvrashchenie* (M: Molodaia gvardiia, 1989), pp. 176–79. Vasil'ev, *Andrei Platonov*, p. 130, comments that in the works following "Gorod Gradov" Platonov writes like a publicist "extremely upset over the gap between all the projects for building a new reality and the actual state of affairs."

3 Platonov was even later to assert, at least on an official questionnaire, that the works in question were *not* satirical. The questionnaire was written in January 1934 for the "Moskovskoe tovarishchestvo pisatelei": "The literary direction within which I work is regarded as satirical. Subjectively I do not feel that I am a satirist, and in my future work I will not preserve any satirical features"; quoted in Chalmaev, *Andrei Platonov* (Voronezh, 1984), p. 144.

4 *Oktiabr'* 6 (1929); quotations from Andrei Platonov, *Gosudarstvennyi zhitel'* (M: Sovetskii pisatel', 1988), pp. 312–19. Langerak points out the curious fact that both this work and "Usomnivshiisia Makar" were published in a RAPP-dominated journal; "Andrei Platonov vo vtoroi polovine," p. 172.

5 *Oktiabr'* 9 (1929); quotations from Andrei Platonov, *Gosudarstvennyi zhitel'*, pp. 93–107.

6 The "doubting" of course alludes to the biblical Thomas, while "Makar" clearly invokes Makar Devushkin of Dostoevsky's *Bednye liudi* (which title Platonov may also be playing on in his theme of poor peasants, *bedniaki*). Dostoevsky's Makar is an impoverished civil servant with a pure heart, who, despite being devoted to his superiors, rebels against social injustice (especially the fact that some are rich and happy, while others are miserable and poor: cf. Platonov's opposition of thin versus fat characters). The dream passage in Platonov's tale may have been inspired by Korolenko's "Son Makara," especially since that work portrays a poor downtrodden peasant who appears before god-as-judge (Toion). *Aleksei* Platonov, Andrei's sometime *doppelgänger*, had also published the story "Makar karaiushchaia ruka" in *Novyi mir* 5 (1929): 27–59. In his notes to a recent Soviet edition of Platonov's works, Chalmaev suggests also Gor'kii's "Makar Chudra," though apart from the deal of a wandering life there would seem to be little connection; see Andrei Platonov, *Gosudarstvennyi zhitel'* (M: Sovetskii pisatel', 1988), pp. 589–90.

7 The invention thus seems to belong to the various images of circularity, associated variously with utopian perpetuity and

stagnation, in Platonov's works: for example *perpetuum mobile*, windmills and whirlpools.

8 Stalin may already be alluded to in the phrase *nauchnyi chelovek* – he was already at this time being lauded as a genius – and perhaps obliquely through the "bronze" of Pushkin's horseman (*stal'*, steel). The reference would seem to be underscored by the tale's subsequent evocation of Lenin as implicit counterexample and advocate of a more "Makarian" approach to socialism (a point not lost on Averbakh in his review of the work). Petr tells Makar he wants to be like Lenin, who saw things *both near and far*, then reads to him some of Lenin's fulminations against creeping Soviet bureaucratism. For examples of laudatory labels for Stalin during the period in question, see Ulam, *Stalin*, p. 339. Clark, *The Soviet Novel*, p. 142, notes the "platonic" mentality underlying the somewhat later stream of praise for Stalin as one who "sees far ahead." For Averbakh's views see his "O tselostnykh masshtabakh i chastnykh Makarakh," *Na literaturnom postu* 21–22 (1929): 10–17.

9 *Krasnaia nov'* 9 (1931); though composed in 1929–1931, see Chalmaev's notes in *Gosudarstvennyi zhitel'*, p. 600. Quotations from Andrei Platonov, *Gosudarstvennyi zhitel'*, pp. 198–250. A. Fadeev, "Ob odnoi kulatskoi khronike," *Krasnaia nov'* 5–6 (1931): 206–9. If true, it is surely one of the oddities of the Stalin era that despite this attack Platonov and Fadeev continued to spend time together "as though nothing had happened"; see Vasil'ev, *Andrei Platonov*, p. 122. Geller, *Andrei Platonov*, p. 293, comments on "Vprok" that in it "the combination in one text of anti-utopia and utopia creates ironic ambivalence; this ambivalence provoked thunder and lightning in the 1930s, and even today allows one to isolate passages in the text appearing to show the writer's political rectitude."

10 See Vasil'ev, *Andrei Platonov*, p. 132, who also notes that the process of collectivization had progressed particularly slowly in the region. For the apology by *Krasnaia nov'*, see the end of Fadeev's review in *Krasnaia nov'* 5–6 (1931): 209.

11 "Golovokruzhenie ot uspekhov," *Pravda* No. 60 (2 March 1930); also in I. Stalin, *Sochineniia* (M: Gos. izd. politicheskoi literatury, 1949), t.12, p. 191–99. For an example of the kind of pronouncement Platonov satirizes, see Stalin's own, "*Ne iasno li, chto avtory etikh iskrivlenii, mniashchie sebia 'levymi', na samom dele l'iut vody na mel'nitsu pravogo opportunizma?*" (p. 195).

12 Platonov in this period also apparently wrote, but failed to publish, a work patently influenced by Radishchev entitled "Puteshestvie iz Moskvy v Leningrad"; see F. Suchkov, "Karavai chernogo khleba," *Literaturnoe obozrenie* 9 (1989): 41.

13 Similar themes also appear in Platonov's "Pervyi Ivan (ocherk)," *Oktiabr'* 2 (1930): 159–68.

14 Fadeev, "Ob odnoi kulatskoi khronike," p. 209. Here again there is an implicit nostalgia for Lenin and lament over Stalin as his successor: the ardent revolutionary Upoev tells how he managed to win an audience with Lenin and, seeing Il'ich's exhaustion, begged him not to die without leaving them "someone like himself, just in case." Somewhat later he declares he is going to see what Comrade Stalin is like (though he speaks positively of him). The narrator reflects elsewhere that "the notion about the oppression of the kolkhoz masses by its leaders" is incorrect – though that "notion" was Stalin's (230)!

15 In this vein Kuchum's policies are labelled "kulak" in essence and destined to rob "the poor and the better part of the middle peasantry of the chance to show its initiative" (222), and the narrator worries, with no apparent irony, that saboteurs might someday take advantage of the well intentioned but naive Kondrov. See also the work's several upbeat tributes to the Soviet worker and Soviet youth (for example, "This spectacle of the industriousness of the young has become routine in our country, because Soviet youth know no reasons for avoiding labor," 225).

16 "Vprok" begins with a justification of its narrative mask which claims that the device should by no means imply that "weak-willed contemplation is more important than tension and struggle," since "in our time" it is impossible to be a mere observer standing "*outside of* labor and the ranks of the proletariat"; one must rather arrive at one's observation *in the midst of* "work on the construction of socialism" (199).

17 The stylistic differences suggest that while the other three were intended for publication, and so linguistically tuned to official expectations, *Kotlovan* was not; following the response to "Makar" and in the climate of attacks on so-called "*iurodstvo*," Platonov must surely have known that *Kotlovan* could not be printed.

18 "Pavel Korchagin," in Andrei Platonov, *Razmyshleniia chitatelia* (M: Sovremennik, 1980), p. 62.

19 The great ironic imitation of this text by real Soviet life came, of course, in the plans for the utopian Palace of Soviets, which was to be built on the site of Moscow's destroyed Cathedral of the Savior but which also yielded only a vacant lot (then, after many years, an enormous outdoor swimming pool). However, since the cathedral was dynamited in 1929, it is possible Platonov had these very plans in mind.

20 Andrei Platonov, *Chevengur* (Moscow: Sovetskii pisatel', 1989), p. 465. Subsequent quotations are from this edition.

21 As Clark points out (*The Soviet Novel*, p. 256), that novel type is the most representative genre of what came to be known as socialist realism. Of the important exemplars, however, only *Tsement* (1925) had appeared by the time Platonov completed *Kotlovan*. Others (such as M. Shaginian, *Gidrotsentral'*, 1931; L. Leonov, *Sot'*, 1930; V. Kataev, *Vremia, vpered!*, 1932; N. Ostrovskii, *Kak zakalialas' stal'*, 1934) all appeared either simultaneously or somewhat later. Novels of collectivization are fewer and virtually all appeared later than Platonov's work (for example, Sholokhov's classic *Podniataia tselina* began appearing in 1931, Panferov's *Bruski* in 1930), though as we have seen there were precedents in journalistic accounts. E. Gnedin's "Na putiakh k kolkhozu," *Krasnaia nov'* 5 (1930): 171–82, may have attracted Platonov with its description of the Voronezh region, while Tolstaia-Segal suggests that the consumption of livestock in *Kotlovan* may have been influenced by A. Shestakov's "'Krestonostsy TsChO," *Novyi mir* 12 (1929): 148–54, in which the similar ritual of a rebellious religious sect in the region is described; "Naturfilosofskie temy," p. 234.

22 See Clark, *The Soviet Novel*, pp. 255–60. Thus the tale's opening, in which Voshchev leaves his former work and ends up at the site of the construction project, represents what Clark calls "Prologue and Separation" (in which the hero arrives at the microcosm of the novel); the discussions of the building's plan and projected construction form an episode of "Setting Up the Task," including even the standard introduction of a more ambitious, utopian plan (here in the ironic form of the foundation pit's move to the larger ravine); the murder of Kozlov and Safronov in the collectivizing village is an instance of "heroic sacrifice"; while the widening pit and the death of Nastia at the tale's close patently invert the standard "Finale," with its twin celebration of the completed task and of "regeneration" (the specific nature of this inversion will be discussed below).

23 On the general theme of "eating" and "food" in Platonov, see Tolstaia-Segal, "Naturfilosofskie temy," p. 234; and Eric Naiman, "The Thematic Mythology of Andrej Platonov," *Russian Literature* 21 (1987): 196, which discusses "eating" in *Kotlovan* as a negative attempt at "filling."

24 Nastia's mother furthermore says she wants to die because "I have exhausted myself" ("*ia umorilas'*," 407). Tolstaia-Segal has pointed out the possible origins of this scene in Pil'niak's *Krasnoe derevo*, where the romantic-revolutionary *okhlomony* take refuge in a similar abandoned factory (itelf a frequent symbol of civil war ruin); see "'Stikhiinye sily'," p. 98.

25 See the discussion in my dissertation, "Linguistic Devices in the prose of Andrej Platonov" (Cornell, 1984), pp. 160ff.

26 See also Naiman's discussion of the interconnected themes of "the void" and "filling" in Platonov's works, in his "The Thematic Mythology of Andrej Platonov"; as well as the provocative discussion of Platonov's void and the peculiarly Russian notion of *toska* in Epshtein.

27 "Givenness" (*dannost'*) is Paramonov's term, "Chevengur i okrestnosti," p. 335. See also Mindlin's remarks, *Neobyknovennye sobesedniki*, p. 431, on Platonov's aversion to any notion of coinciding with the given of one's existence. Like Zakhar Pavlovich, who worries that man is descended from the worm (an empty tube), Voshchev senses within himself a "*tikhoe mesto*" where there is nothing (though there "is nothing to prevent something from starting there", 373).

28 Tolstaia-Segal sees him as the embodiment of a principle of the "inertia of self-governing reason," which has fatally detached itself from the other levels of being and hence embraces a mechanistic view of nature as entirely dead – though this seems to overlook the awareness of reason's limitations with which Platonov endows him; "Naturfilosofskie temy," p. 226.

29 See Clark, *The Soviet Novel*, p. 94, on the period's atmosphere of "fervid industrial utopianism" and deployment of the machine as a dominant metaphor in Soviet culture (a metaphor which, she argues, in the following period of "High Stalinism" gave way to metaphors of nature).

30 See the very similar depictions of "ideal socialism" in the later novels of Il'f and Petrov, as discussed in Iu. K. Shcheglov, "Tri fragmenta poetiki Il'fa i Petrova (mir sotsializma; obraz Bendera; sotsiologizm romanov)," in A. K. Zholkovskii and Iu. K. Shcheglov, *Mir avtora i struktura teksta. Stat'i o russkoi literature* (Tennafly, N.J.: Hermitage, 1986), pp. 85–117.

31 The theme of resurrection appears as well, albeit obliquely. Chiklin asks Prushevskii whether "the successes of higher science will figure out how to resurrect back deceased people," and when Prushevskii says "no" Chiklin retorts that Marxism will figure everything out, which is why Lenin "lies whole in Moscow. He's waiting for science – he wants to be resurrected" (458).

32 For a somewhat later reflection in Platonov's writings of this use of the building as a synthetic metaphor for "socialist construction," see his comments on Ostrovskii's *Kak zakalialas' stal'*, in which he quotes Ostrovskii as referring to "placing the bricks for the foundation of this building we are constructing called socialism" ("Pavel Korchagin," p. 59).

33　For some sense of the commonality of Platonov's theme of the utopian building as a "body," see also Averbakh's insistence in his review of "Makar" that there can be no other approach to socialist construction than "the construction by the ranks of Makars of those new buildings (*domov*) in which will *beat the heart of socialist man*"; "O tselostnykh masshtabakh," p. 12 (emphasis added).

34　This is perhaps a response to some of the specifically "Marxist" emphases of the Five-Year Plan, later attenuated in the period of "High Stalinism"; see Clark, *The Soviet Novel*, p. 95.

35　Cf. the theme of autumn's arrival as the end to utopia in *Chevengur*, and the very similar combination of motifs (complete with falling snow) attending the arrival of the *Revolution* at the close of "Iamskaia sloboda".

36　As Naiman points out, what had promised to be a nurturing womb (or, in my discussion, the sheltering analogue of a perfect body) is here transformed into its opposite, the emptiness of the tomb; "The Thematic Mythology of Andrej Platonov," p. 210.

37　On the "intertextual" nature of many of Platonov's works see, for example, Tolstaia-Segal, "K voprosu o literaturnoi alliuzii v proze Andreia Platonova: predvaritel'nye nabliudeniia," *Slavica Hierosolymitana* Vol. 5–6 (1981): 355–69; and Hans Günther, "Andrej Platonov und das sozialistisch-realistische Normensystem der 30er Jahre," *Wiener Slawistischer Almanach*, Bd. 9 (1982): 165–85.

38　In *Tsement*, for example, one finds, "Here it never used to smell of manure, but now, together with the grass that has crept down from the mountains, a rotten cattleyard has sprung up... And the town beyond the bay, on the foothills, is also different: it looks grimmer, it is covered with mould and dust"; Fedor Gladkov, *Tsement* (M: Khudozhestvennaia literatura, 1967), p. 12. (English references in the body of my text are from F. Gladkov, *Cement*, trans. A. S. Arthur and C. Ashleigh [New York; Frederick Ungar, 1980].) Cf. in *Kotlovan*: "Voshchev lay down in the dusty, downtrodden grasses" (370); "But there already stood a town in the distance...the evening sun lit up the dust above the houses caused by the movement of the populace" (371). The digging which increases the pit may also derive from Gladkov: the workers in *Tsement* dig to extract their raw material from a nearby quarry, and at one point Gleb accuses the footdragging local authorities of having convinced the workers that, "*zavod – ne zavod, a broshennaia kamenolomnia*" (p. 55).

39　Platonov already parodies the content of Gladkov's metaphor –

its likening of people, the working class, to cement – by alluding to a variant of it with which Gladkov heads one of his chapter subdivisions (that describing the purge of the local Party group, "May Our Hearts Be of Stone"). Nastia's dying mother, for example, moans, "I have become like stone...I want to die" (406), "stone" in Platonov's poetic mythology symbolizing the inorganic matter to which life tragically returns at its surcease.

40 See Tolstaia-Segal's comment that the overarching goal of Platonov's prose was to find an intermediary between (traditionally separate) high and low poles of verbal culture, as well as the parallel LEF emphasis on language as potential means of joining city and country ("*smychka*"); "Ideologicheskie konteksty," p. 265. Chudakova, *Poetika Mikhaila Zoshchenko*, p. 52, also points out the frequency with which Soviet literature of the twenties dwelt on folk incomprehension of the literary language (see her examples from the works of Volkov and Shishkov). For linguistic field research see Selishchev, *Iazyk revoliutsionnoi epokhi*; André Mazon, *Lexique de la Guerre et de la Révolution en Russie (1914–1918)*. Bibliothèque de L'Institut Français de Petrograd, tome VI (Paris: Èdouard Champion, 1920); S. I. Kartsevskii, *Iazyk, voina i revoliutsiia* (Berlin: Russkoe universal'noe izd., 1923); Andrei and Tat'iana Fesenko, *Russkii iazyk pri sovetakh* (New York: no publ., 1955); Bernard Comrie and Gerald Stone, *The Russian Language Since the Revolution* (Oxford: Oxford University Press, 1978).

41 For a discussion of Platonov in relation to the late 1920s debate concerning the permissibility of Soviet satire, see Geller, *Andrei Platonov*, pp. 286ff. Regarding critical attacks on Platonov see L. A. Ivanova, "Tvorchestvo A. Platonova v otsenke sovetskoi kritiki 20–30-kh godov," in *Tvorchestvo A. Platonova*, pp. 173–92.

42 A. Fadeev, "Ob odnoi kulatskoi khronike," pp. 206–9.

43 E. Usievich, "Pod maskoi iurodstva (o Zabolotskom)," *Literaturnyi kritik* 4 (September 1933): 78–91. Usievich accuses Zabolotskii of attempting to imitate Khlebnikovian "primitivism" and childish language, and of producing an "amusingly awkward style" behind which is hidden antagonistic class ideology. The article containing Stalin's warning about the enemy's new masks is V. Ermilov, "Iurodstvuiushchaia poeziia i poeziia millionov," *Pravda* (21 June 1933).

44 See, for example, Geller, *Andrei Platonov*, pp. 292ff, for whom Platonov's linguistic theme has primarily to do with the imposition on the Russian folk of alien, Soviet genres of speech.

45 Compare the contrary definition in "Sokrovennyi chelovek,"

which treats awkward malapropism as an inherent property of "simple" speech: "The rest of the people on the locomotive and the snow plow *expressed themselves crudely* in some sort of *home-made* language, *directly baring their innermost thoughts*" (p. 332; emphasis added).

46 As Tolstaia-Segal remarks, "There appears a 'floating' point of view, which adumbrates the various consciousnesses [present in the text]"; "'Stikhiinye sily'," p. 106. Chudakova, *Poetika Mikhaila Zoshchenko*, p. 115, similarly notes that Platonov's prose lacks the "distance between the author and his word" necessary for Zoshchenko's form of satire.

47 See A. P. Tsvetkov, "Iazyk A. P. Platonova" (Diss. Michigan, 1983) especially pp. 92–108; and his definition, in the lexico-semantic terminology of Apresian, of Platonov's "authorial trope" of "substitution" (*podstanovka*).

48 *Chevengur* contains many similar examples of Platonov's style (see my dissertation, "Linguistic Devices," pp. 196–223); but *Kotlovan* is more completely dominated by the devices in question, and still more explicitly engages Soviet political phraseology – no doubt because it finds a specific target in the culture of the Five-Year Plan.

49 This connotative meaning of the passage is reinforced by the verb *predstat'* ("*eshche blizhe predstal pered nim...*"), a bookish term meaning "to present oneself before someone" – Ozhegov's dictionary gives the example "*predstat' pered sudom*," "to appear in court [before a judge]" – which is used here in an unusually literal sense to mean simply standing in front of someone.

50 See the discussion in Clark, *The Soviet Novel*, Chapter 4, "The Machine and the Garden: Literature and the Metaphors for the New Society," pp. 93–113.

51 Bocharov, "'Veshchestvo sushchestvovaniia'," p. 317, comments on the simultaneous urges in Platonov toward metaphor and demetaphorization.

52 In Bocharov's metaphysicalized Formalist reading of Platonov the central theme of the latter's prose thus becomes that of "difficult expression" ("*trudnoe vyrazhenie*"), emblematic of the very "stuff of existence." Tolstaia-Segal suggests the origins of Platonov's attitude in such precedents as Fedorov's notion of "signifying form" ("*znachimaia forma*," which is the personalized expression of spirit) and in Futurism's cult of graphic form; "Ideologicheskie konteksty," pp. 346ff.

53 Zholkovsky, in *Themes and Texts*, observes a similar paradox of verbal iconicity in a limerick involving repeated use of the word

"again": "The fact is that the meaning of the word *again* is only symbolized in [the] text [of the limerick], while the same meaning when enacted by the repetitions of the word, is manifested iconically and therefore quite graphically and palpably. Roughly speaking, the Spanish lady and her intentions are fictional, whereas the repetition of the word *again* is a fact" (p. 220). It is this same paradox of the manifest nature of linguistic elements, versus the "fictional" nature of the world they portray, which makes the irony of semantic disjuncture the primary evidence for disintegration of the utopian ideal in Platonov's work.

54 Walter Redfern, *Puns* (Oxford: Basil Blackwell, 1984), p. 9. My reading of Platonov thus differs somewhat from the essentially post-modernist one offered by Brodsky ("Catastrophes," p. 286), for whom Platonov's "every sentence drives the Russian language into a semantic dead end or, more precisely, *reveals a proclivity for dead ends, a blind-alley mentality in the language itself*" (emphasis added). In my more "modernist" interpretation Platonov posits disjuncture (or dead ends) in language only to the extent that such things obtain in the world itself.

55 On the connection between this and Platonov, see Tolstaia-Segal, "Ideologicheskie konteksty," pp. 247ff.

56 The quotation is from Peter Alberg Jensen, *Nature as Code. The Achievement of Boris Pilnjak (1915–1925)*. Kobenhavns Universitets Slaviske Institut. Studier 6 (Copenhagen: Rosenkilde and Bagger, 1979), p. 311.

57 F. Suchkov claims that Platonov had no liking for "mockery" ("*zuboskal'stvo*") and for that reason disliked Zoshchenko; see "Na krasnyi svet (ob Andree Platonove – mastere prozy)," his introduction to A. Platonov, *Izbrannoe* (M: Moskovskii rabochii, 1966), p. 4.

58 Chudakova, *Poetika Mikhaila Zoshchenko*, pp. 115–16. She also remarks, regarding one of Platonov's early articles, that "he was unable to judge from without, from the position of someone inwardly unassociated with them, the new harsh locutions, whose satirist he was in the process of becoming. It was more characteristic for him to admit his own collusion and take responsibility on himself." Bocharov, "'Veshchestvo sushchestvovaniia'," p. 346, offers a similar account.

59 Boris Grois, "Stalinizm kak esteticheskii fenomen," *Sintaksis* 17 (1987): 108.

5 "SOCIALIST REALIST" PLATONOV (1934–1951)

1 Platonov left an incomplete draft for an apparently socialist-realist novel to have been entitled *Schastlivaia Moskva*. Vasil'ev, *Andrei Platonov*, p. 226, claims that the manuscript breaks off at the sixth chapter, and a Soviet dissertation cites its archival reference as TsGALI f.2124, op. 1, ed. khr. 82 (see L. A. Ivanova, "Lichnost' i deistvitel'nost' v tvorchestve A. Platonova," Diss. na soiksanie uch. stepeni kandidata filologicheskikh nauk, Voronezhskii gos. un-tet, 1973, pp. 195, 249. Olcott, "Andrej Platonov," pp. 188 and 253n, identifies the stories "Liubov' k dal'nemu," "Skripka," and "Iushka" as fragments of the novel.

2 In a 1946 autobiography Platonov admits to having made "crude mistakes" ("*grubye oshibki*"); quoted in F. Levin's introduction to Andrei Platonov, *Izbrannoe*, p. 10. The public declaration of self-reform is contained in "Vozrazhenie bez samozashchity," *Literaturnaia gazeta* No. 69 (20 December 1937): 6. See also V. V. Perkhin, "Dva pis'ma Andreia Platonova," *Russkaia literatura* 1 (1990): 228–32.

3 A. Shcherbakov, for example, objected to the "seriously harmful" idea of "nature's miserliness" in "Takyr"; "Itogi vtorogo plenuma pravleniia SSP," *Literaturnyi kritik* 3 (1935): 7. V. Ermilov declared "Sem'ia Ivanova" (= "Vozvrashchenie") "defamatory" and "harmful" in its suggestion that man is weak by nature and that people must reconcile themselves to that fact; "Klevetnicheskii rasskaz A. Platonova ('Sem'ia Ivanova')," *Literaturnaia gazeta* (4 January 1947). One *Pravda* article denounced "Dve kroshki" as "cheap pacifism"; I. K. Riabov, "K voprosu o poroshnike," *Pravda* (9 January 1948).

4 The note is contained in TsGALI f. 2124, op. 1, ed. khr. 75, l. 1. Along these lines, Geller, who has a keen eye for such things, suggests that "Bessmertie" was the price Platonov paid for getting "Fro" into the same issue of *Literaturnyi kritik*, and that the article "Preodolenie zlodeistva" (*Literaturnaia gazeta*, 26 January 1937), which calls for the death sentence for the accused in the trial of Piatakov, Radek *et al.* (and which, as Geller notes, is omitted from Soviet bibliographies of Platonov) was the price for getting the *Reka Potudan'* (1937) volume into print (*Andrei Platonov*, pp. 360, 363).

5 On this phenomenon in Soviet literature, especially in Pasternak's later poetry, see A. K. Zholkovskii, "Iskusstvo prisposobleniia," *Grani*, No. 138 (1985): 78–98, and "Mekhanizmy vtorogo rozhdeniia," *Sintaksis* 14 (1985): 77–97.

6 The works in question are the *povest'* "Iuvenil'noe more," the story "Musornyi veter," and the plays "Sharmanka" and "14 krasnykh izbushek." Of the four, only "Musornyi veter" was published in the pre-*glasnost'* Soviet Union, no doubt because of its ostensibly anti-fascist theme.

7 In his notes to a recent Soviet publication of the work, Chalmaev remarks that it was part of Platonov's post-"Vprok" efforts to explain himself and win acceptance by the literary establishment. See Platonov, *Gosudarstvennyi zhitel'*, (M: Sovetskii pisatel', 1988), pp. 601–2. A portion of the work under the title, "Stroimaterial i oborudovanie" is contained in TsGALI f. 2124, op. 1, ed. khr. 44.

8 Naiman offers a Freudian interpretation of this episode and suggests that it parallels the scene at the beginning of "Sokrovennyi chelovek" in which Pukhov sits eating sausage on his wife's grave; see Eric Naiman, "Andrej Platonov and the Inadmissibility of Desire," *Russian Literature* 23 (1988): 330. My own view, however, is that Platonov's sense of somatic life is broader than, and consequently inadequately addressed by, that of Freudian thought. Sausage may be indisputably phallic, but this does not necessarily mean that the image of the penis dominates the metaphoric relation between the two. One might argue, for example, that for Platonov the penis is offensive precisely because it reminds him of sausage (that is, food) – not the other way around – and that it thus serves as a double symbol of man's tragic subservience to the corporeal.

9 Andrei Platonov, *Gosudarstvennyi zhitel'* (M: Sovetskii pisatel', 1988), p. 264. Subsequent quotations are from this edition.

10 My quotations are from A. Platonov, *Sharmanka* (Ann Arbor: Ardis, 1975).

11 First published in *Izbrannoe* (M: Moskovskii rabochii, 1966); quotations are from Andrei Platonov, *Sobranie sochinenii v trekh tomakh* (M: Sovetskaia Rossiia, 1984), t.1, pp. 112–28. See Naiman, "Andrej Platonov and the Inadmissibility of Desire," p. 334, for a discussion of the story's parallels with Pil'niak's "Chelovecheskii veter" (1925).

12 Among such aesopian hints in the work – beyond the temptation to see *any* portrayal of totalitarianism as referring back to Stalin's Russia – are the reference to the "workers' clothing" (*prozodezhda*) worn by the Nazis who erect the monument; Likhtenberg's lament that the nineteenth century was "mistaken" (which seems more plausible as a reference to Marx than to any precedent of national socialism); his charge that Hitler has made everyone

serve as his "guard" ("*gvardeitsy*" has a Stalinist-military ring to it); the deserted village where Likhtenberg commits suicide, which seems to refer to the disastrous effects of collectivization; and the origin of the "garbage wind" in the south – here identified as the territory of France, Italy, and Spain, but perhaps really Stalin's Georgia. For further discussion of the parallels, see Geller, *Andrei Platonov*, p. 338.

13 For Naiman it is more narrowly a "society consumed by lust"; "Andrej Platonov and the Inadmissibility of Desire," p. 332.

14 Hence, perhaps, Platonov's use as one of his epigraphs of a passage from the *Thousand and One Nights*. Along these lines it is interesting to consider the description of the bronze monument to Hitler/ Stalin: "*Usta lezhali v nezhnoi ulybke, gotovye k strasti i k gosudarstvennoi rechi*" (117). Platonov's phrasing recalls Maiakovskii's suicidal declaration in "Vo ves' golos" (1930) that his verses stand "*svintsovo-tiazhelo,/ gotovye i k smerti i k bessmertnoi slave.*" Maiakovskii rejects any bronze monument to himself, but by transferring the line to the description of Hitler/Stalin Platonov may be suggesting that his (Maiakovskii's) brand of eager service to the Soviet state is in fact the very kind of "*gosudarstvennaia rech'*" that issues from the lips of the totalitarian idol. His suicide fantasy in "Musornyi veter" would thus seem to present a different, still more troubled notion of the suppression of the writer's voice than that contained in his other works of the late 1920s and the 1930s.

15 Namely, a sketch called "Goriachaia arktika," the story "Takyr," and the *povest'* "Dzhan." Platonov's archives also contain a fragment entitled "Karagez," which appears to be an early variant of "Takyr" (TsGALI f. 2124, op. 1, ed. khr. 66, ll. 1–7).

16 The other, "Takyr," the story of a Persian girl sold into slavery and removed to the wastes of Central Asia, was published in *Aiding-Tiunler. Al'manakh k 10-letiiu Turkmenistana, 1924–1934* (M, 1934); and simultaneously in *Krasnaia nov'* 9 (1934). "Dzhan" was first published in fragmentary form as "Vozvrashchenie na rodinu," *Literaturnaia gazeta*, No. 43 (5 August 1938); and as "Schast'ie vblizi cheloveka," *Ogonek* No. 15 (1947). In the latter the hero's ambivalence is considerably toned down. The work was published posthumously in *Prostor* 9 (1964), in a shortened version which ends roughly a page from what in the longer version is the end of section 16 (with the phrase "*Dostatochno, chto on pomog im ostat'sia zhivymi, i pust' oni schast'ia dostignut za gorizontom*"). A full version was first published only in the two-volume collection put out by *Khudozhestvennaia literatura* in 1978. Quotations are from *Sobranie sochinenii v trekh tomakh*, t.2, pp. 7–115.

17 On this aspect of the story, see V. Turbin, "Misteriia Andreia Platonova," *Molodaia gvardiia* 7 (1965): 295.

18 For example, "Peschanaia uchitel'nitsa" and "Epifanskie shli-uzy." For a discussion of the steppe-desert connection and of the consistent association in Platonov's works of the "east" with the quality of emptiness, see L. A. Anninskii, "Zapad i vostok v tvorchestve Andreia Platonova," *Narody Azii i Afriki*, 4 (1967): 103–15.

19 The *dzhan*'s condition is anticipated in the painting Chagataev sees in Vera's Moscow apartment. One panel of the painting depicts a man standing on earth who has pushed his head through the clouds into the heavens and has gazed so long at the unknown that he forgets the rest of his body. The second panel portrays the separation of the now withered body from its detached head, which roams the heavens in search of a "new infinity" (11). While the painting undeniably casts doubts on the longing for utopian other worlds, Platonov's attention in the tale remains with the lower portion of the panel, the withered body abandoned by reason.

20 On the importance of "borders" to Stalinist culture, see Vladimir Papernyi, *Kul'tura "Dva"* (Ann Arbor: Ardis, 1985), p. 64.

21 The *dzhan*'s wanderings suggest the Israelites' sojourn in the wilderness and their emergence out of diaspora into nationhood, with Chagataev as a Moses figure (hence the reference to the story by some as a "biblical tale"). Other (perhaps related) Near-Eastern myths of nations crossing the desert in search of paradise are relevant as well. The tale explicitly mentions the ancient Persian myth of Ormuzd and Ariman (the former, who rules Iran, a symbol of good and material well-being; the latter, who rules Turan, one of evil and death). Chagataev, who is attacked by surreal, vulture-like birds, suggests an optimistic revision of the myth of Prometheus in which the bearer of modern, Soviet ways to a lost humanity manages to escape his punishment (he eventually kills the birds). At the same time he represents a sacrificial Christ. On these topics see Anninskii; Turbin; Vasil'ev (*Andrei Platonov*, p. 147ff); Chalmaev, *Andrei Platonov* (V, 1984), (pp. 166ff); and Geller (*Andrei Platonov*, pp. 326ff). Tolstaia-Segal also locates an important subtext in Firdawsi's *Shah-Nameh*, which had appeared in 1934 in the commemorative volume *Ferdovsi. 934–1934* (L, 1934); see "Naturfilosofskie temy," p. 231. Platonov's letters to his wife from Turkmenia also reflect this trans-historical vision: in one he describes the ruins of cities 2000–3000 years old, then comments, "We gazed for a long time on the

desert from the height of ruins left by Alexander the Great," and in another speaks of the excavations of Timurlane and the layers of ancient Asian and Greek ruins making the Turkmen region "a graveyard of pre-Turkmen nations"; *Gosudarstvennyi zhitel'*, pp. 560, 562.

22 For this terminology and for many observations regarding Platonov's later works I am indebted to my colleague Alexander Zholkovsky, particularly to his "Fro: Piat' prochtenii," *Voprosy literatury*, 9 (1989): 23–49.

23 *Literaturnyi kritik*, 8 (1936): 114–28. The story has never since been republished, presumably because of Levin's conversation with Kaganovich.

24 See, for example, G. Lukach, "Emmanuil Levin," *Literaturnoe obozrenie*, 19–20 (1937): 55–62. Platonov's ambivalence may in fact have been provoked by this attempt to produce a positive hero representing the "new Soviet man": it has been suggested that the story embodies his response to Stalin's 1935 assertion that technology without men was dead and that socialist construction must now learn to "rely on men," remarks which already revise the relation between socialist "distance" and "the near"; Günther, "Andrej Platonov und das sozialistisch-realistische Normensystem der 30er Jahre," p. 174.

25 Günther, "Andrej Platonov und das sozialistisch-realistische Normensystem," p. 185, suggests that this notion of "love for distant men, vs. for those near at hand" may ultimately derive from Nietzsche's positive valuation of it in *Also sprach Zarathustra*. Zholkovskii points to the idea's possible conduit into the Russian context, S. L. Frank's "Fr. Nitsshe i etika 'liubvi k dal'nemu'," (in P. N. Novgorodtsev, ed., *Problemy idealizma. Sbornik statei*, M, 1902) and notes that Platonov's own, revealingly entitled "Liubov' k dal'nemu" essentially works to undermine the idea (see "Fro: Piat' prochtenii," pp. 41–43). In that story, the hero Bozhko corresponds, in Esperanto, with an abstract "humanity," but finds happiness only when he manages to embrace the young Moskva Chestnova.

26 These appear still more obviously in the very similar "railway" stories "Na zare tumannoi iunosti" and "Strelochnik," in which the heroes are nearly killed in their selfless attempts to avert an accident. Consider also the allusion in "Bessmertie" to the emotional injury Levin received in childhood (the story hints that its cause was an episode of antisemitism), when his soul was so shaken that it "began to fall apart and sensed ahead of time its far-off death" (124). My reading of "Bessmertie" differs here

from that of Günther, who sees in it an allegorical expression of Fedorov's theme of brotherhood.

27 On these themes see Zholkovskii, "Fro: Piat' prochtenii," pp. 34–39. Platonov's familiarity with the myth is evident from his story "Afrodita" (1944–1945?), in which the hero nicknames his beloved – a barmaid – "Aphrodite" because she first appears to him over the foam of his beer.

28 *Sobranie sochinenii v trekh tomakh*, t.2, p. 128; subsequent quotations are from this edition.

29 The allusion to Orpheus is suggested in Naiman, "Andrej Platonov and the Inadmissibility of Desire," p. 345.

30 On these, and especially on their antecedent in readings of Chekhov's "Dushechka" (itself perhaps a model for Platonov's "Fro"), see Zholkovskii, "Fro: Piat' prochtenii," pp. 32–34.

31 First published in the collection *Reka Potudan'* (M: Sovetskii pisatel', 1937) – the only book edition of Platonov's work published in the thirties; quotations are from *Sobranie sochinenii v trekh tomakh*, t.2, pp. 178–204.

32 "*trudnoe preodolenie 'nebytiistvennosti'*"; Tolstaia-Segal, "Ideologicheskie konteksty Platonova," p. 259.

33 On the notion of Platonov's admitting "desire" into the "text" in this work, see Naiman, "Andrej Platonov and the Inadmissibility of Desire."

34 See Chalmaev's notes to the story in *Gosudarstvennyi zhitel'*, pp. 603–4.

35 One scholar calls Nikita's relation to Liuba "maternal"; see Heinrich Riggenbach, "Andrej Platonovs 'Reka Potudan''. Versuch einer Interpretation," *Schweizerische Beiträge zum IX. Internationalen Slavistenkongress in Kiev, September 1983*, Slavica Helvetica, Bd. 22 (Bern: Peter Lang, 1983), pp. 173–92. Platonov's heroes establish similar relations in other stories of the period, for example, "Liubov' k dal'nemu" (where Bozhko looks after Moskva Chestnova) and "Skripka," where Sartorius moves in and takes up chaste relations of caring with Osipova.

36 Both Riggenbach and Naiman ("Andrej Platonov and the Inadmissibility of Desire") note the sexual subtext.

37 Mindlin, *Neobyknovennye sobesedniki*, p. 432, describes a time he and Platonov went swimming in Koktebel' and Platonov timidly hid behind a boat in order to undress, "as embarrassed as if he were a woman." In "Moskovskaia skripka," a draft of the story "Skripka" contained in Platonov's archives, the hero Veshchii (in the published version, Sartorius) even abstains from using the toilet in the apartment of the woman who takes him in, "not

wishing to burden the apartment with his filth or to make noise with the water"; TsGALI, op. 1, ed. khr. 64, l. 83.

38  E. A. Krasnoshchekova, "O poetike Andreia Platonova," *Izvestiia AN SSSR. Seriia literatury i iazyka*, t.38, No. 1 (1979): 49.

39  Tolstaia-Segal makes a similar remark in "Ideologicheskie konteksty," p. 256.

40  A related theme can be found in "Starik i starukha" (1937), in which an old woman convinces her husband that they should try to have a child once again; he eventually acquiesces, but the wife dies in childbirth and the story ends with him being comforted by an official who agrees that the natural order under which people have both to give birth and to die is "bad." "Vozvrashchenie" (1946) is similar to "Reka Potudan'" in that it, too, portrays the relinquishing of a life devoted to the "road" in favor of children and a home (Ivanov is about to abandon his family, but descends from the train at the story's end when his children come running after him); in that work, however, the road is associated with erotic desires (cf. Ivanov's attraction to Masha, whom he meets and flirts with on his way home from war).

## CONCLUSION

1  Platonov's output during the war years was relatively prolific, but adds little new to his poetic other than to absorb the German invasion as yet another hostile force to be endured patiently (for example, "Sredi naroda") or welcomed suicidally (as in "Odukhotvorennye liudi"). So, too, do the later children's stories and adaptations of Russian and Bashkir folk tales form but a footnote to his career, though the children's stories are in the end uniquely "unchildlike" and uttered in an eccentrically plaintive narrative voice. On the latter topic see my "'Childish' Intonation in Platonov's Later Works," forthcoming in *Wiener Slawistischer Almanach*.

2  Apart from the fact that Platonov's earlier stylistic manner would hardly have been tolerated under the aesthetic of socialist realism, which proscribed any such "modernist" excess, he may have found the blander but more "folkloric" speech of Stalin (with its penchant for anaphora and incantory exclamations of "*slava!*") a less intriguing target. The question of whether his own blander and folksier later style latently alludes to Stalin's speech mannerisms might provide an interesting topic for further investigation.

3  To the remark in "Reka Potudan'," for example, that the soldiers

travel home "*smutno pomnia sebia*" ("barely remembering themselves"), which in an earlier work might "oddly" have introduced
Platonov's theme of self-oblivion, is appended the quotidian
explanation, "*kakimi oni byli tri-chetyre goda nazad*" (that is, "barely
remembering what they had been like three or four years ago").

4 See E. P. Korchagina, "O nekotorykh osobennostiakh skazovoi
formy v rasskaze 'Reka Potudan'," in *Tvorchestvo A. Platonova*, pp.
107–16.

5 On the semantic and syntactic attributes of these verbs see
Leonard H. Babby, *Existential Sentences and Negation in Russian*
(Ann Arbor: Karoma Publishers, 1980).

6 I am indebted here to Tolstaia-Segal's analysis of the passage in
"O sviazi nizshikh urovnei teksta s vysshimi (proza Andreia
Platonova)," *Slavica Hierosolymitana* 2 (1978): 172–80.

7 On Russian utopian philosophies in this period, see Richard
Stites, *Revolutionary Dreams. Utopian Vision and Experimental Life in
the Russian Revolution* (New York: Oxford University Press, 1989).

# Select bibliography

The recent proliferation in the Soviet Union of works by Platonov and secondary literature about him has made it gratifyingly difficult to include an exhaustive bibliography. The appended list of works is thus not complete and presents only those sources important to this study. Though they have all been superseded by recent Soviet publications, the following bibliographical sources are particularly useful:

Kiselev, A. "Andrei Platonovich Platonov." *Novyi zhurnal* 97 (1969): 291–301.
Maramzin, V. *et al.* "Andrei Platonovich Platonov (1899–1951). Biobibliograficheskii ukazatel'." *Ekho* 4 (1979): 189–90; 1 (1980): 149–58; 2 (1980): 153–58; 3 (1980): 147–58; 4 (1980): 146–51.
Mitrakova, N. M. *A. P. Platonov: materialy k biobibliografii.* V: Tsentral'no-chernozemnoe knizhnoe izd., 1969.
Olcott, A. C. "Andrei Platonov: the Citizen-Artist." Diss. Stanford University: 1976, pp. 289–388.

## WORKS OF ANDREI PLATONOV

### I. BIOGRAPHICAL MATERIALS

"'... Ia derzhalsia i rabotal'. Stranitsa biografii Andreia Platonova." *Pamir* 6 (1989): 97–118.
Inozemtseva, E. "Platonov v Voronezhe." *Pod"em* 2 (1971): 91–103.
Kornienko, N. and E. Shubina, eds. "O zhivykh i mertvykh." *Literaturnoe obozrenie* 9 (1989): 31–39.
Lasunskii, Oleg. "'V drugikh partiiakh ne sostoial.' Novoe ob Andree Platonove." *Literaturnaia gazeta* No. 23 (5297) (6 June 1990): 6.
Letter to the editors of the newspaper *Trudovaia armiia: Krasnaia derevnia*, 22 August 1920. In TsGALI, f. 2124, op. 1, ed. khr. 109 (1), l. 60.

Litvin, E. "Pis'ma A. P. Platonova 1927–1936 godov." *Volga* 8 (1989): 163–65.

"'Mne eto nuzhno ne dlia "slavy"...' (Pis'ma M. Gor'komu)." *Voprosy literatury* 9 (1988): 174–83.

Perkhin, V. V. "Dva pis'ma Andreia Platonova." *Russkaia literatura* 1 (1990): 228–32.

Platonov, Andrei. "Pis'mo v redaktsiiu." *Literaturnoe obozrenie* 6 (1937): 61.

"Pis'mo Voronskomu." *Vozvrashchenie*, p. 7. M: Molodaia gvardiia, 1989.

"Protiv khalturnykh sudei. (Otvet V. Strel'nikovoi)." *Literaturnaia gazeta* No. 26 (14 October 1929): 2.

"Vozrazhenie bez samozashchity. Po povodu stat'i A. Gurvicha." *Literaturnaia gazeta* No. 69 (20 December 1937): 6.

"Pervoe svidanie s A. M. Gor'kim." *Literaturnaia Rossiia* 32 (188) (5 August 1966): 6.

*Sobranie sochinenii v trekh tomakh*, t.3, pp. 531–50. M: Sovetskaia Rossiia, 1985.

*Gosudarstvennyi zhitel'*, pp. 546–87. M: Sovetskii pisatel', 1988.

Platonova, M. "Zhivia glavnoi zhizn'iu. (A. Platonov v pis'makh k zhene, dokumentakh i ocherkakh.)" *Volga* (9) 1975: 164–78. Reprint. Andrei Platonov. *Gosudarstvennyi zhitel'*, pp. 551–58. M: Sovetskii pisatel', 1988.

Verin, Vladimir. "Platonov nachinaetsia: k tvorcheskoi biografii pisatelia A. P. Platonova." *Literaturnaia ucheba* 4 (1987): 156–58.

"'Ia zhe rabotal sovsem s drugimi chuvstvami'." *Literaturnaia gazeta* No. 17 (5187) (27 April 1988): 4.


## II. POETRY

*Golubaia glubina. Kniga stikhov.* Krasnodar: Burevestnik, 1922.


## III. NOVELS

*Chevengur.* Paris: YMCA Press, 1972 [incomplete].

*Chevengur. Druzhba narodov* 3 (1988): 96–149 and 4 (1988): 43–156.

*Chevengur.* M: Sovetskii pisatel', 1989.

"Tekhnicheskii roman." *Ogonek* No. 19 (3277) (May 1990): 19–23 and No. 20 (3278): 20–23.

IV. SHORTER WORKS OF FICTION

A. *Collections and republications of multiple works*

"Dva rasskaza." *Iunost'* 11 (1988): 2–5 ["Dobryi Kuzia"; "Zabvenie razuma"].

*Gosudarstvennyi zhitel'*. M: Sov. pisatel', 1988.

*Izbrannye proizvedeniia v dvukh tomakh*. M: Khudozhestvennaia literatura, 1978.

*Kotlovan*. Ann Arbor: Ardis, 1973.

*Kotlovan*. *Novyi mir* 6 (1987): 50–123.

*Kotlovan*. In *Kotlovan*. *Iuvenil'noe more*, pp. 3–114. M: Khudozhestvennaia literatura, 1987.

*Kotlovan*. In *Chevengur*, pp. 367–474. M: Sovetskii pisatel', 1989.

*Povesti i rasskazy (1928–1934 gody)*. M: Sovetskaia Rossiia, 1988.

Rvachev, Sergei, ed. "Neizvestnye rasskazy Andreia Platonova." *Pod"em* 12 (1988): 120–29 ["Tam, gde ogon' i zhelezo"; "Rasskaz nesostoiashchego bol'she vo zhlobakh"; "Pop"; "Istoriia Iereia Prokopiia Zhabrina"; "Tiuten', Vitiuten' i Protegalen"; "Chul'dik i Epishka"; "Stranniki"].

*Sobranie sochinenii v trekh tomakh*. M: Sovetskaia Rossiia, 1984–1985.

*Starik i starucha*, edited by Fol'ker Levin. Arbeiten und Texte Zur Slavistik. Bd. 33. München: Verlag Otto Sagner in Kommission, 1984.

Verin, V., ed. "V vozraste 22 let." *Sel'skaia molodezh'*" 4 (1987): 36–40 ["Voly"; "Bog"; "Chelovek i pustynia. Iz ocherka"; "Pop"; "Erik"; "V poliakh"].

*Zhivia glavnoi zhizn'iu*. M: Pravda, 1989.

B. *Publications of individual works*

"Afrodita." *Sel'skaia molodezh'* 9 (1962): 19–22. Reprint. In *Izbrannye proizvedeniia v dvukh tomakh*, t.2, pp. 293–308. M: Khudozhestvennaia literatura, 1978.

"Antiseksus." Published by Thomas Langerak. *Russian Literature* 9 (1981): 281–96.

"Bessmertie." *Literaturnyi kritik* 8 (1936): 114–28.

"Buchilo." *Krasnaia niva* No. 43 (26 October 1924): 1028–32.

"Che-Che-O (Oblastnye organizatsionno-filosofskie ocherki)." *Novyi mir* 12 (1928): 249–58. Reprint. In *Povesti i rasskazy (1928–1934 gody)*, by Andrei Platonov. M: Sovetskaia Rossiia, 1988. [Co-authored by Boris Pil'niak.]

"Chul'dik i Epishka." *Krasnaia gazeta* No. 128 (10 August 1920): 2. Reprint. In *Starik i starucha*, pp. 111–12.

"Detskie vospominaniia." *Voronezhskaia kommuna* No. 176 (6 August 1922). Reprint. In *Starik i starucha*, pp. 105–8.

"Dusha cheloveka – neprilichnoe zhivotnoe. (Fel'eton o stervetsakh)." *Ogni* (V) 1 (18) (4 July 1921): 1.

"Dzhan." First as "Vozvrashchenie na rodinu." *Literaturnaia gazeta* No. 43 (5 August 1938): 5; and as "Schast'e vblizi cheloveka." *Ogonek* No. 15 (13 April 1947): 15–16. First publication of the full text is *Izbrannye proizvedeniia v dvukh tomakh*, t.1, pp. 429–541. M: Khudozhestvennaia literatura, 1978.

"Efirnyi trakt." *Fantastika 1967. Vypusk 1-yi*, pp. 247–302. M: Molodaia gvardiia, 1968. Reprint. In *Sobranie sochinenii v trekh tomakh*, t.1, pp. 151–220.

"Epifanskie shliuzy." In *Epifanskie shliuzy*, pp. 3–62. M: Molodaia gvardiia, 1927. Widely reprinted in collections of Platonov's works.

"Erik." *Krasnaia derevnia* No. 21 (30 January 1921): 2–3. Reprint. In *Kontinent* 10 (1976): 339–342; and in *Starik i starucha*, pp. 28–29.

"Fro." *Literaturnyi kritik* 8 (1936): 129–45. Widely reprinted in collections of Platonov's works.

"Gliniannyi dom v uezdnom sadu." First under the titke "Nuzhnaia rodina." *Krasnaia nov'* 1 (1936). Reprint. In *Izbrannye proizvedeniia v dvukh tomakh*, t.2, pp. 28–40. M: Khudozhestvennaia literatura, 1978.

"Gorod Gradov." In *Epifanskie shliuzy*, pp. 109–70. M: Molodaia gvardiia, 1927. Widely reprinted in collections of Platonov's works.

"Gosudarstvennyi zhitel'." *Oktiabr'* 6 (1929): 70–77. Reprint. In *Gosudarstvennyi zhitel'*, pp. 312–19. M: Sovetskii pisatel', 1988.

"Iamskaia sloboda." *Molodaia gvardiia* 11 (1927): 68–101. Reprint. In *Sobranie sochinenii v trekh tomakh*, t.1, pp. 252–96.

"Istoriia Iereia Prokopiia Zhabrina." *Repeinik* No. 10 (29 April 1923): 3. Reprint. In *Starik i starucha*, pp. 149–151.

"Iuvenil'noe more." In *Gosudarstvennyi zhitel'*, pp. 251–311. M: Sovetskii pisatel', 1988.

"Ivan Zhokh." In *Epifanskie shliuzy*, pp. 79–108. M: Molodaia gvardiia, 1987.

"Kak zazhglas' lampa Il'icha." *Zhurnal krest'ianskoi molodezhi* 21 (7 November 1926): 2–4. Also published under the title "O potukhshei lampe Il'icha." In *Epifanskie shliuzy*, pp. 185–204. M: Molodaia gvardiia, 1927.

"Karagez." TsGALI f. 2124, op. 1, ed. khr. 66, ll. 1–7.

"Liubov' k dal'nemu." *Tridtsat' dnei* 8–9 (1939): 7–15.

"Lugovye mastera." In *Epifanskie shliuzy*, pp. 279–84. M: Molodaia gvardiia, 1927.

"Lunnaia bomba." *Vsemirnyi sledopyt* 12 (1926): 3–15. Reprint. In *Sobranie sochinenii v trekh tomakh*, t.1, pp. 41–59. M: Sovetskaia Rossiia, 1984.

"Markun." *Kuznitsa* 7 (December 1920 – March 1921): 18–22. Widely reprinted in collections of Platonov's works.

"Moskovskaia skripka." TsGALI f. 2124, op. 1, ed. khr. 64, l. 83 [draft of "Skripka"].

"Musornyi veter." In *Izbrannoe*. M: Moskovskii rabochii, 1966. Reprint. In *Izbrannye proizvedeniia v dvukh tomakh*, t.1, pp. 107–26. M: Khudozhestvennaia literatura, 1978.

"Ocherednoi." *Zheleznyi put'* No. 2 (5 October 1918): 16–17.

"Odukhotvorennye liudi." First under the title "Odushevlennye liudi. Rasskaz o nebol'shom srazhenii pod Sevastopolem." *Znamia* 11 (1942): 115–37. Widely reprinted in collections of Platonov's works.

"Peschanaia uchitel'nitsa." *Literaturnye sredy* (28 September 1927): 6–7. Reprint. In *Sobranie sochinenii v trekh tomakh*, t.1, pp. 75–81.

"Pop." *Krasnaia derevnia* No. 206 (16 November 1920): 3. Reprint. In *Starik i starucha*, pp. 113–15.

"Potomki solntsa." *Voronezhskaia kommuna* No. 252 (7 November 1922): 2. Reprint. *Russian Literature* 9 (1981): 297–301 and in *Starik i starucha*, pp. 37–42.

"Reka Potudan'." In *Reka Potudan'*. M: Sovetskii pisatel', 1927. Widely reprinted in collections of Platonov's works.

"Rodina elektrichestva." *Industriia sotsializma* 6 (1939): 6–10. Widely reprinted in collections of Platonov's works.

"Satana mysli." *Put' kommunizma* (Krasnodar) 2 (March–April 1922): 32–37. [The story sometimes appears under the title "Potomki solntsa."]

"Semën (rasskaz iz starinnogo vremeni)." *Krasnaia nov'* 11 (1936): 27–33. Reprint. In *Gosudarstvennyi zhitel'*, pp. 320–28. M: Sovetskii pisatel', 1988.

"Serega i ia." *Krasnyi luch* (Zadonsk) 1 (July 1921): 2–3. Reprint. *Pod'em* 6 (1966): 91–93.

"Skripka." *Sel'skaia molodezh'* 1 (1964): 14–17.

"Sokrovennyi chelovek." In *Sokrovennyi chelovek. Povesti*. M: Molodaia gvardiia, 1927. Widely reprinted in collections of Platonov's works.

"Sredi naroda." First under the title "Ofitser i krest'ianin. Sredi naroda." *Literaturnaia Rossiia* No. 13 (25 March 1966): 18–19. Reprint. In *Izbrannye proizvedeniia v dvukh tomakh*, t.2, pp. 229–39. M: Khudozhestvennaia literatura, 1978.

"Starye liudi." *Krasnaia derevnia* No. 14 (21 January 1921). Also under the title "Ivan Mitrych." In *Epifanskie shliuzy*, pp. 212–13. Reprint. In *Starik i starucha*, pp. 109–10.

"Stranniki." *Kommunisticheskii voskresnik detiam* (6 December 1920): 3.

"Strelochnik." *Kolkhoznye rebiata* 12 (1936): 6–10.

"Stroimaterial i oborudovanie." TsGALI f. 2124, op. 1, ed. khr. 44. [Draft of "Iuvenil'noe more".]

"Svet zhizni." *Tridtsat' dnei* 8–9 (1939): 7–15.

"Takyr." In *Aiding-Tiunler. Al'manakh k 10-letiiu Turkmenistana, 1925–1934.* M: Iubileinaia kommissiia TsIK-TSSR, 1934; and *Krasnaia nov'* 9 (1934): 82–93. Reprint. In *Sobranie sochinenii v trekh tomakh*, t. 1, pp. 129–50. M: Sovetskaia Rossiia, 1984.

"Tiuten', Vitiuten' i Protegalen." *Zori* 2 (August–September 1922): 25–28. Reprint. In *Pod"em* 12 (1988): 125–27.

"Tretii syn." *Krasnaia nov'* 1 (1936). Widely reprinted in collections of Platonov's works.

"Usomnivshiisia Makar." *Oktiabr'* 9 (1929): 28–41. Reprint. In *Gosudarstvennyi zhitel'*, pp. 93–107. M: Sovetskii pisatel', 1988.

"Volchek." *Krasnaia derevnia* No. 174 (8 October 1920): 2–3. Reprint. In *Starik i starucha*, pp. 21–24.

"Voly." *Voronezhskaia kommuna* No. 243 (29 October 1920): 3. Reprint. In *Starik i starucha*, pp. 25–27.

"Vprok (bedniatskaia khronika)." *Krasnaia nov'* 9 (1931): 3–39. Reprint. In *Gosudarstvennyi zhitel'*, pp. 198–250. M: Sovetskii pisatel', 1988.

"V zvezdnoi pustyne." *Ogni* (V) No. 1 (4 July 1921): 2–3. Reprint. In *Starik i starucha*, pp. 30–36. Arbeiten und Texte zur Slavistik b. 33. München: Verlag Otto Sagner in Kommission, 1984.

## V. JOURNALISM

"Bor'ba mozgov." *Krasnaia derevnia* No. 171 (3 October 1920): 2.

"Da sviatitsia imia tvoe." *Krasnaia derevnia* No. 99 (7 July 1920): 2. Reprint. In *Vozvrashchenie*, pp. 13–14. M: Molodaia gvardiia, 1989.

"Dusha mira." *Krasnaia derevnia* (18 July 1920). Reprint. In *Vozvrashchenie*, pp. 15–17. M: Molodaia gvardiia, 1989.

"Gazeta i ee znachenie." *Krasnaia derevnia* No. 163 (23 September 1920): 2.

"K nachinaiushchim proletarskim poetam i pisateliam." *Zheleznyi put'* No. 19 (April 1919): 25–26.

"Khristos i my." *Krasnaia derevnia* No. 77 (11 June 1920): 3. Reprint. In *Vozvrashchenie*, pp. 12–13. M: Molodaia gvardiia, 1989.

"Konets boga." *Prizyv* No. 3 (11) (15 January 1921): 6.

"Krasnyi trud." *Krasnaia derevnia* No. 123 (4 August 1920): 2.

"Meliorativnaia voina protiv zasukhi." *Voronezhskaia kommuna* No. 43 (1583) (no date). In TsGALI f. 2124, op. 1, ed. khr. 109 (1).

"Mir na krasnom shtyke." *Krasnaia derevnia* No. 105 (14 July 1920): 1.

"No odna dusha u cheloveka." *Voronezhskaia kommuna* No. 158 (17 July 1920). Reprint. In "Nachalo soznaniia," by Andrei Platonov. *Literaturnoe obozrenie* 9 (1981): 103–4. [Review of a stage adaptation of Dostoevsky's *The Idiot*.]

"Normalizovannyi rabotnik." *Voronezhskaia kommuna* No. 295 (354) (29 December 1920): 1.

"Novaia mekhanika (uchenie ob absoliutnom dvizhenii)." TsGALI, f. 2124, op. 1, ed. khr. 32, l. 9. Reprint. In "Tri stat'i iz TsGALI." Edited by Thomas Seifrid. *Russian Literature* 23 (1988): 394–95.

"Novoe evangelie." *Nasha gazeta* (13 November 1921).

"O kul'ture zapriazhennogo sveta i poznannogo elektrichestva." *Iskusstvo i teatr* 2 (22 August 1922): 2–3. Reprint. In *Sobranie sochinenii v trekh tomakh*, t.3, pp. 521–22. M: Sovetskaia Rossiia, 1985.

"O liubvi." TsGALI f. 2124, op. 1, ed. khr. 32, ll. 5–8. Reprint. In "Tri stat'i iz TsGALI," edited by Thomas Seifrid, *Russian Literature* 23 (1988): 390–93.

"O nauke." *Krasnaia derevnia* No. 89 (25 June 1920): 2.

"Ob iskusstve." *Zhizn' i tvorchestvo russkoi molodezhi* 19 (1919): 7–8. Reprint. In *Vozvrashchenie*, p. 8. M: Molodaia gvardiia, 1989.

"Ocherki bednoi oblasti." TsGALI, f. 2124, op. 1, ed. khr. 34, ll. 1–2.

"Pervyi Ivan (ocherk)." *Oktiabr'* 2 (1930): 159–68.

"Preodolenie zlodeistva." *Literaturnaia gazeta* No. 5 (26 January 1937): 5.

"Proletarskaia poeziia." *Kuznitsa* 9 (1922): 28–32. Reprint. In *Sobranie sochinenii v trekh tomakh*, t.3, pp. 523–28. M: Sovetskaia Rossiia, 1985.

"Remont zemli." *Krasnaia derevnia* No. 175 (9 July 1920): 2. Reprint. In *Vozvrashchenie*, pp. 10–12. M: Molodaia gvardiia, 1989.

"Revoliutsiia 'dukha'." *Ogni* No. 2 (19) (11 July 1921): 1.

"Slyshnye shagi (Revoliutsiia i matematika)." *Voronezhskaia kommuna* No. 12 (18 January 1921). Reprint. In *Gosudarstvennyi zhitel'*, by Andrei Platonov, pp. 535–37. M: Sovetskii pisatel', 1988.

"Svet i sotsializm." TsGALI, f. 2124, op. 1, ed. khr. 32. Reprint. In "Tri stat'i iz TsGALI." Edited by Thomas Seifrid. *Russian Literature* 23 (1988): 387–89.

"Tvorcheskaia gazeta." *Voronezhskaia kommuna* No. 293 (26 December 1920).

"U nachala tsarstva soznaniia." *Voronezhskaia kommuna* 12 (18 January 1921). Reprint. In "Nachalo soznaniia. O publitsistike Andreia Platonova voronezhskogo perioda." *Literaturnoe obozrenie* 9 (1981): 104–5.

"Velikaia glukhaia." In *Vozvrashchenie*, by Andrei Platonov, pp. 176–79. M: Molodaia gvardiia, 1989.

"Voronezhskaia gidro-elektricheskaia stantsiia." *Voronezhskaia kommuna* 284 (936) (15 December 1922): 2.

"Vospitanie kommunistov." *Krasnaia derevnia* No. 119 (30 July 1920): 2.

"Zhivaia ekhidna." *Krasnaia derevnia* No. 96 (3 July 1920): 2.

"Zhizn' do kontsa." *Voronezhskaia kommuna* No. 189 (25 August 1921): 2.

## VI. PLAYS

"14 krasnykh izbushek." In *Zhivia glavnoi zhizn'iu*, by Andrei Platonov, pp. 311–56. M: Pravda, 1989. Also in *Potaennyi Platonov*, edited by A. Glezer, pp. 132–79. Paris–New York: Tret'ia volna, 1983.

"Duraki na periferii." Synopsis in *Rabis* 46 (31 November 1928). Reprint. In "Andrei Platonov vo vtoroi polovine dvadtsatykh godov (opyt tvorcheskoi biografii). Chast' pervaia," by Thomas Langerak, *Russian Literature* 21 (1987): 170. [Co-authored by Boris Pil'niak.]

"Golos otsa. P'esa v odnom deistvii." *Zvezda vostoka* 3 (1967): 80–85.

*Sharmanka*. Ann Arbor: Ardis, 1975.

"Sharmanka." *Teatr* 1 (1988): 3–28.

"Soldat-truzhenik, ili Posle voiny." In *Sobranie sochinenii v trekh tomakh*, t.3, pp. 271–307. M: Sovetskaia Rossiia, 1985.

"Uchenik litseia." In *Sobranie sochinenii v trekh tomakh*, t.3, 308–84. M: Sovetskaia Rossiia, 1985.

"Vysokoe napriazhenie." In *Iuvenil'noe more*, by Andrei Platonov, pp. 200–36. V: Tsentral'no-Chernozemnoe knizhnoe izd., 1988.

## VII. LITERARY CRITICISM

*Razmyshleniia chitatelia*. M: Sovremennik, 1980.

## CRITICAL WORKS

Akimov, V. "Rabochii klass – eto moia rodina." Afterword to *V prekrasnom i iarostnom mire*, by Andrei Platonov, pp. 402–14. L: Lenizdat, 1979.

Anninskii, L. A. "Zapad i vostok v tvorchestve Andreia Platonova."
   *Narody Azii i Afriki* 4 (1967): 103–15.
"Otkrovenie i sokrovenie." *Literaturnoe obozrenie* 9 (1989): 3–21.
Averbakh, L. "O tselostnykh masshtabakh i chastnykh Makarakh."
   *Na literaturnom postu*, 21–22 (1929): 10–17.
Bazhenova, S. "Avtorskoe povestvovanie v povesti Andreia Plato-
   nova 'Dzhan'." *Russkaia filologiia* (Tartu) 4 (1975): 209–14.
Berlin, Isaiah. "The Energy of Pasternak." In *Pasternak. A Collection
   of Critical Essays*, edited by Victor Erlich, pp. 39–42. Englewood
   Cliffs, New Jersey: Prentice-Hall, 1978.
Bethea, David M. *The Shape of Apocalypse in Modern Russian Fiction.*
   Princeton: Princeton Univ. Press, 1989.
Bocharov, S. G. "'Veshchestvo sushchestvovaniia'. Vyrazhenie v
   proze." In *Problemy khudozhestvennoi formy sotsialisticheskogo realiz-
   ma*, t.2, pp. 310–50. M: Nauka, 1971.
Bogdanov, A. A. [A. A. Malinovskii]. *Filosofia zhivogo opyta. Popu-
   liarynye ocherki.* M: Gosudarstvennoe izd., 1920.
   *Tektologiia. Vseobshchaia organizatsionnaia nauka.* L: Kniga, 1925.
Bogdanovich, Tadeush. "O tvorcheskoi pozitsii i poetike Andreia
   Platonova 20-kh godov (na materiale povesti 'Proiskhozhdenie
   mastera')." *Vestnik Moskovskogo universiteta*, Seriia 9, Filologiia, 2
   (1988): 13–20.
Borovoi, L. "'Radi radosti'. Andrei Platonov." In *Iazyk pisatelia*, pp.
   179–218. M: Sovetskii pisatel', 1966.
Briusov, V. "Sredi stikhov." Review of *Golubaia glubina*, by Andrei
   Platonov. *Pechat' i revoliutsiia* 6 (1923): 69–70.
Brodsky, Joseph. "Catastrophes in the Air." In *Less Than One. Selected
   Essays*, pp. 268–303. New York: Farrar Straus Giroux, 1986.
Brown, Edward J. *Russian Literature Since the Revolution.* Revised and
   enlarged edition. Cambridge: Harvard Univ. Press, 1982.
Bulgakov, S. "Dusha sotsializma." *Novyi grad* 9 (1931): 49–58.
Bürger, Peter. *Theory of the Avant-Garde.* Theory and History of
   Literature, vol. 4. Minneapolis: Univ. of Minnesota, 1984.
Carden, Patricia. "Ornamentalism and Modernism." In *Russian
   Modernism. Culture and the Avant-Garde, 1900–1930*, edited by
   George Gibian and H. W. Tjalsma, pp. 49–64. Ithaca: Cornell
   Univ. Press, 1976.
Catteau, Jacques. "De le Métaphorique des utopies dans la littérature
   russe et de son traitement chez Andrej Platonov." *Revue des études
   slaves* 56:1 (1984): 39–50.
Chalmaev, V. A. *Andrei Platonov.* M: Sovetskaia Rossiia, 1978.
   *Andrei Platonov. Ocherki zhizni i tvorchestva.* V: Tsentral'no-Cherno-
   zemnoe knizhnoe izd., 1984.

Chistov, K. V. *Russkie narodnye sotsial'no-utopicheskie legendy XVI–XIX vv.* M: Nauka, 1967.

Chudakova, M. O. *Poetika Mikhaila Zoshchenko.* M: Nauka, 1979.

Clark, Katerina. *The Soviet Novel. History as Ritual.* Chicago: Univ. of Chicago, 1981.

Clark, Katerina and Michael Holquist. *Mikhail Bakhtin.* Cambridge: Harvard Univ., 1984.

Dragomiretskaia, N. V. "Stilevye iskaniia v rannei sovetskoi proze." In *Teoriia literatury*, vol. 3, edited by G. L. Abramovich *et al.*, pp. 139–43. M: Nauka, 1965.

Drozda, Miroslav. "Khudozhestvennoe prostranstvo prozy A. Platonova." *Umjetnost Riječi* 2–4 (1975): 99.

Eidinova, V. V. "Rasskazy A. Platonova 20-kh godov (stil' i zhanr)." In *Problemy stilia i zhanra v sovetskoi literature*, pp. 83–100. Sverdlovsk: Ural'skii gos. un-tet im. Gor'kogo, 1976.

"K tvorcheskoi biografii A. Platonova." *Voprosy literatury* 3 (1978): 213–28.

Elsworth, J. D. *Andrey Bely: A Critical Study of the Novels.* Cambridge Studies in Russian Literature. Cambridge: Cambridge Univ., 1983.

Epshtein, Mikhail. "Teoreticheskie fantazii." *Iskusstvo kino* 7 (1988): 69–81.

Ermilov, E. "Iurodstvuiushchaia poeziia i poeziia millionov." *Pravda*, 21 July 1933.

"Klevetnicheskii rasskaz A. Platonova ('Sem'ia Ivanova')." *Literaturnaia gazeta*, 4 January 1947.

Fadeev, A. "Ob odnoi kulatskoi khronike." *Krasnaia nov'* 5–6 (1931): 206–9.

Fedorov, N. F. *Filosofiia obshchego dela.* In *Sochineniia.* Filosofskoe nasledie, t.85. M: Mysl', 1985.

Fesenko, Andrei and Tat'iana Fesenko. *Russkii iazyk pri sovetakh.* New York: no publ., 1955.

Fomenko, L. P. "Tvorchestvo A. P. Platonova (1899–1951)." Diss. na soiskanie uch. step. kand. fil. nauk, Moskovskii pedago-gicheskii institut im. N. K. Krupskoi, 1969.

"O nekotorykh traditsiiakh russkoi prozy v povestiakh A. Platonova 20-kh godov." In *Sovetskaia literatura. Traditsiia i novatorstvo*, vypusk 1-i, pp. 99–110. L: Izd. leningradskogo un-ta, 1976.

Furman, D. E. "Sotvorenie novoi zemli i novogo neba." *Voprosy filosofii* 3 (1989): 34–36.

Geller, Mikhail. *Andrei Platonov v poiskakh schast'ia.* Paris: YMCA Press, 1982.

Golomstock, Igor. *Totalitarian Art.* New York: Harper Collins, 1990.
*Gor'kii i sovetskie pisateli. Neizdannaia perepiska.* Literaturnoe nasledstvo, t.70. M: Izd. Akademii Nauk SSSR, 1963.
Grois, Boris. "Stalinizm kak esteticheskii fenomen." *Sintaksis* 17 (1987): 98–110.
*Gesamtkunstwerk Stalin. Die gespaltene Kultur in der Sowjetunion.* München: Carl Hanser, 1988.
Gumilevskii, Lev. "'Nepravil'naia prelest' iazyka'." *Literaturnaia gazeta* No. 42 (16 October 1974): 7.
Günther, Hans. "Andrej Platonov und das sozialistisch-realistische Normensystem der 30er Jahre." *Wiener Slawistischer Almanach* 9 (1982): 165–86.
"Andrej Platonov: Unterwegs nach Tschevengur." In *Literarische Utopien von Morus bis zur Gegenwart*, edited by Klaus L. Gerghahn and Hans Ulrich Seeber, pp. 191–202. Königstein/Ts.: Athenäum, 1983.
Gurvich, A. *V poiskakh geroia.* M-L: Iskusstvo, 1938.
Hartman, Geoffrey H. *The Unmediated Vision.* New York: Harcourt, Brace, and World, 1966.
Heller, Leonid. "Les chemins des artisans du temps: Filonov, Platonov, Hlebnikov et quelques autres." *Cahiers du monde russe et soviétique* 25:4 (October–December 1984): 345–74.
Iakusheva, Genrika and Aleksei Iakushev. "Struktura khudozhestvennogo obraza u Andreia Platonova." In *American Contributions to the Eighth International Congress of Slavists. Zagreb and Ljubljana, September 3–9, 1978.* Vol. 2, Literature, edited by Victor Terras, pp. 746–78. Columbus, Ohio: Slavica, 1978.
Ivanova, L. A. "Lichnost' i deistvitel'nost' v tvorchestve A. Platonova." Diss. na soiksanie uch. stepeni kand. fil. nauk, Voronezhskii gos. un-tet, 1973.
"Tvorchestvo A. Platonova v otsenke sovetskoi kritiki 20–30-kh godov." In *Tvorchestvo A. Platonova*, edited by V. P. Skobelev et al., pp. 173–92. V: izd. Voronezhskogo un-ta, 1970. Reprint. Ann Arbor: Ardis, 1986.
*Iz istorii sovetskoi literatury 1920–1930-kh godov.* Literaturnoe nasledstvo, t.93. M: Izd. Akademii Nauk SSSR, 1983.
Jakobson, Roman. "Randbemerkungen zur Prosa des Dichters Pasternak." In *Selected Writings*, vol. V, edited by Stephen Rudy and Martha Taylor, pp. 416–32. The Hague: Mouton, 1979.
Jensen, K. M. *Beyond Marx and Mach. Aleksandr Bogdanov's 'Philosophy of living experience'.* Sovietica vol. 41. Dordrecht, Holland: D. Reidel, 1978.
Jensen, Peter Albert. *Nature as Code. The Achievement of Boris Pilnjak*

(*1915–1925*). Kobenhavns Universitets Slaviske Institut, Studier 6. Copenhagen: Rosenkilde and Bagger, 1979.

"The thing as such: Boris Pil'njak's 'Ornamentalism'." *Russian Literature* 16 (1984), 81–100.

Kantor, K. M. "Bez istiny stydno zhit'." *Voprosy filosofii* 3 (1989): 14–21.

Kartsevskii, S. I. *Iazyk, voina, i revoliutsiia*. Berlin: Russkoe universal'noe izd., 1923.

Korchagina, E. P. "O nekotorykh osobennostiakh skazovoi formy v rasskaze 'Reka Potudan'." In *Tvorchestvo A. Platonova*, edited by V. P. Skobelev, *et al.*, pp. 107–16. V: izd. Voronezhskogo un-ta, 1970. Reprint. Ann Arbor: Ardis, 1986.

Kornienko, Natal'ia Vasil'evna. "Filosofskie iskaniia i osobennosti khudozhestvennogo metoda Andreia Platonova." Diss. na soiskanie uch. stepeni kand. fil. nauk, Gos. Pedagogicheskii Institut im. Gertsena, L, 1979.

Kozhevnikova, N. A. "Iz nabliudenii nad neklassicheskoi ('ornamental'noi') prozoi." *Izvestiia AN USSR. Seriia literatury i iazyka*, t.35, 1 (1976): 55–66.

Krasnoshchekova, E. A. "A. Platonov i Vs. Ivanov (vtoraia polovina 20-kh godov)." In *Tvorchestvo A. Platonova*, edited by V. P. Skobelev, *et al.*, pp. 147–56, pp. 107–16. V: izd. Voronezhskogo un-ta, 1970. Reprint. Ann Arbor: Ardis, 1986.

"O poetike Andreia Platonova." *Izvestiia AN SSSR. Seriia literatury i iazyka*, t.38, 1 (1979): 42–51.

"Ob odnom literaturnom fenomene." *Novyi zhurnal* 171 (1988): 150–69.

Langerak, Thomas. "Andrei Platonov v perelomnom periode tvorchestva (Zametki ob 'Antiseksuse')." *Russian Literature* 9 (1981): 303–22.

"Andrei Platonov vo vtoroi polovine dvadtsatykh godov (opyt tvorcheskoi biografii). Chast' pervaia." *Russian Literature* 21 (1987): 157–82.

"Kommentarii k sborniku A. P. Platonova, 'Epifanskie shliuzy'." In *Dutch Contributions to the Tenth International Congress of Slavists. Sofia, September 14–22, 1988. Literature*, edited by André van Holk, pp. 139–68. Amsterdam: Rodopi, 1988.

"Andrei Platonov v Voronezhe." *Russian Literature* 23–24 (1988): 437–68.

"Nedostaiushchee zveno 'Chevengura'. Tekstologicheskie zametki." *Russian Literature* 22 (1987): 477–90.

"Andrei Platonov i levoe iskusstvo (Zametki ob 'Antiseksuse' 2)." In *Festschrift für Herta Schmid*, edited by Jerry Stelleman and Jan van der Meer, pp. 191–204. Amsterdam: Universität von Amsterdam 1989.

Lenin, V. I. *Materializm i empiriokrititsizm*. M: Izd. politicheskoi literatury, 1984.

"Ob ochistke russkogo iazyka." In *Sochineniia*, t.30, p. 274. M: Politicheskaia literatura, 1952.

Levin, F. "Andrei Platonov." Preface to *Izbrannye rasskazy*, by A. Platonov. M: Sovetskii pisatel', 1958.

Liubushkina, Sh. "Ideia bessmertiia u rannego Platonova." *Russian Literature* 23–24 (1988): 397–424.

Locher, Jan Peter. "Zur Poetik des Andrej Platonov." In *Slavica Helvetica. Band 22: Schweizerische Beiträge zum IX Internationalen Slavistenkongress in Kiev, September 1983*, edited by Peter Brang, Georges Nivat, and Robert Zett, pp. 75–93. Bern: Peter Lang, 1983.

Lotman, Yury. "Language and Reality in the Early Pasternak." In *Pasternak. A Collection of Critical Essays*, edited by Victor Erlich, pp. 21–31. Englewood Cliffs, New Jersey: Prentice-Hall, 1978.

Lukach, G. "Emmanuil Levin." *Literaturnoe obozrenie* 19–20 (1937): 55–62.

Lukashevicz, Stephen. *N. F. Fedorov (1828–1903). A Study in Russian Eupsychian and Utopian Thought*. New York: Associated University Presses, 1977.

Maizel', M. "Oshibki mastera." *Zvezda* 4 (1930): 195–202.

Makedonov, A. *Nikolai Zabolotskii. Zhizn, tvorchestvo, metamorfozy*. L: Sovetskii pisatel', 1968.

Malygina, N. M. "Ideino-esteticheskie iskaniia A. Platonova v nachale 20-kh godov ('Rasskaz o mnogikh interesnykh veshchakh')." *Russkaia literatura* 20: iv (1977): 158–65.

*Estetika Andreia Platonova*. Irkutsk: Izd. Irkutskogo un-ta, 1985.

Markstein, Elisabeth. "Der Stil des 'Unstils': Andrej Platonov." *Wiener Slawistischer Almanach* 2 (1978): 115–44.

"Dom i Kotlovan, ili mnimaia realizatsiia utopii (Chitaia Andreia Platonova)." *Rossiia/Russia. Studi e ricerche a cura di Vittorio Strada* 4 (1980): 245–69.

Mazon, André. *Lexique de la Guerre et de la Revolution en Russie (1914–1918)*. Bibliothèque de L'Institut Français de Petrograd, tome VI. Paris: Èdouard Champion, 1920.

McClelland, James C. "Utopianism versus Revolutionary Heroism in Bolshevik Policy: The Proletarian Culture Debate." *Slavic Review* 39:3 (September 1980): 403–25.

Mindlin, E. *Neobyknovennye sobesedniki*. M: Sovetskii pistatel', 1968.

Morson, Gary Saul, *The Boundaries of Genre. Dostoevsky's 'Diary of a*

*Writer' and the Traditions of Literary Utopia*. Austin: Univ. of Texas Press, 1981.

Naiman, Eric. "The Thematic Mythology of Andrej Platonov." *Russian Literature* 21 (1987): 189–216.

"Andrej Platonov and the Inadmissibility of Desire." *Russian Literature* 23 (1988): 319–66.

Nikonova, T. A. "Kommentarii k povesti A. Platonova 'Epifanskie shliuzy'." In *Tvorchestvo A. Platonova*, edited by V. P. Skobelev *et al.*, pp. 204–20. V: Izd. voronezhskogo un-ta, 1970. Reprint. Ann Arbor: Ardis, 1986.

*Ocherk istorii russkoi sovetskoi literatury*. M: Izd. Akademii Nauk SSSR, 1954.

Olcott, Anthony Charles. "Andrej Platonov. The Citizen-Artist." Diss. Stanford Univ. 1976.

Papernyi, Vladimir. *Kul'tura "Dva"*. Ann Arbor: Ardis, 1985.

Paramonov, Boris. "Chevengur i okrestnosti." *Kontinent* 54 (1987): 333–72.

Pil'niak, Bor. "O teorii sotsial'nogo zakaza." *Pechat' i revoliutsiia* 1 (1929): 70–71.

Piskunova, S. I. "Mudrost' zabroshennykh knig." *Voprosy filosofii* 3 (1989): 32–34.

Podoroga, V. A. "Evnukh dushi (Pozitsii chteniia i mir Platonova)." *Voprosy filosofii* 3 (1989): 21–26.

Pollak, Nancy. "Mandel'shtam's *Mandelshtein* (Initial Observance on the Cracking of a Slit-Eyed Nut OR a Couple of Chinks in the Shchell)." *Slavic Review* 46: 3/4 (Fall/Winter 1987): 450–70.

Poltavtseva, N. G. *Filosofskaia proza Andreia Platonova*. Rostov-na-Donu: Izd. Rostovskogo un-ta, 1981.

Pronin, V. A. and L. N. Taganov. "A. Platonov – poet (sbornik *Golubaia glubina*)." In *Tvorchestvo A. Platonova*, edited by V. P. Skobelev, *et al.*, pp. 130–39. V: Izd. voronezhskogo un-ta, 1970. Reprint. Ann Arbor: Ardis, 1986.

Reck, Vera T., translator and editor. "Excerpts from the Diaries of Korney Chukovsky Relating to Boris Pilnyak." *California Slavic Studies* 11, 1980: 187–99.

Redfern, Walter. *Puns*. Oxford: Basil Blackwell, 1984.

Riabov, I. K. "K voprosu o poroshnike." *Pravda*, 9 January 1948.

Riggenbach, Heinrich. "Andrej Platonovs 'Reka Potudan''. Versuch einer Interpretation." In *Slavica Helvetica. Band 22: Schweizerische Beiträge zum IX Internationalen Slavistenkongress in Kiev, September 1983*, edited by Peter Brang, Georges Nivat, and Robert Zett, pp. 173–92. Bern: Peter Lang, 1983.

Rose, Mark. *Alien Encounters*. Cambridge: Harvard Univ. Press, 1981.

Rozanov, V. *Liudi lunnago sveta. Metafizika khristianstva.* 2-e izdanie. St. Petersburg: no publisher, 1913.

Schulte-Sasse, Jochen. "Foreword: Theory of Modernism versus Theory of Avant-garde." In *Theory of the Avant-Garde*, by Peter Bürger. Theory and History of Literature, vol. 4, pp. vii–xlvii. Minneapolis: Univ. of Minnesota, 1984.

Seifrid, Thomas. "Linguistic Devices in the Prose of Andrej Platonov." Diss. Cornell Univ. 1984.

"Writing Against Matter: On the Language of Andrej Platonov's *Kotlovan.*" *Slavic and East European Journal* 3 (1987): 370–87.

"On the Genesis of Platonov's Literary Style in the Voronež Period." *Russian Literature* 23–24 (1988): 367–86.

Selishchev, A. M. *Iazyk revoliutsionnoi epokhi.* M: Rabotnik prosveshcheniia, 1928. Reprint. Leipzig: Zentralantiquariat der Deutschen Demokratischen Republik, 1974.

Selivanovskii, A. "V chem 'somnevaetsia' Andrei Platonov." *Literaturnaia gazeta,* 10 June 1931.

Semenova, S. G. "N. F. Fedorov i ego filosofskoe nasledie." Introduction to N. F. Fedorov. *Sochineniia.* Filosofskoe nasledie, t.85, pp. 5–50. M: Mysl', 1985.

"'Ideia zhizni' u Andreia Platonova." *Moskva* 3 (1988): 180–89.

"Mytarstva ideala. K vykhodu v svet 'Chevengura' Andreia Platonova." *Novyi mir* 5 (1988): 218–31.

Shcheglov, Iu. K. "Tri fragmenta poetiki Il'fa i Petrova (mir sotsializma; obraz Bendera; sotsiologizm romanov)." In *Mir avtora i struktura teksta. Stat'i o literature,* by A. K. Zholkovskii and Iu. K. Shcheglov, pp. 85–117. Tennafly, N.J.: Hermitage, 1986.

Shcherbakov, A. "Itogi vtorogo plenuma pravleniia SSP." *Literaturnyi kiritk* 3 (1935): 7.

Shekhanova, T. S. "V 'Prekrasnom i iarostnom mire' slova A. Platonova." *Russkaia rech'* 6 (1979): 36–42.

Shepard, Joe Willwerth. "The Origin of a Master: the Early Prose of Andrej Platonov." Diss. Indiana Univ. 1973.

Shklovskii, Viktor. *Tret'ia fabrika.* M: Artel' pisatelei "Krug," 1926.

Shubin, L. "Andrei Platonov." *Voprosy literatury* 6 (1967): 26–54.

*Poiski smysla otdel'nogo i obshchego sushchestvovaniia. Ob Andree Platonove.* M: Sovetskii pisatel', 1987.

Skobelev, V. P. *et al.,* eds. *Tvorchestvo A. Platonova.* V: Izd. voronezhskogo un-ta, 1970. Reprint. Ann Arbor: Ardis, 1986.

Śliwowska, Wiktoria and René Śliwowski. *Andrzej Płatonow.* Warszawa: Czytelnik, 1983.

Stalin, I. "Golovokruzhenie ot uspekhov." *Pravda* No. 60, 2 March 1930. In *Sochineniia,* t.12, pp. 191–99. M: Gos. izd. politicheskoi literatury, 1949.

Stites, Richard. *Revolutionary Dreams: Utopian Vision and Experimental Life in the Russian Revolution.* New York: Oxford Univ. Press, 1989.

Strel'nikova, V. "'Razoblachiteli' sotsializma." *Vecherniaia Moskva,* 28 September 1929.

Striedter, Jurij. "Journeys Through Utopia. Introductory Remarks to the Post-revolutionary Russian Utopian Novel." *Poetics Today* 3:1 (1982): 33–60.

Suchkov, F. "Na krasnyi svet (ob Andree Platonove – mastere prozy)." Introduction to *Izbrannoe,* by A. Platonov, pp. 3–14. M: Moskovskii rabochii, 1966.

Svitel'skii, V. A. "Konkretnoe i otvlechennoe v myshlenii A. Platonova-khudozhnika." In *Tvorchestvo A. Platonova,* edited by V. A. Skobelev, *et al.,* pp. 7–26. V: Izd. voronezhskogo un-ta, 1970. Reprint. Ann Arbor: Ardis, 1986.

Terts, Abram [Andrei Siniavskii]. *V teni Gogolia.* Paris: Syntaxis, 1981.

Teskey, Ayleen. *Platonov and Fyodorov. The Influence of Christian Philosophy on a Soviet Writer.* Amersham, UK: Avebury, 1982.

Tolstaia-Segal, Elena. "O sviazi nizshikh urovnei teksta s vysshimi (Proza Andreia Platonova)." *Slavica Hierosolymitana* 2 (1978): 169–212.

"'Stikhiinye sily': Platonov i Pil'niak (1928–1929)." *Slavica Hierosolymitana* 3 (1978): 89–109.

"Naturfilosofskie temy v tvorchestve Andreia Platonova 20–kh– –30–kh gg." *Slavica Hierosolymitana* 4 (1979): 223–54.

"K voprosu o literaturnoi alliuzii v proze Andreia Platonova: Predvaritel'nye nabliudeniia." *Slavica Hierosolymitana* 5–6 (1981): 355–69.

"Ideologicheskie konteksty Platonova." *Russian Literature* 9 (1981): 231–80.

"Literaturnyi material v proze Andreia Platonova." In *Voz'mi na radost': To Honor Jeanne van der Eng-Leidmeier,* pp. 193–205. Amsterdam: no publisher, 1980.

Tsvetkov, A. P. *Iazyk A. P. Platonova.* Diss. Univ. of Michigan 1983.

Turbin, V. "Misteriia Andreia Platonova." *Molodaia gvardiia* 7 (1965): 293–307.

Ulam, Adam B. *Stalin. The Man and His Era.* New York: Viking, 1973.

Usievich, E. "Pod maskoi iurodstva (o Zabolotskom)." *Literaturnyi kritik* 4 (1933): 78–91.

Utechin, S. V. "Philosophy and Society: Alexander Bogdanov." In *Revisionism: Essays on the History of Marxist Ideas,* edited by Leopold Labedz, pp. 117–25. New York: Praeger, 1962.

Vakhrushev, V. "Platonov – tragicheskie paradoksy gumanizma." *Volga* 8 (1989): 166–74.

Varshavskii, V. "'Chevengur' i 'Novyi grad'." *Novyi zhurnal* 122 (1976): 193–213.

Vasil'ev, Vladimir. *Andrei Platonov. Ocherk zhizni i tvorchestva.* M: Sovremennik, 1982.

Verin, Vladimir Aleksandrovich. "Gazetnaia publitsistika Andreia Platonova (1918–1925 gg.) i ee znachenie dlia khudozhestvennogo tvorchestva pisatelia." Diss. na soiskanie uch. stepeni kand. fil. nauk. Moskovskii gos. un-tet im. Lomonosova, 1987.

"Istoriia odnoi komandirovki." *Sever* 10 (1986): 103–5.

"Andrei Platonov – publitsist. Po stranitsam voronezhskikh gazet dvadtsatykh godov." *Literaturnaia gazeta* No. 2 (5210) (7 January 1987): 5.

"Videt' zvuki, slyshat' zvezdu." *Tekhnika – molodezhi* 5 (1987): 52–54.

Vinokur, G. "O revoliutsionnoi frazeologii (odin iz voprosov iazykovoi politiki)." *LEF* 2 (April–May 1923): 104–18.

Walicki, Andrzej. *A History of Russian Thought from the Enlightenment to Marxism.* Stanford: Stanford Univ. Press, 1979.

Yakushev, Henryka. "Andrei Platonov's Artistic Model of the World." *Russian Literature Triquarterly* 16 (1979): 171–88.

Zadonskii, N. "Molodoi Platonov." *Pod"em* 2 (1966): 145–48.

Zalygin, Sergei. "Skazki realista: realizm skazochnika." *Voprosy literatury* 7 (1971): 120–42.

Zamoshkin, N. Review of *Sokrovennyi chelovek*, by Andrei Platonov. *Novyi mir* 3 (1928): 270.

Zholkovsky, A. K. "The Window in the Poetic World of Boris Pasternak." *New Literary History* 9:2 (Winter 1978): 279–314.

*Themes and Texts. Toward a Poetics of Expressiveness.* Ithaca: Cornell Univ. Press, 1984.

"Tekhnologiia chuda i ee razoblachenie." *Russkaia mysl'* No. 3600 (20 December 1985): 9.

"Iskusstvo prisposobleniia." *Grani* 138 (1985): 78–98.

"Mekhanizmy vtorogo rozhdeniia." *Sintaksis* 14 (1985): 77–97.

"Fro: Piat' prochtenii." *Voprosy literatury* 12 (1989): 23–49.

Zolotonosov, Mikhail. "Usomnivshiisia Platonov." *Neva* 4 (1990): 176–90.

# Index

267

*Joseph Brodsky*
VALENTINA POLUKHINA
*Petrushka: the Russian carnival puppet theatre*
CATRIONA KELLY
*Turgenev*
FRANK FRIEDERBERG SEELEY
*From the idyll to the novel: Karamzin's
sentimentalist prose*
GITTA HAMMARBERG
'*The Brothers Karamazov*' *and the poetics of memory*
DIANE OENNING THOMPSON